Anisur Rahman

SOCIOLITERARY CULTURES IN SOUTH ASIA

PAPER MISSILE

NIYOGI BOOKS

Published by
NIYOGI BOOKS
Block D, Building No. 77,
Okhla Industrial Area, Phase-I,
New Delhi-110 020, INDIA
Tel: 91-11-26816301, 26818960
Email: niyogibooks@gmail.com
Website: www.niyogibooksindia.com

Editor: Sukanya Sur
Design: Nabanita Das

ISBN: 978-93-86906-95-3
Publication: 2019

Printed at: Niyogi Offset Pvt. Ltd., New Delhi, India

To Tabassum

for all her care and consideration

There hangs in the space a red bowl of gold
A bright, a beautiful, a happy bowl of gold
Neither the Vedas, nor the Purana, nor the Quran mention it
This bowl is neither here upon this earth, nor there in the skies
No craftsman can ever draw its figure, my friend!
Drunk to the brim, one day Shiv Shankar spoke to Parvati:
Only from your prime powers, I got this red bowl of gold.

—An extract from a *kajri*, translated by Anisur Rahman

Contents

REALISTIC CONFIGURATIONS

Preface

There is a general perception that South Asia, apart from being a geographical entity, is a conglomeration of mutually compatible nations, which together constitute a larger whole. Reiterated over time, this perception has now matured enough to be accepted as a truism with little realization that it has contributed towards effacing the real identity of South Asia. A repudiation of this supposed truism may, however, be possible by posing certain questions which would, in turn, help us appreciate the richness of South Asia as a space characterized by richness of diversity rather than by illusion of unity. In order to make my point, I may ask whether all South Asian nations are really a compatible whole in terms other than geographical, and if they are so, then there must be a centre to bind them together. The answer to this question has to be in negative. Further, I may ask that if there is a centre, there must also be margins to go along with it. Again, the answer cannot be in positive. If that be the case, I may assert that the essential spirit of South Asia clearly denies a single centre because the very strength of South Asia, as an assembly of nations, lies in the self-evolved centrality of each location, and all of them taken together impart uniqueness to a broader South Asian identity. This argument may be carried forward by positing that the writers of different South Asian locations speak in their own voices without the echoes of the other, and they also address others in the same manner. This is well borne-out by the way they have negotiated with their history and also dealt with their secondary and tertiary states of existence in their individual ways. Although South Asia has been relegated to the generic 'third space', it has, with the passage of time, turned out to be a larger location of great interest to social and political scientists, cultural theorists and anthropologists, literary writers and critics, historians and philosophers, and technocrats and industrialists. As it appears now, South Asia is everyone's point of reference.

In addition to their social, cultural, economic, and political variables, South Asian nations have had a shared history of underdevelopment. For the reasons of their physical proximity, they have always impacted each other both directly and indirectly, but even while they have done so, they have maintained their intrinsic differences. Since South Asia is now a site of growing economic strength, political power, and upward social mobility in the postcolonial era, there has been a flourishing of literary activities in five of its major sites like India, Pakistan, Bangladesh, Sri Lanka, and Afghanistan. The literary writers of these sites have drawn upon their literary traditions to write their texts of affection and disaffection. The growing number of subaltern and women writers is a significant feature of this literary scenario. Today, South Asia is visiting its past, strengthening its medial space between the past and the present, and writing its present in order to stress upon its cultural autonomy and define its socioliterary canon for a readership within and outside its own locations.

This book presents studies on authors, texts, and issues under three different sections that represent different secular traditions, imaginative landscapes, and realistic configurations of South Asia as a socioliterary space. Four studies in the first section present a case for the reading and reception of Kabir and Rumi, Sufi music of India and Pakistan, a regional folk music of India, and Indian court poetry and its patrons. While they spell out different aspects of secularity in retrospect, two other studies examine modern cinematic representations of Muslims in Bombay/Mumbai cinema with reference to language and culture, and the twentieth-century constructions of Indian Muslims in sociopolitical texts. All the six studies cumulatively underline the comprehensive sociocultural and political configurations of a given South Asian space. The second section explores the imaginative landscapes of India and Pakistan with reference to modernist representations in Urdu poetry, sociopolitical poetry of Faiz Ahmad Faiz, feminist poetry of Pakistani women poets, romantic configurations of Sarojini Naidu, indigenously rooted poetry of Kamala Das, and multiple associations of Agha Shahid Ali's poetry. These studies focus upon the rich variety of poetical expressions with reference to historical exigencies and their literary reception. The third section on realistic configurations evaluates the tradition of Indian English fiction writing over decades, premises of Premchand, subversive art of Michael Ondaatje, poetry and politics of Afghani warrior-poet Khushal Khan Khattak, and the historical fiction of Tahmima Anam. All the texts and issues selected from the five South Asian sites—India, Pakistan, Afghanistan, Bangladesh, and Sri Lanka—represent a larger kaleidoscope of South Asian socioliterary capital. They represent personal and collective biographies in terms of history, memory, and myth, as they spell out stages in the formation of identity and also appraise the problematic of survival as projected in literary texts. They examine their imagery, metaphor, and symbol, their versions of femininity and feminism, their ideological bases, indigenous expressions, and structures of hybrid thought patterns and linguistic structures.

Anisur Rahman

SECULAR TRADITIONS

Rumi and Kabir: Reading and Reception

Identifying Rumi and Kabir

Jalaluddin Rumi (1207–1273) and Kabir (1338–1448/1398–1448/1398–1518/1440–1518) have emerged unquestionably as figures of deep reverence. They have also emerged, with unanimity of critical opinion, as poets of extraordinary merit. This is rather unusual, since poets are always read and appreciated essentially for their worth as poets and not for extra-literary merits where personality seems to predominate over poetic expression. The reason for such a response which evolved rather instantly and got reiterated over various historical periods could be traced in the instantaneous appeal of the message they imparted and the unassuming method with which they chose to do so. This dual identity based on the spirit of reverence for these poets and respect for their poetry started evolving even while they lived, and it got reiterated in every literary/historical period without any break. It may be justifiably argued that a major reason behind their broader acceptance lies as much in the validity of the spiritualist content they delivered as in the unassuming stance they developed towards their poetry and poetics. A survey of their larger acceptability across time and place would show that the two poets have appealed in equal measure to the common folk and the elite for their relevance to the broader perceptions of life, as well as for the artistic merit of their poetry. Any reading of the two poets would, therefore, bring three central issues to the fore that relate with the problematic of their identity, their spiritualist predilections, and the myriad contexts of their reading and reception. I would like to examine these aspects in order to contextualize the two poets in a comparative perspective.

Rumi and Kabir, the two iconic poets of our richly ambiguous Orient, widely separated in terms of time and place,[1] and clearly differentiated in terms of their cultural identity, are both subjected to the enigmatic interplay of hagiographies, biographies, and stereotypes. Even without contextualizing them in their times and examining the supposedly consequential events in their lives, it may be safely asserted that both these poets have been mystified in about the same measure, as they have been studied for their literary merit. We have had a variety of readings both from the Eastern and Western scholars[2] over a large period of time, which establish their location in the great tradition of spiritualist poetry. These readings concern especially the problematic of their birth and lineage, their affiliations with Sufism[3] and bhakti,[4] their shariat[5] and tariqat[6] , *saguna*[7] and *nirguna*[8], *shabda*[9] and *sahaja*[10], and pir[11] and guru[12]. More importantly, they problematize their idea of divinity and the divine power represented through Ram and Rahim as the emblems of kindness, beneficence, and mercy.[13] In spite of these readings available to us, we may still explore certain newer frames of references to appreciate and evaluate their overall worth as poets and seers. These frames of references may be used to develop a comparative perspective on the two poets on a number of accounts. This chapter seeks to identify some of those frames and, to posit that, they may be used profitably to read the two poets together in a newer and broader perspective.

In order to substantiate the aforementioned readings, and to extend the frontiers of Rumi and Kabir studies, let me make ten precise propositions to underline the levels of their proximity:

First, even though it might sound naïve to present it as an issue, there is much to the epithets of *maulana* and *sant* that were prefixed to Rumi and Kabir at certain stages of their canonization in their respective locations. These epithets became the marks of their essential identity that also defined the nature of their lives and their poetical utterances. They defined their character and assigned them a place in the social imagination and also secured a space for them in the larger spiritual hierarchy. I would like to suggest that instead of essentializing them, these epithets determine the broader contexts of their belonging and individuality which go to explain their proximity with each other in a spiritualist tradition.

Second, both sought their individual methods of developing their communion with the divine as seers in the form of a sant and a Sufi. In spite of the fact that Kabir disaffiliated from the constraints of organized faith and Rumi followed a given system of religious faith and practice, they were liberal humanists at the very core. They brought their basic beliefs to bear upon life and to discover their own levels of spiritualist signification. They developed an understanding of life that verged on the mystical (Sufi–Bhakti) in their own ways and extended the proceeds of their apprehension to their addressees. In this manner, both of them believed in the philosophy of love, and both strove for love, with love, and by love, which is frequently demonstrated by their poetic utterances.

Third, both sought and met their spiritual masters who helped them realize their longing and attain their vision. The place of a pir, murshid, ustad, mentor, or guru is well acknowledged in the spiritual yearning of the seekers and is well borne out by the way the seekers of truth learn to aspire and achieve their goals in the quest of their selves. It is testified by the way Rumi met his pir in Shams-i-Tabrizi[14] and Kabir his guru in Ramananda[15], who ultimately defined their spiritualist hankering and helped them find their path.

Fourth, both were teachers at large and had their own sets of addressees. Rumi taught a large section of disciples formally, and Kabir spoke to an open house of keen listeners who drew closer to him for his verses of wisdom. In spite of the differences in the composition and levels of their addressees, both sought to share the moments of spiritualist enlightenment with a curious set of receivers of their spoken words. In this act of sharing, the word, the speaker, and the audience became one and together validated the value of speech and the act of speaking. They developed a discourse of spiritual wisdom in a process of sharing with their addressees.

Fifth, both developed a poetic diction and a tone and tenor that drew significantly on the oral–aural nature of their idiom. Since their message had an intended spiritualist meaning and power, they made way for instantaneous communication with the audience. Apart from the value of their word, their magic lay in the form their message was moulded into. As such, their verses created a kind of music that transcended formal rhyme and appealed directly to the listeners for their spontaneity and spiritual worth.

Sixth, both believed in a formless God. Rumi had the medium of *tawheed,* the idea of one and the only one God that is formless, and Kabir practised a liberal way of reaching the divine by apprehending the spirit rather than the matter through Ram and Rahim, both being the supreme power to regulate individuals' lives and the material world. Both of them approached the divine in a manner that was essentially personal, and both believed in the spirit behind all the manifestations by experimenting with the bare truth.

Seventh, both believed in the unity of beings as a credo. For doing this, both experimented with truth as a way of discovering the concrete through the maze of the abstract. This, too, was an essentially personal way of establishing a rapport with the divine being. It was for them a philosophical way of understanding the myriad manifestations of being and of establishing a link between objects and their metaphoric/symbolic representations.

Eighth, both left behind their grand legacies in two institutions of reverence. Rumi's followers developed the Mevlevi Order[16], and those of Kabir came up with Kabir Panth[17] that reiterate and carry forward their message. They have thus left behind their legacies that help their descendants and readers to relate with them beyond time and space. These institutions have, thus, created and taken forward a tradition of sharing reverence for their spiritual icons.

Ninth, both emerged as canonical figures, both discovered an interface between faith and art, and both left behind flocks of singers and performers to revisit and reformulate their work after them. They have, thus, been institutionalized through various forms and kinds of performing arts. These forms have developed in different locations along the aesthetic principles practised there.

Tenth, and finally, both Kabir and Rumi survive in their physical spaces that they inhabited during their lifetime. Rumi's shrine in Konya and Kabir

Chaura Math in Benaras stand as testimonies of reverence for the two poets where they remain idolized and canonized, more for spiritual than for other reasons. These have also emerged as institutions and have stood as testimonies to their medium and message beyond time and space.

With reference to the points made earlier, it may be argued that both Kabir and Rumi have remained the constant points of reference with respect to their iconicity and canonicity, as well as their mythic stature and their appeal to both the common and the scholastic imagination through ages. Even though they offer adequate and justifiable grounds for comparison with each other, they also show certain oppositional stances with respect to their basic methods of apprehending the physical and the non-physical, the material and the mystical, as well as the illusory and the realistic. It might be asserted that Rumi drew upon a strong spiritual and intellectual tradition based on Islam, and emerged as a religious scholar, a jurist, a discourser, and a writer of thoughtful letters,[18] but Kabir had no such resources to draw upon or develop.[19] It may also be added that a large part of Rumi's poetry is the direct annotation of The Holy Qur'an and the life and teachings of the prophet of Islam, whereas Kabir did not have any such verifiable sources for attaining a stance of his own kind. It may be claimed further that Rumi wrote in the elitist Persian language, but Kabir drew largely upon the vernacular Hindi with dependence upon Braj, Awadhi, and Bhojpuri. The oppositional reasonings with reference to their basic modes of apprehension and verbal expression may also be seen in the following two arguments. Afzal Iqbal, a Rumi scholar, lays down Rumi's method of apprehending reality even as he compares him with the characteristic mode of another major Persian poet Faizi in the following terms:

> Both Ghazali and Rumi were essentially mystics, but their mysticism was always accompanied by an orthodox insistence on the five articles of faith and the five pillars of practice. Their mysticism led them to emphasise the spiritual side of worship. The mere form is nothing. (72)
>
> Rumi recognises one leader, follows one guidance, looks towards one goal. The leader is the Prophet, the guidance is of the Holy Qur'an,

> and the goal is Allah! His belief in the limitless capacities of man is indeed inspiring, his scorn for death and tragic suffering raises you to heights unknown and in his incessant quest for unravelling the mysteries of life he is satisfied with nothing less than Heaven itself. Even that is not considered a prize worth ending the glorious quest of man for he stops at nothing less than the presence of God himself—and here too this tiny creature display the unique confidence of holding his own in the presence of the Supreme Reality before which he does not simply wither away! Pessimism and despair do not find any place in Rumi's scheme of life—he weeds out every vestige of fear which arrests the urge for growth and the expression of life. (148)

Iqbal has tried to mark the major aspects of Rumi's credo and practice by drawing upon his mysticism, his subscription to the pillars of faith and practice, his adherence to the prescriptions of the holy Qura'n, the primacy of Allah, and the guidance of the prophet. This is different from the way Kabir apprehended his mode of faith and practice. Sadiq-ur-Rahman Kidwai, a scholar of Urdu literature, has underlined Kabir's characteristic method as follows:

> Islamic mysticism does not depart from the basic tenets of religion. The Sufi claims to represent the true spirit of Islam. He traces the origin of his system of thought to the Koran and the *hadis*. He never rejects the *shari'a* but calls upon to even go beyond it. According to him, while form as prescribed by the *shari'a* is essential, it is not enough as it is the bare prescribed minimum. As for the substance of religion, for him it is as much more than formal adherence to prescribed tenets. Also the Sufi stresses the importance of attaining the true path to God through personal endeavour. For him to observe the *shari'a* is one thing and to imbibe the spirit of religion, another. Sufis stress the supremacy of personal experience over the mere observance of formal rules.
>
> The concept of God as we find it in Urdu Sufi poetry is similar to that of Kabir. *Wahdat al wujud* or 'unity of existence', according to which the ultimate reality exists in every particle of the universe,

> is the most common concept. Thus God resides in all human beings. To them, treating all fellow human beings with respect and tolerating even those who differ is the way to find ultimate reality or to commune with God. (166–67)

The way Kidwai charts out the basic tenets of Islamic mysticism and places Kabir in that context, he also provides us a way that may help us appreciate the methods that Rumi sought for his purposes. As such, it may be justifiably argued that in spite of their differences that appear on the surface, the practices of both the poets may also be appreciated in a liberal framework. It may, thus, be possible to assert that while Rumi was a cultivated spiritualist, Kabir was a naturalist, a yogi without practising yoga as a discipline. Compared with Rumi, Kabir grew naturally and spoke naturally to his addressees and, both of them taken together, moved towards the same goal of a purely human understanding of the divine. All these propositions that situate Rumi and Kabir in two apparently distinct positions may also lead us to assert that the question of the authentic or inauthentic text, more in the case of Kabir than in Rumi, do not limit the significance of their quest for the truth. Similarly, the problem of mixed dialects becoming a language, as in the case of Kabir, and a language getting refined and charged further, as in the case of Rumi, stress the point that language can also be subservient to spiritual experience in order to acquire its extra edge and appeal to the readers and listeners alike. Instead of examining as to how they called on language, it is important to note that it was language that called on them, which means that they chose to express themselves without any irritable reaching after the contrived nuances of words and idioms. Their poetic utterances bear it out that their words and idioms got metamorphosed into metaphors and symbols in a natural process of impassioned speech. From this position, it should only be proper to assert that in identifying their leitmotifs, both these poets were engaged essentially with evolving the dialectics of the particular and the universal, developing the tropes and trajectories of life lived as natural quest, and art practised as pure devotion.

Spirituality: Sufism and Bhakti

Rumi's *Mathnawi* and *Divan*[20] and Kabir's *shabda* (or pada), *beejak, sakhis* (or *dohas*), and *ramaini*[21], preserved variously, are the essential sources for our reading of the two poets. There is an underlying unity in the works of the two poets, and the two poets taken together verbalize and philosophize, annotate and exemplify their urge to identify with the divine. Let us illustrate these with examples from their texts.

In his *Divan*, Rumi describes the man of God as one who is 'drunken without wine', 'full without meat', 'distraught and bewildered'. He has no 'food or sleep', is a 'king beneath dervish-cloak', and a 'treasure in a ruin'. Further, he is 'not of air and earth', not even 'of fire and water'. He is, in fact, a 'boundless sea', who 'rains pearls without a cloud', and has 'hundred moons and skies', and 'hundred suns'. This man of God is 'made wise by the Truth'; he is 'not learned from book', he is 'beyond infidelity and religion', he knows that 'right and wrong are alike', is 'ridden away from Not-being', and is 'gloriously attended'. Finally, at the end of the verse, Rumi addresses his pir and says:

> The man of God is concealed, Shamsi Din;
> The man of God do thou seek and find! (RAN 30–31)

Kabir refers to this man of God as a 'yogi' who has 'no sky or earth', no hand, foot, form or shape', and 'where there is no market he sets up shop'. He 'weighs things and keeps the accounts', has 'no deeds, no creeds, no yogic powers, not even a horn or gourd'. This yogi has 'no healing herbs', 'looks and looks at the juggler's tricks', and such a one makes it to the 'King's land' (LH and SS 66). Further, this yogi is 'solitary'. 'He doesn't go on pilgrimages' or 'to religious fairs' and attends no 'congregations'. He 'doesn't keep fasts', 'doesn't have a travel bag', or 'utensils' or 'plate' or a 'purse'. He 'doesn't rub his body with ash', has no 'alms bowl', and 'ever goes hungry'. Finally, he says:

> You can't meet him
> Says Kabir
> He's left the country
> We're citizens of
> And he's not coming back. (AKM 135)

What brings the two perceptions of Rumi and Kabir closer to each other is their negation of the earthly and their firm belief in the power of the divine. Equally important to note is their ability to create metaphors and symbols that extend the spheres of their spiritual reference and help recognize the ultimate mover. Both in Rumi and Kabir, this divine is defined through a metaphor of the horizon. Rumi says:

> O skeptic who sees nothing in empty space
> Think now of infinity as God's face. (FD 46)

The same metaphoric expression may also be seen in Kabir:

> I offer myself to an image:
> the great being beyond boundaries
> and beyond beyond. (LH and SS 50)

Thinking of the divine power as inalienable, indefinable, and formless, they come to believe in the unity of beings. This philosophy of the ultimate being as one, and only one, is expressed emphatically in both of them. Rumi says:

> The Muslim and the unbeliever share
> This world of joy, this world of shame and care
> Beyond, there is a place without Islam
> Or disbelief—come, let me take you there. (FD 13)

Kabir echoes similar sentiments:

> Turks and Hindus have one way
> The guru's made it clear.
> Don't say Ram, don't say Khuda,
> So says Kabir. (LH and SS 46)

In yet another instance, Rumi reiterates this idea of the unity of beings:

> O Muslim, when you stand in the rank of prayer,
> You are the fabric of all others, indivisible as the air

The Messenger of God has made you as one
You who were divided, son against son. (FD 46)

Kabir comes up with his own logic for the same:

Hindus prefer cremation,
Turks burial.
But in the end, one way or another,
Both have to leave home. (LH and SS 61)

In the spirit of total submission, while Rumi dispenses with the temple and the mosque to 'drown in the divine lust' (FD 111), Kabir confesses that he is 'Ram and Allah's foolish baby' and that Ram and Allah is his 'guru and pir' (LH and SS 74).

These kind of utterances help them problematize both the idea and the receptacle of the idea—known as language.

Rumi says:

A pen is an instrument
it does not know how to write. (FD 42)
Opposites are identical and logic is in vain. (FD 43)
To wear a crown lightly is to be a king. (FD 48)
All kings are only servants to their slaves (FD 101)
So Jalaluddin identify
Yourself as one who says that you are I. (FD 125)

Similar instances are there in Kabir, where he plays both with his idea and his language:

The question that's killing me, says Kabir,
Is whether the pilgrim
Or the pilgrim town is greater? (AKM 131)

Colour is born of colour
I see all colours one,
What colour is a living creature? (LH and SS 92)

What a marvel, seekers:
a corpse ate death. (LH and SS 104)

Where speech was: the syllable.
Where the syllable was: a firm mind.
Speech and silence are the same.
A knower is hard to find. (LH and SS 113)

I'm watching you,
you are watching him.
Kabir says, how to work it out—
I—he—you? (LH and SS 126)

While playing effortlessly with their ideas, they are able to philosophize on the major aspects of life and living in ways that approximate the pithiness of proverbs and sayings.

Rumi says:

And so my friends, to be remade and whole
Prepare to desecrate your very soul. (FD 9)
To be born you must first renounce each breath. (FD 11)
The bird in hand is that one which has flown. (FD 13)
The false draws its sustenance from the true. (FD 123)
To crave the light is to accept the sun. (FD 36)

Kabir also speaks in the same vein:

Life is a sort of guest
you don't meet twice. (LH and SS 90)

Do one thing completely, all is done;
try to do all, you lose the one. (LH and SS 122)

When the guru is blind,
what can the student do? (LH and SS 107)

> Don't display your diamond
> in the vegetable stalls. (LH and SS 109)

> The body is a ship, the mind's a crow
> that flies a million miles. (LH and SS 119)

The realities concerning the seeker and the sought, truth and untruth, rationality and sentimentality, soul and body, temporal and eternal, and the manifold ways of life and living engage their attention invariably in all their verses. Coming from Rumi and Kabir, the two unassuming poets of primeval concerns, these verses read now like sermons, now like sayings, and develop a characteristically Sufi–Bhakti perspective and idiom. They accept monism as the essential article of their personal belief and the divine as formless. Their poetry engages primarily with the dichotomies of life, while developing a discourse on the myriad manifestations of life, death, and eternity. Both Rumi and Kabir have often been read as iconoclasts who interrogate orthodoxies and hierarchies of all kinds, but it may be relevant to note that they seek their individual ways, and that their ways intersect frequently as they point towards the same goal.

Reading and Reception: Myriad Contexts

In discussing the Sufi–Bhakti connotations of their word, critics have often referred to the spontaneity of their verses, their larger appeal among the informed and the uninformed readers and listeners, the adaptability of their verses to music and performance, and quite prominently to their twilight or upside-down language. To extend the Rumi–Kabir scholarship further, it should be possible to argue that their poetry is a mode of developing a discourse on oppositional ideas and aesthetics, where allusions and antithesis, inversions and irony, metaphors and mixed metaphors, paradoxes and pathetic fallacies, and sarcasm and satire play significant roles. Their poetry works through extending the symbols of affiliation and disaffiliation, and by evolving dialogic patterns. It gathers its vitality in the written word, the oral idiom, and the performative gesture. In a larger perspective, their poetry is a discourse on the tropes of orality, language, and performance. It presupposes an addressee who might be a listener, a reader, or a participant-performer. Both Rumi and Kabir evolve and pursue an argument, which is intended essentially to be shared with their addressees. It may be posited further that their poetry is yet another way for them to deny the mundane and the stereotypical, and to assert an independent stance of their own in matters of faith, philosophy, and their verbal execution.

In order to contextualize the above-stated discussion, it may be suggested that the texts of both Rumi and Kabir evolved in a given cultural milieu, and that they sought their strength in the residual capital of their respective locations. As they illustrate the evolution and growth of a spiritual tradition of the Orient, they also identify the evolution and growth of a literary culture. From this perspective, while it is important to mark the Oriental nature of their poetry, it is equally significant to identify the contours of their text and the evolution of their readerships in relation to time and place. In this respect, the texts of Rumi and Kabir may be read as texts of inheritance that draw upon the religio-cultural milieu of their time and place. Extending this logic further, it should also be suggested that while they inherit from their respective traditions, they also hand over the same to the subsequent readership that has preserved it for seven hundred years in the case of Rumi, and five hundred years in the case of Kabir. As such, these texts have their acute contemporary meaning, and they make way for contemporary texts of similar nature or milieu.

With reference to the points made so far, the reading and reception of Rumi and Kabir can be assessed in several contexts. At one level, it is the formation of the text, its mechanics, its language, and its varied tropes that hold our attention, and, at the other, it is the content carried in that language that merits consideration. Though formed in their given places and times, the texts of Rumi and Kabir may be considered to have evolved in and beyond place, time, and the larger contexts of time called history. As they move beyond time and place, they also go beyond the generic constraints and, thus, become a part of broader textual formation, as also the history of their reception.

While considering the essential contents of Rumi and Kabir, it may be suggested that it is the Sufi–Bhakti nature of their teachings that accounts for their larger acceptance over the vast expanses of time and place. Both Sufi and Bhakti, as the two modes of liaison with the divine, have had a great romantic appeal during all times and places, in and beyond the Orient.[22] As liberal interpretations of faith, they have moved beyond the Hindu or the Islamic way of life and established their relevance even in sites dominated by Western faith and philosophy. The relevance of their expression, which I should like to call the Rumi–Kabir *bani*, lies in its universality rather than its particularity, which it emphatically negates. This *bani* holds both on emotion and reason—it infuses ecstasy, approximates music, draws upon action,[23] and remains at best a liberal source of larger mediation among human beings with themselves, as also with the divine.

Endnotes

1. While Rumi lived in the thirteenth century in Persia, Kabir is supposed to have lived in the fifteenth century in India. It is agreed upon that Rumi was born in 1207 and died in 1273, but there is no such agreement in the case of Kabir. The four dates recorded in various critical texts, biographies, and miscellaneous writings vary widely. These are 1338–1448 which means that he lived for 110 years, 1440–1518 which accounts for 78 years, 1398–1518 which comes to 120 years, and 1398–1448 which implies that he lived for 50 years. The variations in dates are wide and they give a lifespan of 50 to 120 years to Kabir. The important point to note is that no authentic reading of Kabir in any given historical time or perspective can be possible except that he has to be read in terms of his poetic output and its larger affiliations with liberal faith and philosophy.
2. With reference to Rumi, some of the more prominent critical works and translations that may be referred to include those by R.A. Nicholson (*The Mystics of Islam*, 1914), A.J. Arberry (*Classical Persian Literature*, 1958), Annemarie Schimmel (*The Triumphal Sun: A Study of the Works of Jalaloddin Rumi*, 1978), William C. Chittick (*The Sufi Path of Love: The Spiritual Teachings of Rumi*, 1984), Coleman Barks (*The Essential Rumi*, 1995), Fatemeh Keshavarz (*Reading Mystical Lyric: The Case of Jalal al-Din Rumi*, 1998), and Kabir Helminski (ed.) (*The Rumi Collection*, 1998). For Kabir, reference may be made to works by G.H. Westcott (*Kabir and the Kabir Panth*, 1907), David N. Lorenzen (*Kabir Legends and Ananta-Das's Kabir Parachai*, 1991), Winand M. Callewaert, Swapna Sharma, and

Dieter Taillieu (*The Millennium Kabir Vani,* 2000), Linda Hess and Sukhdev Singh (trans.) (*The Bijak of Kabir*, 2001), Vinay Dharwadker (Kabir: *The Weaver's Songs,* 2003), Charlotte Vaudeville (*A Weaver Named Kabir,* 1993), Robert Bly (*Kabir: Ecstatic Poems,* 1976), and David Masterman (*Kabir Says,* 2011).

3. Associated with Islamic mysticism, Sufism is an institution of spiritualist devotion practised by a sect of Muslim devotees who follow the path of abstinence and strive to establish a direct rapport with the Almighty. There are several kinds of Sufi orders or Sufis. While some of the Sufis follow the prescribed tenets of Islam, others choose to disengage from the constraints of the organized faith and roam like dervishes in the eternal quest for truth.
4. Associated with Hinduism, bhakti is another institution analogous to Sufism and is suitably studied together with Islamic mysticism to mark the similarities and differences between them. It underlines devoted or engrossed action by the spiritually charged individuals. Bhaktas, who practice bhakti, are divinely ordained and develop, like the Sufis, their own manners of developing a liaison with the divine power.
5. Shariat refers to the revealed laws, statutes, ordinances, or practices that determine the religious practices of the faithful and regulate their actions and responses in everyday life. This prepares the sinful mortals for rewards on the day of judgement and the life hereafter.
6. Tariqat refers to the ways, manners, and modes of Islamic religious behaviour. The faithful practice the defined rules that relate to right observances, and it is with following the defined tariqa that the practising men and women fashion their lives and seek divine blessings.
7. *Saguna*, in the Hindu view of life, implies positive attributes that qualify a believer. Such believers embody personal properties and qualities, which define them as virtuous beings and help them live a life of proper form and right values.
8. *Nirguna,* unlike *saguna,* refers to a condition devoid of all qualities and properties. It is a state of void, a kind of worthlessness, which is caused by the loss of all positive attributes that helps man to deserve being a man.
9. *Shabda* (also *shabad*) has multiple implications. Literally, it stands for a word, but it also refers to the science of words. A word, or a *shabda,* in combination with another word acquires a halo of meaning and is manifested through various kinds of sounds, songs, hymns, or verbal communication. It has a deep spiritual implication where *shabda* becomes the medium to communicate with the divine.
10. *Sahaja* refers to an expression, action, or feeling that is essentially facile. It is a state of ease, softness, assimilation, and larger human catholicity that brings about a state of calmness and composure.

11. Pir or murshid in Islamic tradition is the spiritual master, a pathfinder for the *mureed* or disciple. He is a holy man, a saint, and a guide who initiates his disciple on the right path and blesses him.
12. Guru is basically a mentor of his *shishya* or disciple. He can be a mentor or a teacher of worldly knowledge and wisdom and also be a spiritual master like a pir. Kabir attributes greater power to the guru when he says: *Guru Govind dono khadey kakey lagoon paaye/Balihaari guru aap ne jin Govind diyo bataaye* (My Teacher and my God are both in front of me/Whose feet shall I touch first?/My sacrifice to you my teacher if you told/Which God's feet I shall touch first?).
13. Ram represents a number of meanings. It stand for the beauteous, the charming, and the delightful, as also for the mythological figures being the incarnations of Vishnu, namely Parashurama, Ramachandra, and Balaram. The hero of the epic poem *Ramayana,* Ram is a religious, social, and cultural symbol representing truth, virtue, power, bravery, kindness, and similar other attributes without end. Interestingly, Rahim, meaning the kind and the merciful, is one of the ninety names of Allah, each one representing an attribute. Ram–Rahim has thus come to stay on as a common refrain for the divine, who keeps and sustains humanity with kindness.
14. Shams-i-Tabrizi (1185–1248) was Rumi's spiritual master, his pir. He was a wanderer and a mendicant of profound spiritual vision. There are several stories about their encounter with each other. Rumi's indebtedness to him was so immense that he named his *diwan* (poetry) after him, *Diwan-e Shams-e Tabrizi.*
15. Ramananda (1300–1411) revived the philosophy propounded by Ramanuja (1017–1137), who strove to rid Brahminism of orthodoxy. Kabir found a spiritual ally in him, who also wanted to lend his ears to the call of the heart than of intellect. The story of how Kabir met Ramananda is one of spiritual romance of a seeker for the guru.
16. The Sufi order established in Konya is also known as the order of Whirling Dervishes, who seek a condition of proximity with God through whirling dance attuned to a certain kind of music. The Mevlevi Order is now spread over in other parts of the world like the US and the UK.
17. It is a community of those who believe in bhakti, unity of faith, and salvation through good deeds. This, too, has travelled beyond finding its followers in African and South Asian countries, apart from UK, US, Canada, and Australia.
18. Rumi's *Fihi Ma Fihi* ('It Is What It Is' or 'In It What Is in It'), *Majalis-e Sab'a* ('Seven Sessions of Discourses'), and *Makatib* (*Maktubat al-Rabbani*) ('Letters') are his non-poetical works where he developed religio-philosophical discourses on human life and letters, as well as on faith and spirituality.
19. Unlike Rumi, Kabir was unlettered, had no formal education, grew up entirely on his own, and also engaged himself in vocations for his livelihood. His spiritual awareness, however, distinguished him from others, and he came to compose verses that drew people around him.

20. Rumi's *Mathnawi*, a poem of epic scale, was composed in chaste Persian which earned him a place of pride in the canon of Persian poetry. His other important work in verse is *Diwan-e Shams-e Tabrizi*, which is a collection of spiritual odes and is named after his pir Shams-i-Tabrizi.
21. Kabir's works have been recorded and preserved variously. The more important of them include *Kabir Granthavali* (1961) by Parasnath Tiwari, *Kabir Granthavali* (1969) by Mata Prasad Gupta, *Kabir Vangmaya* (1981) by Jaydev Singh and Vasudev Singh, and *The Millenium Kabir Vani: A Collection of Pad-s* (2000) by Winand M. Callewaert *et al.*
22. Both Rumi and Kabir have reached out to a larger readership in various languages of the world. The translations of their work in English have been done by several hands. See note 2 earlier.
23. Rumi has been represented by musicians in concerts, whirling dervishes in theatres and open spaces, and skilful readers in recitations. In recent times, he has made it to the list of Billboard's top 20 and has been performed by Madonna, Goldie Hawn, Philip Glass, and Demi Moore. With reference to Kabir, mention may be made of the huge Kabir Project that represents him in myriad ways through films, recitations, performances, music, etc.

References

Dhondy, Farrukh, trans. 2011. *Rumi: A New Translation.* New Delhi: Harper Perennial (referred to as FD).

Hess, Linda and Sukhdev Singh, trans. 2001. *The Bijak of Kabir.* New Delhi: Motilal Banarsidass Publishers (referred to as LH and SS).

Iqbal, Afzal. 1991. The *Life and Work of Jalaluddin Rumi* (sixth edition). Islamabad: Pakistan National Council of the Arts.

Kidwai, Sadiq-ur-Rahman. 2002. 'Kabir and Mystic Poetry in Urdu.' In *Images of Kabir*, ed. Horstmann, Monika. New Delhi: Manohar.

Mehrotra, Arvind Krishna, trans. 2011. *Songs of Kabir.* Delhi: Hachette (referred to as AKM).

Nicholson, Reynold A., trans. and ed. 1898. *Selected Poems from the Divani Shamsi Tabriz.* Cambridge: Cambridge University Press (referred to as RAN).

Love Songs to the Divine: Sufi Music in India and Pakistan

Sufi Music: Form, Function, and Nature

Music marks the nature of a people and bears the rhythm of their lives. It characterizes them by the modes of their living and determines their location in a culture. Sufi music in the Indian subcontinent, which has had its origin in the deep classical past of which the dates are difficult to ascertain, has developed over ages into various forms and genres. It has grown and flourished in different gharanas, or schools of music, from the classical to modernist and postmodernist styles of composition and performance. Of the various kinds of music, one of the most popular in India and Pakistan has been the Sufi music. Arguably, these two locations that closely bear upon one another for reasons of cultural proximity have developed their own styles, representing similarities and differences in sensibilities and oral-aural systems. As Sufi music, by its nature, has a deep cleansing and therapeutic effect on the listeners, it has found its ways in regions, dialects, and languages across a remarkably huge sociocultural matrix. It has been practised with greater resilience in the past and the present times than studied for its meaning and comparative worth. Let us examine the essential marks of Sufi music with respect to its form and function, its composers and consumers, as also its sites of performance, to underline how, in spite of the fading glory of the classical languages and styles of music, it stays on in the contemporary linguistic and musical framework and prospers as a significant art form.

We are all in the midst of music, all our lives, from birth to death.[1] We may not notice, but it makes a certain difference to our personal and communal lives, although none of us are sure of the extent of our sensitivity to its nuances. Music resides in the air; it has no physical form and connects universally. In a given vocal form, it speaks through a language, caters to a people, marks a culture, and carries a message. In one of its most powerful expressions, it creates a condition for an individual's relationship with the divine. It is in this domain of the human hankering for the spiritual that we have a variety known as 'Sufi music,' different from all other kinds of religious music.[2] It broadly refers to a special kind of music rooted in the traditions of the East, more especially of the Arab world, Persia, Turkey, India, and Pakistan. It uses language as gesture and gesture as language, the two primordial modes of expression, to offer obeisance, sing praise, seek grace, and perish in a state of rewarding nothingness.

In its essential nature, Sufi music varies from being an impassioned speech to an inspired imploring addressed to the divine. Essentially secular in its spirit, it shuns all differences between different faiths and their followers, even to the extent of embracing all orders[3] and sects[4] within the Islamic structure of faith, which it seemingly aspires to represent. It is liberal in its approach to reality and existential in its apprehension of truth. It addresses issues related to *baqaa* (existence) and *fanaa* (annihilation) by controlling the *nafs* (self) and indulging in *zikr* (remembrance). In its character, Sufi music is gnostic as it shuns the material and embraces the spiritual; in its method and make-up, it is ontological insofar as it explores the nature of being and nothingness; in its apprehension, it is ascetic because it shows preference for an unassuming way of life. It leads to a moment of epiphany[5] as it engages with the semiology of faith, its signs and symbols, marks and metaphors, and hermeneutics of belief in relation to an elemental approach to the words of religio-philosophical intent. Interestingly enough, it develops its own frames of reference as it explores spiritualist hankering through the ambiguous symbolism of love and wine. In such a rendering, the physicality of love and wine is transcended and they become the source of reaching the divine in a state of rare ecstasy.

Sufi music functions variously and at various levels. In one of its essential roles, it is ameliorative and therapeutic as it restores the individuals and strengthens them to face the existential angst. At a broader level, it helps evolve a syncretic tradition as it obliterates all distinctions between human beings and their spiritual practices. While it performs at personal and communal levels, it negotiates between word and image, sound and message, singer and performer, and listener and onlooker. In doing this, it represents a social milieu, as much as it signifies a cultural and spiritual condition. In this respect, Sufi music incorporates multiple texts of faith, literature, culture, and performance into one. In its larger role, it interrogates the established agencies of power and communities, languages and texts, traditions and sects, faiths and beliefs, and regions and people. Representing the religio-philosophical cultures of the East, it emerges as a fine blend of medium and message.

Like its roles that are various, the forms and genres of Sufi music are multifarious too. It is conceived and performed as *hamd* (the praise of God), or as *na'at* (the praise of the last prophet of Islam), or as *manqabat* (the praise of the prophet's companions), or as expression of reverence to the pir (the spiritual master), or as mystical representations in various states of reverence and rapture. All these are rendered in various styles of qawwali and folk music, popular compositions and film lyrics, combining divergent traditions of the local and lesser-known modes of musical expressions. Qawwali, being one of its major modes of expression, has come to stay on as a site where a rich variety of subjects become the matters of concern. Regula B. Qureshi, a scholar of Urdu and Hindi language, writes:

> Indeed, issues of spiritual and socio-economic priority, of dominance and submission, of hierarchical order and individual assertion, of conformity and creativity, are being negotiated audibly, in the language of music, throughout a Qawwali performance....The Qawwal 'speaks' musically not only for himself, but for all his listeners, articulating, in structure and dynamic, the multiplicity of relationships between all participants including himself. (231)

Many of these qawwalis are rendered in a classical style by properly trained qawwals, both in India and Pakistan. In his book *Pakistani Culture: A Profile*

(1992), M. Yusuf Abbasi pertinently remarks in his chapter on 'Pakistani Music' that the 'classical discipline of Pakistani music is a continuation of the Indo-Muslim musical tradition which evolved as a result of the centuries of Hindu-Muslim cultural inter-action' (362). The Sufi singers in both the locations belong to different gharanas, or schools, and sing in various genres among which the qawwali, kaafi, and ghazal stand out as the most prominent ones.

A major question that relates all art forms, as it does the Sufi music much more pertinently, is the question as to who is the addressee of this special kind of rapturous singing. To answer, it must be posited that Sufi music has multiple addressees. At the primary level, it is addressed to God, the last prophet, and also the pir, or the spiritual master; but it addresses several others as well, like the spiritually inclined, the morally stricken, and the emotionally ravaged. Equally important is the fact that it is an address to one's own self, that is, when the poet imparts words to his feelings, he addresses his own self before he addresses others, just as the musician who sets the poet's words to music sings first to himself before he reaches out to an audience. Thus, the Sufi music addresses the egalitarian and the elitist, the philistine and the philosopher, and the anguished and the afflicted. The intention in all the cases is to soothe and to seek, to redress and to rejuvenate the addressees, irrespective of their social, political, cultural, and religious affiliations.

Sufi music is also distinguishable for its amenability to performance along with singing. This may be testified by watching it at the sites of its performance and by ascertaining how it gains in strength in the company of those sitting around to see it sung and performed. It may be appreciated that the Sufi *kalaam*, or poetry, acquires remarkable power once it is brought to music and supplemented by the singers' gestures to reach out to an audience. In this process, the message created and the image invoked coalesce together to create a condition of appeal and acceptance. It has been sung and performed by trained musicians in classical and modernist styles, as also by the spiritually charged dervishes, wandering fakirs, liberal mystics, as well as the common man. The sites of its performance also vary immensely from Sufi shrines to folk festivals, popular musical soirees to high-profile concerts, and from films to open spaces like the streets, marketplaces, and such other sites of common congregation.

Sufi Music: Poets, Performers, and Audience

Sufi music may be appreciated in a triangular relationship of the poets, performers, and audience. While the performers and the audience remain in the foreground, the poet who provides the staple word, or the *kalam*, most often goes unnoticed. It is essentially because the performer creates a condition of music, which sways the audience and gives them an occasion to relate with that condition naturally, spontaneously, and urgently. However, the significance of the *kalaam* may not ever be relegated to the background, even though the performers and the audience occupy the foreground. It would be pertinent to mention here that a very respectable amount of the finest Sufi *kalaam* is available to us in some of the major Eastern languages like Arabic, Persian, Turkish, Urdu, and Punjabi. While many compositions are by canonical poets in these languages, there are works that remain of unknown authorship and have been handed down through generations as poetic aphorisms of a larger human appeal. We have the Sufi *kalaam* of the highest order coming down to us from widely acknowledged poets of the past since the ninth century. Mansur Al-Hallaj (858–922), Muhyiddin Ibn 'Arabi (1165–1240), and Umar Ibn al-Farid (1181–1235) created their masterpieces in Arabic; as Sanai Ghaznavi (1080–1131), Fariduddin Attar (1145–1220), Jalaluddin Rumi (1207–1273), Saadi Shirazi (1210–1291), Mahmud Shabistari (1288–1340), and Hafiz Shirazi (1325/26–1389/90) did in Persian; and Ahmed Yesevi (1093–1166) and Yunus Emre (1240–1321) in Turkish. In India, we have works from Amir Khusrau (1253–1325) who wrote in a mixed dialect, Bulleh Shah (1680–1757), and Khwaja Ghulam Farid (1845–1901) who wrote in Punjabi. While Sufi *kalaam* has been traditionally sung at mausoleums, in the modern age it has found new sites in urban centres where it is performed for the elite audience in private and public spaces. At all the sites, the performers, rather than the poets, earn greater applause from the audience for the obvious reason that they establish an immediate rapport with them. The performers combine the poet's message with their method, as they bring their classical style to bear upon the semi-classical, the semi-classical upon the romantic, and the romantic upon the modernist pop rock. Such works are now available for listening and viewing in CDs, DVDs, films, and documentaries.

While discussing Sufi music in India and Pakistan, it would be pertinent to qualify that even though there are variations in the styles of singing, owing to the impact of linguistic variations and their intermixing in the two locations, the spirit of Sufi singing remains the same at both the locations. M. Yusuf Abbasi comments on this aspect:

> How is it that the same music is called Indian music in India and is styled as Pakistani music in Pakistan, ask some people. Most of the objections are raised by foreigners. However there is no dearth of people in India who deny the existence of Pakistani music as they tend to minimise the Muslim contribution to music. This is a complex question which is rooted not only in history but in political attitudes. (359)

While he discusses this aspect in some detail, he also says that, 'Pakistani culture is a new concept as the country itself' (i) and further that the 'starting point of history of Pakistani culture, necessarily has to be the date of Pakistan's independence' (vii), and also that 'Pakistan's culture is older than Pakistan' (1) which implies that what is considered as Pakistani culture has had its origins in the Indian culture spread over centuries in the past. In sum, it may appropriately be posited that both the cultures have their points of intersection, which is as evident in Sufi music as it is in other aspects of the two cultures.

Keeping this in mind, when one considers the case of singer-performers in India and Pakistan whose works are available in their albums, one is struck by a swarming number of them who have authenticated Sufi music in various genres like the qawwali[6], and the popular numbers created for films and music bands.[7] Some specific examples will make the point. A number of Pakistani compositions like *Tu maane ya na maane* (Whether you believe or you don't) by Wadali Brothers, *Yaar ko humne jaa ba jaa dekha* (I saw my love wherever I looked) by Abida Parveen, *Aafreen aafreen* (Praise be to you) by Nusrat Fateh Ali Khan, *Taajdar-e Haram, ho nigaah-e karam* (O, the prince of Harem, be kind to me) by Sabri Brothers, *Allah hi jane kaun bashar hai* (Only God knows who this creature is) by Aziz Mian, and *Allahu Allahu* (O God, my God) by Rahat Fateh Ali Khan, just to pick a few from a huge mass of examples, represent the major concerns of the seekers for God's grace. These are marked by non-linear articulation of sentiments with creative interpolations to dramatize and take the cadence to climax. Equally haunting numbers from the Indian performers balance the great tradition of Sufi singing in Pakistan. *Khwaja mere Khwaja* (O Khwaja, my Khwaja) by A.R. Rahman, *Mere haal da mehram tu* (You know my state of being) by Jaswinder Singh, *Khuda wahi hai* (He alone is God) by Kavita Seth, *Munh apna jo tune dikhaya mujhe* (When you showed me your face) by Zila Khan, and *Shah-e mardaan* (The bravest of the brave) by Dhruv Sangari represent various other facets of spiritual hankering and fulfilment. Certain questions concerning one's own identity, the image of God as the beloved, the pains of separation, and the craving for union mark these compositions generally. These issues, in turn, constitute the spirit of Sufi *kalaam.*

There are some all-time favourite Sufi songs that have been repeatedly performed by some of the most celebrated singers. *Chhap tilak sab chheeni re mose naina milai ke* (Your glance has robbed me of my looks, my identity) has been rendered, one after another, by Sabri Brothers, Nusrat Fateh Ali Khan, Abida Parveen, Shujaat Husain Khan, Kavita Seth, Richa Sharma, Dhruv Sangari, and Kailash Kher with clear variations in crescendo and stress. Similarly, another well-known composition *Man kunto maula* (Whoever accepts me as a master) has been rendered by Sabri Brothers, Nusrat Fateh Ali Khan, Abida Parveen, Aziz Mian, Zila Khan, and Atif Aslam, who bring their individual talent to emphasize the different notes in different orders and create a different impact each time. Similarly, another all-time favourite *Damaa dam mast qalandar* (O, the red-robed, God-intoxicated being) has been worked upon by Noor Jahan, Wadali Brothers, Nusrat Fateh Ali Khan, Reshma, Runa Laila, and Abida Parveen to create varying moods of ecstasy and ultimate assimilation into a higher being. They are characterized by alternate accents and balance. Yet another preferred number, *Bulla ki jaana main kaun* (Who knows who I am) has been done by Wadali Brothers, Rabbi Shergill, and Harshdeep Kaur with remarkable tonal modulations of high and low pitch with which they charge the primal refrain to pose an eternal question regarding one's identity. Apart from these, one of the most remarkable musicians to make his mark in Sufi singing, A.R. Rahman, has carved a space for Sufi *kalaam* in and outside the films. His creations *Khwaja mere khwaja* (Master, my master), *Arziyan* (Supplications), and *Piya Haji Ali* (My love, Haji Ali) in films like *Jodhaa Akbar, Delhi-6*, and *Fiza* respectively, and his other much more charged numbers like *Kun faya kun* (Let there be, and there it was), *Marhaba ya mustafa* (Welcome, my prophet), and *Zikr* (Remembrance) create a definite niche for him in conceiving and composing Sufi music of an unprecedented kind. Rahman's music is marked by sonorous articulation of words with adequate cadence and pauses in rendition. In the recent years, Sufi music has found a special place in popular films. Some of these like *Sajdaa* (Prostration) in *My Name is Khan, Ali Maula* (Ali, my master) in *Kurbaan, Haan reham, haan reham* (Mercy, yes mercy) in *Aamir, Aaya tere dar par* (I stand at your door) in *Veer-Zaara*, and *Maula mere le le meri jaan* (Lord, take my life) in *Chak De! India* bring this genre to common people and create a condition for the acceptance of this category of songs. As they do this, they also broaden the scope of film songs and styles of singing.

The development of Sufi music in India and Pakistan underscores the validity of this genre and the conditions for its natural reception in both the countries. As the genre has matured in both the sites, it has also emerged as the repository of their broad cultural markers. Furthermore, this music has eminently borne out the similarities and differences in the very nature of the two peoples. No less important is the fact that Sufi music in both the sites has drawn upon the local traditions of music in order to create new tones of voice. With these, the two places eminently qualify to be studied for their individual merits with respect to their regional, cultural, and linguistic variation. While one may profitably study the two regions and their traditions for these reasons, one may also mark how this music can make way for breaking the barriers and getting the two peoples together with their individual sociocultural and political affiliations. It may help compose, in this process, a kaleidoscope of enormous linguistic and cultural variety. Sufi music is the panacea, the most appropriate medium, mode, and manner to reach this end.

Endnotes

1. It welcomes the newborn and bids farewell to the dead. As long as one lives, music keeps company. Imagine being in a variety of situations and places like a patient in a hospital, a passenger in a train, a customer in a mall, a guest in a party, or a phone caller in waiting, or one driving a vehicle, music is perennially present with us in all these and umpteen other situations.
2. To illustrate the point, mention may be made here of some of the major religions of the world and their music like the bhajan and kirtan of Hindu music; mass, carol, and hymnody of Christian music; piyyut, *zemirot, nigun, pizmonim*, and *baqashot* of Jewish music; and chanting and *honkyoku* of the Buddhist music.
3. This refers to the four major Islamic Sufi orders found in South Asia: Naqshbandi, Qadri, Chishti, and Suharwardi. Naqshbandi order is named after Bahauddin Naqshband Bukhari (1318–1389), Qadri is named after Abdul Qadir Jilani (1077–1166), Chishti is named after Khwaja Moinuddin Chishti (1142–1236), and Suharwardi is named after Shahabuddin Suhrawardi (1154–1191).
4. For example, the Shia and Sunni sects, being the major ones. Also, there are schools of jurisprudence and theology, apart from several movements and branches of faith.
5. Sufi singers, in a state of rapture, pass into a state of trance and lead the listeners to a similar condition. There is a culture of listening to music known as *sama*, which applies to Sufi music more appropriately than other forms of music. For *sama* and related concepts in Islamic order, see Arthur Gribetz, 'The Sama Controversy: Sufi vs Legalist,' in *Sufism: Critical Concepts in Islamic Studies*, Vol III, ed. Lloyd Ridgeon (London and New York: Routledge, 2008), pp. 1–17.
6. For a detailed account of qawwali, see Regula Burckhardt Qureshi, *Sufi Music of India and Pakistan: Sound, Context and Meaning in Qawwali* (Cambridge: Cambridge University Press, 1986).
7. Some of the finest specimens of Sufiana qawwali from Pakistan come from the Sabri Brothers, Nusrat Fateh Ali Khan, Rahat Fateh Ali Khan, Shafqat Amanat Ali Khan, Aziz Mian, and a host of others. The Sufiana folk is remarkably rendered

by Abida Parveen, Alam Lohar, Arif Lohar, Farida Khanum, Wadali Brothers, and several others. While in Atif Aslam, Adnan Sami, Ali Haider, Ali Zafar, Sajjad Ali, Bilal Saeed, Ali Azmat, and Javed Bashir, to name a few, we have the important practitioners of Sufiana *kalam* in film and popular media, there are music bands like Noori and Junoon that have imparted an entirely new form for greater popular consumption in pop and rock style. In India, we have another host of Sufiana *kalam* singer-performers like Zila Khan, Harshdeep Kaur, Kavita Seth, Rabbi Shergill, A.R. Rahman, and Dhruv Sangari, who sing in classical and semi-classical styles, and others like Kailash Kher who sings in more popular styles for a larger section of listeners.

References

Books

Abbasi, M. Yusuf. 1992. *Pakistani Culture: A Profile*. Islamabad: National Institute of Historical and Cultural Research.

Qureshi, Regula Burckhardt. 1986. *Sufi Music of India and Pakistan: Sound, Context and Meaning in Qawwali*. Cambridge: Cambridge University Press.

Films

Amin, Shimit (Director). 2007. *Chak De! India*. Yash Raj Films.

Chopra, Yash (Director). 2004. *Veer-Zaara*. Yash Raj Films.

D'Silva, Rensil (Director). 2009. *Kurbaan*. UTV Motion Pictures.

Gowariker, Ashutosh (Director). 2008. *Jodhaa Akbar*. UTV Motion Pictures.

Gupta, Raj Kumar (Director). 2008. *Aamir*. UTV Motion Pictures.

Johar, Karan (Director). 2010. *My Name is Khan*. 20th Century Fox.

Mehra, Rakeysh Omprakash (Director). 2009. *Delhi-6*. UTV Motion Pictures.

Mohamed, Khalid (Director). 2000. *Fiza*. UTV Motion Pictures.

When Black Clouds Hang: Rethinking *Kajri*

A Folklorist Interlude

Every culture is characterized by the rhythm of its spoken and written word as also its physical and emotional gestures. These words and gestures ultimately define the nature of a culture and determine its place in the larger matrix of national culture(s). The folk constitutes a major part of the larger cultural manifestations; it opens a way to develop a view on a particular cultural expression, which might have lost much of its resilience, yet remains a significant marker of a culture in a state of constant flux. A.K. Ramanujan has drawn upon the various facets of the rich folklorist tradition in general, which provides us a way to approach *kajri* for all its individual merit expressed through words and gestures:

> Anyone studying the culture of India needs to study not only its written classics but its oral traditions, of which folklore is an important part. Folklore pervades childhoods, families, and communities as the symbolic language of thee nonliterate parts of the people and the culture....Verbal folklore, in the sense of a largely oral tradition with specific genres (such as proverb, riddle, lullaby, tale, ballad, prose narrative, song), nonverbal modes (such as dances, games, floor or wall designs, artefacts from toys to outdoor clay horses in villages) and composite performing arts (such as street magic and street theatre, which combine prose, verse, song, dance, various local objects, costume, etc.)—all of these expressive folk forms weave in and out of every aspect of city, village, and small town life. (xiii)

Ramanujan's reference to verbal, non-verbal, and composite performing arts can be quite appropriately developed as major points of reference to study *kajri* as a folk text and folk performance. Before I do that, let me relate an episode in which a charismatic musician, Ustad Bismillah Khan, made a frank and justifiably fair statement in a musical soiree in Jammu.[1] He said: '*Aap ko achha lagey ya nahin ... hum to kajri bajayengey....*' (Whether you like it or not, I will play *kajri*...). He was enamoured by the beauty of the valley and wanted to play the various tunes of nature. He thus chose *kajri* as one of his offerings to the charmed audience, completely undeterred by the fact that the acoustics of the hall were poor.

In order to justify why a reputed musician was enamoured by this art form, let me briefly introduce *kajri* as a verbal and performance text. *Kajri* is played, staged, or sung when black clouds, announcing the rains, literally hang in the sky. When the ustad chose to play, there were no such clouds. He probably wished to make a metaphoric statement to suggest that we all live in times of great anguish and need soothing. Today, even though black clouds hover all over and we exist in various states of uneasiness, we have little hope that we shall get the redeeming rains. The ustad's offering may, thus, be taken as a folklorist interlude of hope, faith, and redemption that his music might bring to listeners.

Music has a healing touch. The same is true of literature. The two may sometimes join together to reinforce the modes of human expression, both through words and performance, and become a source of deliverance. The folk forms of tales, fables, legends, myths, sagas, songs, or even proverbs and riddles have long been known to have the capacity to rejuvenate human beings. We relate to folk arts rather naturally, as they represent our history, memory, and myth, both in direct and imaginative/creative terms. While they do so, they also allow us to connect with our environs and ourselves. In this process, they help us live, imagine, and dream, and seek roots in our race and culture. They reaffirm our identity and provide opportunities to extend ourselves beyond time and space. Folk arts and forms also call the past to bear upon the present and make the two points of time mutually relevant. They offer us with a principle of sustenance that proves vital in how they operate upon us and impart meaning to our existence.

The inimitable players and singers like Ustad Bismillah Khan and Begum Akhtar have rendered *kajri* in such a way that it has acquired the potential of being a major point of reference in culture studies. When Begum Akhtar sang *Chha rahi kari ghata...* (The black clouds are gathering...) in the 1930s, she did so in a manner that was more spontaneous and less embellished. However, when she sang the same *kajri* in the mid 60s for All India Radio, it was quite artfully conceived and proficiently delivered. The two renditions of the same *kajri* represent two modes of artistic apprehension—one marked by immediacy and the other by deliberation. While the tonal and musical impact of the two renditions differed greatly, they remained united in one way: they represented the essential pathos associated with the plight of the sufferer in a particular season of the year.

Many classical, semi-classical, and popular musicians and singers have found their appropriate medium in *kajri*. This has been happening over a long period of time. In its classical rendition, it may be set, for example, to a play of *keharwa* (eight beats) and other styles. It may also be sung in Misra Piloo, which is a light raga. *Kehana va Madho* by Mala Ramadorai is an example of this. Even though a large number of *kajri*s have been lost forever (because they were not recorded and lived only in the memories of the singers), the institution has not been dead altogether. They have existed in a variety of languages and dialects, composed on a variety of themes, and sung in innumerable styles. In all these manifestations, *kajri* has provided an emotionally fulfilling and aesthetically sound interlude in the humdrum existence of human beings. Other folk songs like *chaitri* (*chaita*, *chaiti*), *sohar*, and *malhar*, sung by men and women, and the fine satirical comedies of the *bhaands*[2] also provide similar interludes and supplementary source of emotional sustenance.

Kajri: Origin, Form, and Value

There are various views about the origins of *kajri*. According to a popular belief, *kajri* had its origin in the black clouds of Sawan, which has a stock symbolic significance with respect to love and longing. The days of scorching heat that gave birth to *chaitri* look forward to the arrival of black clouds and rains. These clouds and rains raise the songs of love and longing in what we know as *kajri*. Traditionally, it is a folk song composed and sung in the regions of eastern Uttar Pradesh, Bihar, and in parts of Rajasthan on the eve of Teej[3] of Shravan Shukla Paksha.

As a folktale of Mirzapur (the home of this song) would have it, *kajri* had its origin in the story of a woman called Kajli, whose husband had gone to a far-off land. Even when monsoon arrived and her love did not return, her suffering grew unbearable. She wept at the feet of Goddess Kajmal and her imploring turned into pathetic songs known as *kajri*. The story sounds familiar. There are many such tales in the literatures of the East and the West, but this one goes so well with the story of *kajri*.

Bhartendu Harishchandra, one of the greatest Hindi writers of modern India, has enumerated three sources of *kajri*.[4] *First*, he has related it to the death of King Dadu Rai of central India and the sati of his widow queen, Nagmati. These two tragedies brought immeasurable pain to the people of the kingdom. They, thereafter, evolved a new form of expressing their woes in a song that came to be known as *kajri*. *Second*, he has related *kajri* to the beautiful wild forests in the kingdom of Dadu Rai. The forests were called Kajli, and the songs, named after them, later came to be known as *kajri*. *Third*, he has proposed that the songs sung on the eve of Teej in the months of Sawan and Bhadon were known as *kajli* or *kajri*. The given explanations often bring the two expressions *kajli* and *kajri* together. It could be proposed that many of the expressions in the regions of eastern Uttar Pradesh and Bihar replace 'i' with 'r' as they fit well with the spoken dialect of the people in these regions. As such, *kali badli* (black cloud) is often spoken or sung as *kari badariya* and *kajal* as *kajar*, etc. It is only natural, therefore, that *kajli* was called *kajri*.

The origin and development of *kajri* as a folk art form is almost impossible to ascertain, as it has mostly been a manifestation of impassioned speech, an oral art *par excellence*. The composers were neither self-proclaimed poets, nor were they otherwise acknowledged as such to form a possible part of any literary history. Hardly aware of the remarkable literary feat that these composers (better called poets) were achieving, they did not make any conscious effort to write or preserve their creations. They did not also consciously follow the norms of poetic composition, yet their *kajri*s emerged as fine creations of remarkable literary worth. As it kept emerging and consolidating as an independent folk genre, it posed several important questions, hitherto unattended, regarding spontaneity in verbal expression, vigour, and vitality of the spoken lexicon, cultural roots, musicality, drama, and community entertainment.

*Kajri*s may be read as eminent examples of secular poetry rooted in history, culture, region, spirituality, and patriotism. Apart from other constituents, nature and woman remain at the centre of this composition. *Kajri* is an emotional and dramatic representation of village life. It spells out the longings and despairs of a community of people enjoying close emotional bondage. *Kajri* represents an individual history as forcefully as it does the history and geography of a people, its sociology, and its philosophy of existence. *Kajri*s may also be read as the dream indices of the village men and women living their lives passionately and in an environment of their own. They spell out the beat of life, its internal rhythm, and association with the lives around. *Kajri* has had various forms since its origin at some point of time in the past and has passed through several variations in techniques of composition and styles of rendition. They may best be read as written or recorded songs for their broad rhetorical and prosodic, cultural and historical, philosophical and religious significance, and also as a text in performance with adequate emphasis on the principles of presentation like *tek udan* (techniques that singers use to create impact as they sing), off-and-on stage presentation, and community participation. There are regional variations in the styles of singing that may clearly be noticed in the way *kajri*s are sung in Ramnagar (Kashi) and Mirzapur. In this respect, *kajri*s may also be read as manifestations of the tones and tunes characteristic of a community of people living in two areas of the same region.

While Ramnagar has been the home of Ramlila, Mirzapur has been the home of *kajri*: *Leela Ramnagar ki bhari/Kajri Mirzapur sarnam/sardar*

(Ramnagar excels in Ramlila, Mirzapur in *kajri*). Sometimes, it holds close to *jhoola*, another form of folk devotion to Radha and Krishna: *Jhoola lagal kadam ki dari/ Jhoolein Krishna Murari na/ Radha jhoolein Kanha jhulawein/ Kanha jhoolein Radha jhulawein, Pari-pari na* (There is a swing on the *kadam* branches/Krishna enjoys swinging/Both Krishna and Radha swing each other/one by one). As men and women sit in swing in the month of Sawan and sing *kajri*, so are the gods made to sit in a swing and listen to *kajri* sung in great devotion and delight. *Kajri* and *jhoola*, therefore, appear to be holding close to each other, as both represent facets of romantic love and also complement the acts of singing and listening.

As a typical example of a folk song sung in Sawan, a *kajri* by the prominent Hindi poet Badrinarayan Chaudhary Premghan[5], as quoted by Abdul Bismillah in *Lok Kavya Vidha: Kajri*[6], is produced here as follows:

Rimjhim rimjhim barsey re badariya
More chadariya bhiji jai.
Kahan jai ab hai bachaun mein
Daiyya jiya ghabrai.
Lai chhata tar chhati se lagi
Preeti reet barsai.
Priya Premghan Paiyan lagaun
Begi bachawa aiye. (13)

The clouds send drizzles; my sheet is drenched
Where shall I hide myself; I'm wet, I'm scared
He drew me close under the umbrella
He embraced; he showered his love
Dear Premghan! I must touch his feet
How soon he appeared to save me from distress.[7]

At Home in Mirzapur

Ever since Kajli sang her song of separation at the feet of Goddess Kajmal in the folk tale mentioned earlier, Mirzapur, a small town in eastern Uttar Pradesh, has been the real home of *kajri*. It has become synonymous with the place and is more than a folk song for its people; it is Mirzapur's culture icon. Many of the landmarks here, including a pond, have been named after *kajri*. On the occasion of Naga Panchami, women bathe in this pond every year and come back home singing *kajri*. *Kajri* is also sung on other religious occasions and has become a kind of ritual for the people who have been practising it for a long time now.

Following the forlorn Kajli, women in Mirzapur sing *kajri* while working in the fields or swinging on *jhoola*s. They also do so behind a curtain by the roadside. On the eve of Anant Chaturdashi, these performances from behind the curtains increase in number as more women join in. A popular couplet says that the women of this place would not go to their husbands' homes in the month of Sawan, for that is when the sons of the soil would return and *kajri* would be sung. It is a very special occasion when one participates in festivity and enjoys oneself in a community of kindred souls.

Men join in singing *kajri* in a different manner. They form groups and sing their chosen songs in a number of *akhaadaa*s spread all over the town and even in the peripheries. The two *akhaadaa*s of Jehangir and Siddhnath are better known than others, as these groups pose questions, seek answers, and try to establish their supremacy over each other. Singers also change their parties or groups with the exchange of cardamom. The *kajri* composers or poets pass on their creations to the singers, who earn praise and pride for themselves as also the poets.

Kajri in Mirzapur is sung and performed in three different ways. Men sing it in a classical, semi-classical, or popular manner with nostalgic fervour and enjoy its emotional flavour. Women sing in folk tunes in the fields, on the *jhoola*s, or behind the curtains. Then there are actors who perform them enthusiastically in local *dangal*s. Turning their gestures into language and language into gestures, they add to the given text and perform in *dangal*s with a keen sense of competition. This sense of competition is heightened when *kajri*s are presented as questions and answers. As the imagination of the poets is required to soar high to seek gems of questions and jewels of answers, the actors, too, have to keep pace and sound overpowering. Parties lose and win, receiving public applause and criticism for the quality of their performance. An example may be seen here:

Question song:
Chaat rahi chakchhu se chakori kora katora chandi ka
Bhara hua lau hai amrit se weera katora chandi ka (tek)
Lagaiga kya koi use jo bada anal se laga hua
Dhalengey kis sanchey mein jo chheer Sindhu mein dhala hua
Tab se suraj tapayega kya tar karai usey jo tala hua
Churayega kya chor usey wah khud choron ka bala hua
Meley ke mehfil mein ghoomein chunh ora katora chandi ka (udan) (16–17)
The chakori is licking with eyes the empty bowl of silver
It's filled with amrit to the very brim, that bowl of silver
Who can fill it better; it's already filled with fire
In which cast shall it be moulded; it's already moulded in Sindhu
With what heat would the sun burn; it's already soaked in frying
How can the thieves steal it; it's already a bane for them
I wish to stroll in the fair all around with an empty bowl of silver.

Answer song:
Latka hua adhar mein hai ek lal katora soney ka
Lalit prathat paaya Shankar khushhal katora soney ka (tek)
Nahi baid na puran mein na kuran mein iska barnan
Na ye katora zameen mein na na yeh rahta yaar gagan
Naqsha jiska duniya ke karigar na paye mitran
Nashey mein ek din Shiv Shnakar thhe Parvati se lagey kahan
Liya pratham sakti se terey yeh lal katora soney ka (udan) (17)
There hangs in the space a red bowl of gold
A bright, a beautiful, a happy bowl of gold
Neither the Vedas, nor the Purana, nor the Quran mention it
This bowl is neither here upon this earth, nor there in the skies
No craftsman can ever draw its figure, my friend!
Drunk to the brim, one day Shiv Shankar spoke to Parvati:
Only from your prime powers, I got this red bowl of gold.

The questions and answers are presented in complex ways and as riddles to the rival party. The intention is to make it too difficult to answer and bring defeat to the rival party. More than mere exercises in *kajri* singing, these competitive items create a keen sense of participation by training and sharpening the sensibility of the listeners.

These exercises not only underline the creative vitality of the poets; they also bear witness to their sharp logic, deep knowledge, and command over the art of rhetoric. The lexicon used in the *kajri*s of Mirzapur is a rich admixture of the Hindi–Sanskrit and Urdu–Persian expressions in addition to those drawn from Bhojpuri and Awadhi. *Kajri*s are not written in any particular style or form; they are composed in any metre, line, or text length, and in any manner that might appeal to the poet. These are the free expressions of untutored imagination, but deserve to be read as serious literary texts.

The *Kajri* Protagonist

Considering how *kajri* had its supposed origin and what seminal references it grew with, it would not be improper to assert that *village* is the essential protagonist in a typical *kajri* handed down to us through generations of poets and singers. The village does not exist in isolation; it is lively as it enjoys and suffers, and has a whole lot of references associated with it. It represents various facets of romantic love, sociopolitical concerns, historical situations, cultural manifestations, linguistic registers, mystical apprehensions, and patriotic expressions.

The female persona in the romantic *kajri* is composed of delicate material that makes the lover pine for her. She often wears a bright costume, and nature envies her youth and beauty. This is the stock character of a romantic folklore. Both in image-making and phrase-formation, some *kajri*s exhibit strong Persian influence. Written in the couplet form, they represent a gesture on the part of the narrator. It is on this account that the couplets acquire a certain dramatic/melodramatic tone and tenor, and that is how they become suitable enough to be sung on the stage. Following are some examples of Mirzapuri *kajri*s characterized by overt Urdu–Persian influence, as most of the poets and performers in that region belonged to the Muslim community, spoke Urdu, and represented that culture in its localized form. Two examples are quoted further on to confirm these readings. In the third example, a different image may be seen where the beloved pines for the lover who is away; her tattered, thatched roof leaks, the night is dark, and she is too scared to step out of the house. All these examples, taken together, represent romance, gesture, pathos, and the courage to live life.

Wo nazneen jab libas badley
Sitaaron ke dil jigar phatengey
Jo chashm-e khooni lagaley surma
Hazaron ke sar yahan phatenge. (19)

When that dainty love shall change her dress
The heart and soul of the stars shall tear
When those killing eyes shall put in *surma*
Many injuries the heads shall bear.

Aaj terey majnoo ki tasweer sarasar roti hai
Bigad gayi taqdeer meri tadbeer sarasar roti hai. (20)

Your lover's image cries unstopped today
I have a bad fate; all my methods fail today.

Mori tutahi madaiyya chuwai bun mori sajni
Mohi chhad balamua de gailein dukh dun mori sajni.
Chadhat Asadh gagan ghan chhaye boond birah ki barse ho
Sawan jhoole sakhi hindola birhan baithhi tarsey ho
Bhadon andhyari dar se ho, kadam na nikle ghar se ho
Pi pi papeeha boley uthai junoon mori sajni. (20)

My thatched roof leaks; repair it my friend
My love has left me alone; I am in pain my friend
Asadh is there, the sky is full of clouds, drops of separation fall

My friends swing in Sawan; I pine for love alone
I am scared of the dark Bhadon; I can't step out of home
I hear papeeha's *pi pi*; I grow wild.

Several examples may be quoted to show the variety of moods in romantic love that pertain to hope, despair, and ultimately a sudden recuperation to face the odds. The female protagonists in all these conditions of being hail from different points of times. The poets also recall the images of Gaura, Shaivya, Ahalya, and Draupadi, Urvashi, Uttara, apart from those of Sita and Radha, who are the stock characters of the ideal woman and ideal beloved respectively. While thinking of Radha, the poet is naturally drawn towards Krishna and His playfulness. Both become one, as if in a moment of magic realism. Opposed to them are the women who belong to modern times and wish to be treated differently. These divergent images may be seen in the following lines:

Urvashi sun re Dhananjaya kaha bigad ke batiya ho
Sawatia such ke dahey jiyara.
Aayi saja ke saj sab nakhra dikhaney ko yahan
Lagi na aiko chal tohri maan ja m era kaha. (22)
Listen Urvashi, said Dhananjaya in anger
Your heart burns in jealousy against the other woman;
You have come here so embellished to have your way
Nothing would work; you should better understand what I say.

Sajjano aaj Ahalya nari ki laachaari suniye
Indra ki atyachari suniye (23)
Gentlemen! Hear today how helpless was Ahalya
Listen! How cruel Indra was to her.

Aadhe Radhika aadhe Nand ke lal ba re balmu
Ek roop mein dono roop bisal ba re balmu (tek)
Aadhe sir per mukut biraje aadhe mein beni chamkey
Aadhe math mein chandan sohe aadhe mein bendi damkey

Ek aankh mein dor gulabi ek aankh mein mohini damkey
Ek kan mein kundal ek mein bari aur jhumka jhamkey
Ek sanwaro ek hain gore gaal ba re balmu (udan) (25)
Half Radhika half Nand, shine bright in one image
In one image are two united, the image looks splendid
On half the head sits a crown, on half is a plait of hairs
On half the crown dazzles *chandan*, on half the *bindiya*
In one eye a line of pink, in another a rare enchantment
In one earlobe hangs a *kundal*, in another dangles a *jhumka*
One is brown, another a fair-cheek, my love.

Hamein cycle pe chadhhna sikhai da piya
Mirjapur ghumai da piya na. (24)
Love! Teach me how to ride a bicycle
Take me around and show me Mirjapur.

Maheen kapda badan ke ooper pehnai khatir karai jatan
Darjan darjan sabun mangwai lagwai ghas ghas ke badan
Powder, alta, othh ka lali, ingur kajar karai rachan
Latka ke choti peeth ke ooper khol ke sar ghumai banthhan (24)
She makes efforts to put on a thin material on her body
She gets dozens of soaps; she rubs them on her body
She applies powder, nail polish, lipstick, kohl
She dangles a *choti* at her back, walks bareheaded as a painted doll.

Along with references to Hindu mythology and religious personages, *kajri* has enough space for Islamic thought and mysticism. The poets have referred to man's spiritual yearning and the desire to know the eternal truth. As stated earlier, *kajri* is a purely secular form of folk tradition and both the Hindu and Muslim poets have executed their own mythical and religious references to construct their individual apprehension of the impending reality. References to *burraq, Karbala, advait, shariat, tariqat, marifat, haqiqat, lahoot, fanaa,* and *baqaa* recur in poems with Islamic backgrounds. These references, however, do not limit the appeal of their creations, as all of them can be most appropriately sung with tonal variations or performed on the stage with gestures and lively action. Some examples would bear this out:

Baba duwariya dhum machal hoor-o ghilman karti mujra
Panhuchi barat meraj ki raat dayi jhimjhimat gherey badra (28)
Baba! There is festivity in the yards as the sylphs dance,
The *barat* has arrived on the night of Meraj,
The clouds have gathered all around.

Din juma mubarak masjid mein azaan pukari jaati hai
Karbala mein Bibi Zohra ki looti phulwari jati hai (28)
It's a holy Friday; the call to prayer comes from the mosque
Ah! In Karbala, Bibi Zohra's garden is being ravaged.

Tod chuke zunnar Brahman taj baithhe butkhanon ko
Bana liya zahid ne masjid ab merey maikhane ko (29)
The Brahmin has broken his thread; he has deserted the temple
The *zahid* too has turned the tavern into a mosque.

Mai pee kar Mansur anal-haq kehta thha bazaron mein
Sarmad ne sar katwaya mashhoor thha jo maikhwaron mein (29)
Mansur drank his cup and said in the marketplace: I am God
Sarmad got himself beheaded; his name spread
Among those who drank from this cup.

Hai paish-e nazar tasweer-e sanam guftar hai apne aap se
Ajpa jap hota hai apna apne aap ke japey se (29)
I have my beloved's face before me; I speak to my own self
The best worship is the worship when you worship your own self.

Saaf nazar aati hai amaan ab khuda ki qudrat shishey mein
Chashm-e haqeeqat se dekha hai yaar ki surat sheeshey mein (30)
I can clearly see God's magic in the glass

I have the eyes that see reality
And I have seen my beloved's face in the glass.

Maraz ishq ki dawa dair aftaar se nikley Allahu
Lahoot ki manzil tai ho dil-e afkaar se nikley Allahu
Noor se nikle Allahu aur naar se nikle Allahu (30)
Love's patient needs to wait; he would himself utter Allahu
When the stage of lahoot is crossed, the heart will cry Allahu
Heavens would utter Allahu; hell would echo Allahu.

Baqa fana se kaam nahin kucch gharz na marne jeeney se
Mit gaya khud bekhudi mein ek jam wasl ka peeney se (31)
I have nothing to do with eternity or with annihilation
There is nothing for me in life or in death
My self got merged with selflessness
After I drank a cup of union.

These verses deny the impression that the *kajri* poets depended on sheer inspiration and on merely developing the art of spontaneous utterance. In fact, these poets were quite informed and chose their references with considerable critical sense and discrimination. Their renditions remind the common readers and listeners of Tulsi, Sur, Jaisi, and Kabir. They may, in this respect, be considered the descendants of these poets. The thesis proposed earlier that *kajri* poets were no less intellectually aware gains further ground here. These poets did not assume an intellectual stance, as they were much too rooted in the folk tradition of composing and sharing rather than the elitist literary tradition of constructing a self-conscious text and getting it canonized. There are various other manifestations of deep religious and philosophical apprehensions on the part of the poets hailing from both the traditions of Hinduism and Islam, including their mutual acceptance and secular understanding for each other.

Many of the *kajri* poets have been truly concerned with constructing their nation, a matter that has occupied the postcolonial writers in the recent past. These poets have been engaged with events in history and their impact on the making of the new India. They are aware of the contemporary relevance of new developments and the sacrifices of Gandhi for creating a political democracy. They also reflect upon the partition of the country, the suffering of the people in the wake of this event, and the importance of vote banks for narrow personal ends. Some examples are quoted here:

Jhula pada ahimsa ka, Bharat ke lalanwa jhool gaye
Liye hatheli paranwa jhool gaye, kata kata gardanwa jhool gaye (37)
The swing of *ahimsa* is swinging
The sons of soil have swung in them—
They all have sacrificed their lives.

Naye chhe paise mein purana ek aana ba
Badla bhai jamana ba na.(38)
There is an old anna in the new six paise
See how the times have changed, my dear.

Hey bhagwan kawan gati hoihein yenhan ghuskhoran ke
Chalbaj au chorwan ke na (39)
O God! What will happen to these bribe seekers?
These deceitful ones, these thieves?

Garib janta se vote lekey ban ge aflatoon suna
Kahen pahunchtai assembly banwaub kanoon suna (39)
I hear he would thrive on the poor man's vote
He says he would reach the assembly and have the laws made.

Kajri as a folk form has moved beyond the confines of the village and brought into the outside world to bear upon it and vice versa. It has drawn upon a world of broad references, images, symbols, and archetypes. It has created its own lexicon and absorbed the contemporary diction of the village and the town. *Kajri* has long been a cultural icon of the village, and the two have bonded the people together. They have helped them tell a tale, and taught them to be keen and sensitive listeners. *Kajri* and the village together provide a mode of acculturation and a way of holding hands.

A Case for *Kajri*

Folk literatures deserve serious critical attention. There is a postcolonial need to remember one's history and identify one's cultural heritage. These literatures help us do that precisely. The sprawling industrial city has pushed the village out of sight. The city stands next door as a dark, impending reality, claiming all that the village stood for once. The village is now rewriting itself; it is revisiting its myths and acquiring new references. Its ethnicity and iconography have all undergone drastic changes. With all these happening and with such speed, the folk tradition is in a state of neglect and would, subsequently, stay only as a point of reference while talking of our rich cultural heritage.

Kajri is a far cry from the complicated, artful, urban text. It would sound hollow and remain isolated if severed from the roots. Far from being a song of the Sawan, *kajri* may be read as a cultural text, a performance text, an artistic text, and a text of history, society, and politics. In brief, it may be approached as a meta-text that reflects our primeval associations. It may broadly strengthen other texts that fail to seek their sustenance from the soil and have been looking for readers who elude them again and again. While other texts, including the elitist ones, may elude the reader for a number of reasons, *kajri* can only help connect and justifiably seek its space in our collective psyche.

In spite of all its virility, *kajri* has lived in handwritten manuscripts and human memory. Both are subject to decay and may be effaced in due course of time. Even those texts that have been recorded and preserved suffer the indifference of general readers, and certainly of those who have remained isolated from the essential sources of human sustenance.

It would be wholly erroneous to say that an art form like *kajri* is a weak literary form, devoid of literary merit, or that it refers to a certain community of less educated beings. In fact, there are a number of compositions that call for informed interventions. It may be easily marked that those written in classical and semi-classical styles, as also those composed for the popular taste, have their individual merits and affirm the poets' ability to command the form. Their artistic vitality may only be verified by referring to the tools that the *kajri* poets employ to make their compositions meaningful, both for the popular and the informed literary reader. A critical reading of *kakahra*, which, in Hindi poetry, is known as Akhrawati and had been employed by poets like Kabir, would show how keenly conscious the *kajri* poets were of their tools and techniques. It would also establish how sensitive they have been to sound, as much of their appeal depends on the modulation of music and tones of voices. Similarly, many of their alliterations are not conceived on the repetition of certain sounds alone, but on the arrangements of alphabets in order of their appearance, and with emphasis on a certain sound at the beginning of each line. Some poets have also composed *kajri*s of mixed lexicons and created a unique linguistic and auditory impact upon the listener.

We may relate to *kajri* rather naturally. We may approach it as a literary text, a song, and also as a potential reference to our heritage, fauna, and flora. The variety of themes as reflected in the titles[8] of some of the *kajri*s and the rhythm that they create could be the two simple reasons for us to approach them. Once we do that, it would open up a world of strange mysteries and rare delights, a condition many literary texts aspire to achieve. There are a thousand merits, but lesser number of seekers. The following couplet tells it in no uncertain terms:

Kabiyon ke kavita sey kahoon hoteen hain kalaein ek hazar
Khabar karo hain kalp vriksha ki sakhaaein ek hazar (tek) (88)
Let me tell the poets' creations
There are a thousand arts in them
As there are thousand branches
In the *Kalp* tree.

The strange world of *kajri* awaits exploration. That is surely why Ustad Bismillah Khan said, 'I will play *kajri* whether you like it or not.'

Endnotes

1. The event was organized by Jammu and Kashmir Academy of Arts, Culture and Languages in collaboration with University of Jammu and SPIC MACAY, Jammu Chapter at Abhinav Theatre, Jammu on 8 September 2005.

2. *Bhaands* were a kind of strolling players who, like jesters, buffoons, or non-serious actors, sang songs of eulogy, or narrated episodes or events in a light manner but with satirical overtones. They turned into institutions, although they have now almost vanished from the folk life of the regions where they were appreciated once for their merit.
3. Teej refers to the monsoon festivals, observed in the western and northern states of India.
4. In his essay titled 'Hindi Bhasha: Kajli ki Kavita' (1890), Bhartendu Harishchandra has mentioned three sources of *kajri*. These include (a) the *kajris* of Mirzapur which stand apart from all others (b) a jungle in the kingdom of Dadu Rai known as Kajli Bun which was its home, and (c) the Teej festivals in which *kajris* were sung. This essay is included in Hemant Sharma, ed., *Bhartendu Samagra* (Hindi Pracharak Sansthan: Varanasi, 1987).
5. Badrinarayan Chaudhary Premghan had considerable space for *kajris* in his poetry. He also published an anthology called *Kajli Kadambini* (1889). The *kajri* by Premghan, quoted in the text, is included in Abdul Bismillah (ed.), *Lok Kavya Vidha: Kajri* (Delhi: Anang Prakashan, 2000). Extracts of other *kajris* quoted in the text with page numbers are all taken from this anthology.
6. The anthology of *kajris* edited by Abdul Bismillah contains sixty-two compositions on a variety of themes and experiences. They were mostly written for dramatic presentations in *dangals*, where people gathered to enjoy themselves and encourage the performers. The scenario presented a great sense of excitement and festivity. Some of them draw heavily upon Persian–Urdu vocabulary and relate to religious and philosophical themes. This reader-friendly volume also contains an introduction and annotations to words and concepts that many of the readers may need to know. Extracts of *kajris* quoted in the text have been taken from this book.
7. All translations of the extracts quoted are by the author of this book.
8. Some of the *kajris* included in *Lok Kavya Vidha: Kajri* has titles like: 'It Ut Nain Niharey Pant', 'Ichhuk Prasang Pee Mai Anang', 'Kalpat Birah Biyogin', 'Adhey Radhika Adhey Nand Ke Laal', 'Aainey Mein Hai Aaina Saaz', 'Pauwwan Pauwwan Hari ke Gauwwan', 'Brahm Roop Brahmand Alakh', 'Neek Nipun Nutan Nartat', 'Hud Hud Har Har Shor Machawey', and 'Bhaiwa Milal Faisani Humkey Ek Mehraroo Ba'. The first line of each *kajri* has been used as its title for the convenience of identification, as *kajris* do not have titles like other poetic compositions.

References

Bismillah, Abdul, ed. 2000. *Lok Kavya Vidha: Kajri*. New Delhi: Anang Prakashan.

Ramanujan, A.K. 1994. *Folktales from India*. New Delhi: Penguin Random.

The Making of a Literary Culture: Patrons and Urdu Poets

The Making of a Literary Culture

Let me begin by making a reference to a couple of statements made by C.M. Naim, an American academic and critic of Urdu literature. In Appendix V to Mir Taqi Mir's *Zikr-i Mir*, entitled 'Mir's Patrons', he wrote: 'Being a poet was an occupation in the pre-modern times, no different from soldiering or accountancy. Poets and patrons sought out each other with certain well-understood expectations' (167). While discussing Mir and Ghalib, he extended his argument further in 'Mughal and English Patronage of Urdu Poetry: A Comparison' in *Urdu Texts and Contexts* (2004):

> There were many shared traditions between these poets and their patrons, including many implied or overt obligations to each other. Honour begat honour, loyalty received loyalty. Just as the patron assured the physical well-being of the poet, so did the poet contribute to the perceived sense of success and prosperity of the patron; one specific human being interacted with another, no matter how perfunctorily (169).

I would like to extend these arguments further and relate it with the origin and development of Urdu as a language and then of Urdu becoming a site for literary expression. I would suggest that both the trajectories of language and literary expression represent two different narratives of history, even though they remain interrelated at the core. It may be justifiably asserted that one draws upon material history that takes note of the conditions in which this language grew, while the other engages with the making of its literary tradition in the larger contexts of time and place where it materialized. I should like to engage here with both of them together, as they intersect and constitute a larger narrative that ultimately accounts for the formation of multiple literary cultures. These cultures, as is borne out by the twin histories of Urdu language and literature, signify the defining moments in a continuing literary tradition. They are characterized by the imaginative vitality that the authors possessed to represent their times, the graph of linguistic maturity that the texts exhibited age after age, and the essential spirit that the readers embodied in every generation to be able to identify with the past and the present authors together. In problematizing this argument, I should add further that while history engaged with the presentation of physical realities of the changing times, literature engaged with the representation of those shifting realities. Further, while history used language to construct its narrative, literature used metalanguage to configure its metanarrative. I would like to carry this argument forward by underlining the simultaneous growth of Urdu language and its literature with reference to select Urdu poets and their patrons in medieval India.

With reference to this central argument, the account of the patronized poets must begin with Amir Khusrau (1253–1325) and come down to Asadullah Khan Ghalib (1797–1869), and of the patrons with the fifth ruler of the Qutb Shahi dynasty of Golconda, Muhammad Quli Qutb Shah (1565–1612) and end with the last Mughal emperor, Bahadur Shah Zafar (1775–1862). Although multiple canons and literary cultures have appeared during the past four hundred years from various schools of poetry,[1] locations of culture,[2] forms of poetic expression,[3] and genres of special kind,[4] I should like to engage here with one of them particularly, constructed by patrons and their poets, as they carried language beyond literariness and history beyond historicity. While literary criticism has taken note of these aspects rather sparingly, details of the poets and their patrons may be seen in some biographical writings and literary histories in Urdu.[5]

A Poet of Many Patrons: Amir Khusrau

Amir Khusrau marks the beginning of Urdu's literary history, but he is not even partly considered to be so, in spite of all his tone, tenor, and temperament that brings him close to the spirit of Urdu language and literature. An early avatar of Hindavi, which later matured into Urdu only in the late eighteenth century, is quite clearly traceable in the literary works[6] of Khusrau way back in the late thirteenth and early fourteenth centuries. About four hundred years in advance, he wrote in a language that approximated Urdu in many ways and laid the foundation of a secular language, culture, and literature. An accomplished poet, musician, and a celebrated disciple of the great Sufi saint Hazrat Nizamuddin Auliya (1238–1325), Khusrau is also known for his association with several nobles and rulers. This association started when he was only twenty, and, by the time he reached his forties, he was conferred the title of *amir*, meaning a commander or a noble man, by one of this patrons Jalaluddin Khalji. Of all the poets who cultivated, craved, or developed their bond with their patrons, Khusrau stands apart as he enjoyed respect like no one else during his own times or even afterwards. His association with Nasir ud din Mahmud (1246–1266), Ghiyas ud din Balban (1266–1287), Jalaluddin Khalji (1290–1296), Alauddin Khalji (1296–1316), Qutbuddin Mubarak Shah (1316–1320), Ghiyasuddin Tughlaq (1320–1325), and Muhammad bin Tughlaq (1325–1351) is spread over a larger portion of his life and shows his keen understanding of society, culture, and politics of his times. Apart from leading a life which, in the modern times, would be known as that of a career diplomat, Khusrau evolved a language out of a unique synchronization of dialects to create a rich paradigm of meaning. His short poems, long poetical narratives, historical accounts in verse, riddles, and prose discourses bear testimony to his genius as a literary figure of exceptional reach and range. While he eulogized Jalaluddin Khalji for his four conquests in his *masnavi Miftah-ul-Futuh* (Key to the Victories) (1290), he celebrated the accomplishments of Ghiyasuddin Tughlaq in *Tughlaq Nama* (1320). *Nuh Sipihr* (Nine Skies) (1318), written in nine different metres to describe nine different spheres, is a unique work in which Khusrau wrote a panegyric for Mubarak Shah. In his prose work entitled *Khazain-ul-Futuh* (The Treasures of Victories) (1296), also known as *Tarikh-i-Alai*, he described Alauddin Khalji's conquests with pride. Apart from putting all his patrons in good humour with complete clinical detachment, he developed his narratives in a manner that might also be read as sources for understanding the larger political and cultural life of medieval India. This apart, Khusrau is remembered today as a poet and an icon of popular culture having great contemporary relevance. Let me quote three different kinds of examples to show how he modulated his counters of expression to evolve a literary language, even while he continued his association with his patrons at sociopolitical levels. His knowledge of Arabic, Persian, Turkish, and Hindi empowered him to draw upon the vitality of these languages and configure a secular medium of poetic expression. When he mixed Persian with Hindavi, he invented a unique language for himself which matured later into Urdu. Here is an example of this mode of expression:

Ze haal-e miskeen makun taghaful doraye nainan banaye batiyan
Chu tab-e hijran na darm ai jaan, na lehoo kahey lagaye chhatiyaan[7]
Ignore not this wretch, turn not your eyes away, make no excuses,
No longer can I bear this separation, why don't you come and embrace me, my love?[8]

In this particular ghazal, the first line of each couplet is in Persian, while the second line is in Hindavi, for instance: *kisey padi hai jo ja sunawey pyare pee ko hamaari batiyaan* (who would bother and tell my love in what state I lie now), *sakhi piya ko jo main na dekhoon to kaisey katoon andheri ratiyaan* (how shall I live through the dark nights if I don't see my love), *na neend nainan na ang chainan na aap aawey na bhejey patiyan* (neither sleep in eyes, nor limbs at rest—my love neither comes nor sends a word).

When he portrayed the folk life and manners, he configured his language as differently as this:

Amma merey bawa ko bhejo ri ke sawan aayaa
Beti tera bawa to buddha ri ke sawan aayaa[9]

After mother send my father; Sawan is here
How can I, dear daughter? Your father is old and Sawan is here.

And when he described his separation from his spiritual master who had drawn a curtain between life and death, he brought yet another dimension to his understanding of human existence, as a mystic would do:

Gori soye saij per mukh per daarey kais
Chal Khusrau ghar aapne saanjh bhayi chaundes[10]
My love lies asleep on his pyre, tresses of hair cast over his face
Now you too leave for your home, Khusrau; it's dark all around.

Several examples like *chhap tilak sab cheeni ray mosay naina milaikay*[11] (you looked at me and snatched indeed all my bridal glory), *Khusrau darya prem ka, ulti wa ki dhaar*[12] (Khusrau, it's the river of love, its streams flow backwards), *sakal bun phool rahi sarson*[13] (all over the woods, the mustard plants are abloom), *bahut kathin hai dagar panghat ki*[14] (not easy; it's so hard indeed to walk the path to the riverbank), and numerous other songs and riddles make him an iconic figure representing the spirit of conciliation between life and art, as well as society and politics. It would be pertinent to draw that it was the versatility of this poet that earned him his patrons, and, as it happened, the gain accrued on both the sides of the poet as also the patrons.

Poets and Patrons in Deccan

Poets have had their patrons in almost all ages. Even before the Urdu poets received patronage, we have examples of the Persian poets drawing upon the munificence of Mughal emperors. We are aware of the Mughal emperor Akbar (1556–1605) appointing Ghazali Mashhadi (d. 1572) and Faizi (1547–1595), the two Persian poets, in his court. We are also aware of Abu'l Fazl (1551–1602) recording in *Ain-i-Akbari* that fifty-nine poets were associated with his court at one point of time. Although Akbar had little taste for poetry, he took pride in patronizing poets, and which seemed to suggest that his patronage of poets reflected well on him as well as his statecraft. Compared with Akbar, Jahangir (1605–1627) had better appreciation for poets which is reflected in *Tuzk-e Jahangiri* (1609). Like his two predecessors, Shah Jahan (1628–1658) too liked patronizing poets in his court. Even though none of these three Mughal emperors were poets themselves, they took pride in promoting poetry. While Akbar introduced the title of *Malik-us Shu'ara* (the king of poets), Jahangir and Shah Jahan got some poets weighed in gold.

The tradition of these Mughal emperors was also carried further by the contemporary Deccan rulers of the Qutb Shahi and Adil Shahi dynasties of Golconda and Bijapur, although with lesser prominence. Unlike the Mughals, at least four Qutb Shahis like Muhammad Quli Qutb Shah (1580–1611), Muhammad Qutb Shah (1611–1625), Abdullah Qutb Shah (1625–1672), and Abul Hasan Qutb Shah (1672–1686) were poets themselves and pursued the craft of poetry with the same devotion as they did the craft of state. The most remarkable of them all is Muhammad Quli Qutb Shah who wrote in Persian, Telugu, and Deccani—a variant of Urdu—and came to be acknowledged as the first poet in Deccani Urdu with at least fifty thousand *sher*s and a complete *divan* to his credit. Acclaimed to be a major poet, he practised all poetic forms. He wrote on a variety of issues concerning communal life and the sentiments of the common people, their festivals and faiths, and the love and pleasures of union in a frank and disarming manner. Drawing upon Hindu culture, as also upon the Persian culture and its literary tradition, he developed a secular view of love, life, and literature. He blended the best traditions of the two streams of thought and life to impart a new halo to his poetry. His poetic merit lies in his simplicity and musicality, which he appropriated to project an inclusive view of life and art. Essentially a poet of his own flora and fauna, Quli Qutb Shah was a kind-hearted ruler, a passionate lover, and a great patron of arts and architecture. A legend goes that Quli Qutb Shah founded a city called Bhag Nagar, after one of his beloveds called Bhagmati, which later became Hyderabad once Bhagmati came to be known as Hyder Mahal. Quli Qutb Shah, who had appointed Mullah Asadullah Wajahi

(1551–1660) as Poet Laureate, wrote a poetical narrative called *Qutub Mushtari* (1953), celebrating his love for this lady called Mushtari who was no one else but Bhagmati herself. Let me quote two different examples to show both the spiritual and the amorous nature of his verse, and the two kinds of diction he employed for each one just as Khusrau had done earlier. When he wrote his hymn to God, he drew upon one kind of idiom:

Chunder soor terey noor they, nis din koon noorani kya
Teri sifat kin kar sakey, tu aapi hai mera jiya
Tuj nam munj aaram hai, munj jiu so tuj nam hai
Sab jug koon tuj soon kam hai, tuj nam jap mala hua
Tuj yad mein jug muhiya, hai jug upar tera maya
Jo jug mangey so toon diya, toon hi jagat ka hai diya
Bhautik maya seetey apan, deta Qutub koon sab dakhan
Seesoon nabi ka nit charan jab lag hai tan mayaney jiya[15]

The moon and the sun bear your glow;
Your glow turns the dark night into day.
None can ever be as you are
All life and soul to this man of clay

Only your name brings me comfort;
In comfort, I offer my life to you.
I count your name; you are my rosary
The world worships you as I do.

They remember you; they are all yours,
Your love is greater than the world's love.
You bestow what the world desires
The sky sends its rays from above.

I look up to you; I know you are kind
A kind God of heavens who sends His grace.

You have what I need; provide all I want
And all you confer, I always embrace.

Deccan showers all its love on Qutb,
Qutb adorns his head with the prophet's feet.
He only prays to you—to you—who else
As long as the soul and the body meet.

In expressing love and longing, he appropriated an entirely different diction which must have led literary historians to proclaim him as the first Urdu poet:

Piyaa baaj pyaala piyaa jaaye naa
Piyaa baaj yek til jiyaa jaaye naa

Kaheethey piyaa bin saboori karoon
Kahhiya jaye amma kiyaa jaaye naa

Nahi 'ishq jis wo badaa kood hai
Kadhein us se mil biseeyaa jaaye naa

Qutub Shah na de mujh diwaaney ku pand
Diwaaney ku kucch pand diyaa jaaye naa[16]

I can't ever drink my drink without my love
I can't ever breathe, I sink without my love

I should be patient, you say, without my love
How unfair! I can't even blink without my love

A boor indeed is one who can't be in love
I'm no boor; I'm on the brink without my love

No counsels, Qutb Shah, none to this crazy one
I'm the one, I can't even think without my love

Several other examples show that while Quli Qutb Shah was performing his role as a ruler, he was evolving his idiom as a poet at the same time.

From the Adil Shahi dynasty of Bijapur, we have the example of Ali Adil Shah (1558–1580) who patronized Muhammad Nusrat Nusrati (d. 1674) by appointing him as Poet Laureate. Like him, Ibrahim Adil Shah II (1580–1626) too patronized poets, although those poets did not prove their potential to earn their place in literary history. Nusrati wrote panegyrics for his patron, which could also be read as the histories of Deccan. Noted for his skill as a poet and his appeal to the ruler, Nusrati was later appointed as Poet Laureate once again by Emperor Aurangzeb (1618–1707) when he gained control over Bijapur in 1686. While Nusrati revelled in this pride, he also earned enemies and wrote lampoons on them only to be killed by his staunch critics. This underlines the problem of rivalry among court poets and their followers of which several cases appeared later also, but none as heinous as this one.

Although the Mughal Empire had started declining by the end of the seventeenth century, Persian remained the language of the court, the nobility, and the poets. Poetry in the new-fangled and the so-called Urdu language was still in its infancy, but it was vying for a place alongside the poetry written in the canonical Persian. As a developing language, Urdu had closely drawn upon other languages like Arabic, Persian, Turkish, and Braj, and had come to be known variously at various points of time and at various places as Deccani, Gujari, Hindi, Hindavi, Dehlavi, Rekhta, and Urdu-i-Mu'alla before it finally got canonized as Urdu. As against this, poetry in the northern parts of India had a different set of conditions to fall back upon. It reflected the cultural norms defined by the continuity of Muslim rule, its courts and nobility, refinement and elitism and, finally, the unitary dominance of the Persian literary culture. This was best represented by the poets and their patrons, who, together, were contributing to the emergence of a new literary culture in the northern part of India.

Poets and Patrons: Delhi and Lucknow

Poets and patrons in Delhi and Lucknow wrote the most remarkable chapters in Urdu literary history, as did those who stayed outside the courts.[17]

Muhammad Rafi Sauda (1713–1781), an Urdu poet, offers an important case in point who chose to refuse the title of Poet Laureate from Emperor Shah Alam II (1759–1806), as he could not abide by his growing demands to advise him on his verses. Instead of bowing down to the one who dictated, he chose to accept the patronage of other nobles who respected him and gave him his due. His many patrons included Basant Ali Khan, Nawab Saifuddaulah, Nawab Ghazi ud-Din Khan Imad-ul-Mulk in Delhi and Meharban Khan 'Rind' in Farrukhabad, and Nawab Shuja-ud-Daulah in Faizabad, apart from Nawab Asaf-ud-Daula in Lucknow who rewarded him with a monthly stipend of rupees two hundred, which was later converted to a *jagir* of rupees six thousand per annum. He wrote panegyrics for them, as also for some others like Alamgir II, Nawab Hasan Raza Khan, and Mir Muhammad Kazim. Sauda wrote in Persian before coming to Urdu, and distinguished himself as a panegyrist. He wrote forty-three panegyrics, celebrating his patrons and historicizing his times. John Borthwick Gilchrist (1759–1841), the famous linguist and Indologist, acknowledged rather profusely that he learnt his Urdu from Sauda's *divan*. The Persian literary tradition helped him acquire a tone and tenor, which he adopted to his benefit for writing his poetry in Urdu. Marked for his vitality of imagination, precise turns of phrases, and compact expressions, he practised various forms of poetry like panegyric, satire, and elegy, and emerged as one of the canonical poets in Urdu. In spite of all the oddities that life presented, Sauda retained his optimism:

Jo guzri mujh pe mat us sey kaho huaa so huaa
Balaa kashaan-e-muhabbat pe jo huaa so huaa

Mubaadaa ho koyee zaalim teraa garebaangeer
Merey lahoo ko to daaman se dho huaa so huaa

Pahunch chukaa hai sir-e zakhm dil talak yaaro
Koyee siyo koyee maraham dharo huaa so huaa[18]

What befell me just don't mention, whatever happened, happened
To the love-stricken one; whatever happened, happened

Lest a tyrant hold you guilty for not a fault, my friend
Just wash my blood from your garb; whatever happened, happened
Wound's head has made a way, has reached the heart, my friends, at last
Sew up the wound, put a balm; whatever happened, happened.

This was Sauda's way of striking a balance, or seeking a reconciliation, which speaks of his objectivity even while being a recipient of his patrons' favours. This further underlines the individual strength of the poet who did not stoop low enough to sing praises, irrespective of the stark realities of the times which the common people had to confront.

We have a very different example in Mir Taqi Mir (1723–1810), who migrated from Agra to a shattered Delhi to seek the sources of his sustenance, but could meet his ends with great difficulty. In spite of certain patronage he received from the nobles like Riayat Khan, Raja Jugal Kishore, and Raja Nagar Mal, with whom he maintained a cordial relationship for fourteen years, his relationship with Nagar Mal came to an end when he felt that he did not really respect him as much as he deserved.[19] He was also associated with Shah Alam II and, at the ripe age of sixty, Mir left Delhi for Lucknow where he received sustenance from Nawab Asaf-ud-Daula (1775–1797) and Saadat Ali Khan (1798–1814) till his death, while still thinking of Delhi as a lost home. Mir lived in a period of great political crisis. Both Delhi and Lucknow, the two literary centres and two ways of life and letters, had failed him. Mir always remained an unyielding genius, hardly ever making a compromise to retain his courtly position, even though he had written panegyrics for his patron Nawab Asaf-ud-Daula. He lamented over the fate of Delhi, as he did over his own predicament. When asked to introduce himself on his arrival from Lucknow to Delhi, he spoke about both Delhi and himself rather mournfully:

Kya bood-o baash poochho ho poorab ke sakinon
Hum ko ghareeb jan ke hans hans pukar ke
Dilli jo aik shahr thha 'aalam mein intekhab
Rahtey jahan thhe muntakhab hi rozgar ke
Jis ko falak ne loot ke barbaad kar diya

Hum rahney waaley hain usi ujaday dayar ke[20]
Don't ask me my dress and dwelling, you, the dwellers of East
They laughed at me; they thought I was so tattered.
Delhi, that was once a chosen place in all the world was the place where lived the chosen ones alone.
With the skies unkind, that's now a place shorn of all glory
I come from there—that very ransacked place.

In his autobiography *Zikr-i Mir* (1999), his impressions of Delhi are even murkier. In his verse, he found his own metaphors to identify and situate himself:

Main kaun hoon ai hamnafasan sokhta jaan hoon
Ek aag merey dil mein hai so sholafeshan hoon[21]
Who am I, my friends, I'm bereft of life
There's a fire in my heart, so I burn in that fire.

Jis sar ko ghuroor aaj hai yaan taajwari ka
Kal us pe yaheen shor hai ek nauha gari ka[22]
The head that's so proud to wear a crown today
For that are the sighs of lament only tomorrow.

Dono haathon se thamiye dastar
Mir sahib zamana nazuk hai[23]
Hold your headgear with both your hands
Times are bad, Mir sahib, bad indeed.

Shaam se kucch bujha sa rahta hoon
Dil hua hai chiragh muflis ka[24]
It's put out since the evening
My heart is only a poor man's lamp.

Dekh to dil k jaan se uthhta hai
Ye dhuan sa kahan se uthhta hai[25]

See from where it rises, from heart or body
From where does this smoke rise.

Is 'ahd mein ilahi muhabbat ko kya hua
Chhoda wafa ko un ne murawwat ko kya hua[26]
What happened to love in these times, my God
They washed their hands off love, they cared little for courtesy.

Mir experienced misery both in life and death. It is reported that his grave in Lucknow is untraceable, as a rail line has been laid over the spot where he was buried once. His pride is as remarkable as the poetry he wrote with genuine concern, without caring if it irked the mighty and the powerful. This only underlines the unyielding nature of the poet, which also distinguishes him from those who made compromises for personal benefit.

Poetry in the age of Sauda and Mir made remarkable strides in two directions: *first,* it refined and enriched Urdu as a language of poetry in a face-to-face interaction with Persian; and *second,* it cultivated poetry as a precious art evolved with a great care for craftsmanship. This age saw the cultivation of Urdu as a virile medium of poetic expression in several parts of northern India. The poetry of this age, characterized by a move towards enlightenment, expressed a sense of acute emotional and physical dislocations borne by the poets in their bid to reconcile with their times. Their discontent was born out of the conditions that contemporary history brought forth in terms of conflicts, invasions, battles, and acquisition of political power ever since the death of Emperor Aurangzeb in 1707. The poets lamented in metaphoric and symbolic ways the fallout of what in physical terms may be identified as invasion of Nader Shah (1738–39), the seven expeditions of Ahmad Shah Durrani (1748–67), the Maratha onslaughts (1758–1804), the arrival of Warren Hastings as the first Governor General of India (1773), and the attack by Rohilla chieftain Ghulam Qadir (1788), all of which have stayed on as the terms of reference of eighteenth-century India.

Yet another example of a patronized poet is that of Insha Allah Khan Insha (1757–1817) who got admittance in the court of Shah Alam II. He was despaired at the failing powers of the Mughal Empire and left for Lucknow, where Nawab Saadat Ali Khan employed him as a poet and a personal companion. Later, he resented the growing demands of the nawab for writing more verses and remaining in constant attendance. Unable to yield or strike a deal, he chose to relinquish his job as he could not check his defiant nature, nor keep his unsparing wit against the nawab in abeyance. He spent the rest of his life in misery, penury, and silence. His bitterness was further deepened with the ongoing literary brawls he had with his contemporary Ghulam Hamdani Mus'hafi (1750–1824), who could not get admittance in the court, even though his talent as a poet was well acknowledged for his great command over diction and the degree of spontaneity in which none could match him then. Insha was a scholar, a talented poet, a prose writer, and a linguist who knew Arabic, Persian, Braj, Turkish, Pashto, Kashmiri, Punjabi, Marwari, and Rekhti. This helped him towards developing an idiom for his ghazal, which had been growing and maturing continuously at the hands of the contemporary poets. Interestingly, he also brought the Hindi idiom to bear upon his Urdu, which added yet another dimension to his urge for making experiments with language and broadening its frontiers in poetry. Insha has left behind a literary capital marked by rich variety, which include his *divan,* a major exemplar of literary, cultural, and linguistic nuances and prose works like *Silk-e Gohar,* a work of elegant Urdu fictional prose, *Rani Ketki ki Kahani,* a tale told without dependence on Persian idiom, and *Daryaa-e-Latafat,* a discourse on language and rhetoric. A sampler would bring out his easy negotiation with language and conditions of life:

Kamar baandhey huey chalney ko yaan sab yaar baiththey hain
Bahut aagey gaye baaqi jo hain taiyyar baitthey hain[27]
Set to leave, all the fellows here are set to leave
Many have gone ahead, the rest are set to leave.

Na chchaid ai nikhat-e baad-e bahaari raah lag apni
Tujhey atkheliyaan soojhi hain hum bezaar baiththey hain[28]
Don't tease me, the fragrant breeze of spring! Don't!
You are toying with me; I'm tired now, set to leave.

Kahaan gardish falak ki chain deti hai hamain Insha
Ghanimat hai ke hum soorat yahaan do chaar baiththey hain[29]
The skies don't spare me a moment to think, Insha
Enough for us to sit apart and set to leave.

The lineage of Khusrau, Nusrati, Sauda, and Insha reached its end with Sheikh Muhammad Ibrahim Zauq (1789–1854) and Mirza Asadullah Khan Ghalib (1797–1869), who received patronage from Bahadur Shah Zafar. Let me refer to Bahadur Shah Zafar first.

A poet, a kind patron of poets, an aesthete, and a man of religious leanings, Zafar, the crown prince, was a disciple of lesser poets like Shah Naseer and Mir Kazim Husain 'Beqarar' in the early years, and of Zauq and Ghalib in the later years. For him, composing poetry was cultivating a difficult art that called for perseverance and devotion. This also explains his choice for multisyllabic lines and difficult *qaafiyaa* (the rhyming syllable at the end of a two-line verse) and *radif* (repeated after rhyme). He is remarkable for the typical Indianness of his poetry and his apprehension of the musical that helped him modulate his tone of voice. Zafar wrote the characteristic poetry of love and despair in his early phase and of more serious concerns like the failings of human fate and the mystic apprehensions of life during the later period of his dethronement and exile. It has been claimed that he was not such a faithful portrayer of human sentiments, and that he exploited language only to his limited gain, but it may also be posited that in drawing upon the potential of the same language and the same poetic skills, he emerged as a sensitive commentator on the fall of the royalty. Zafar had completed four *divan*s before 1857, although much was lost during the terrible events of the year. The feelings of loss, sadness, and resignation mark his poetry:

Ya mujhe afsar-e shaahana banaayaa hotaa
Ya mera taaj gadayaana banaayaa hotaa[30]
You had better made a royal mover of all
Or turned my crown into a beggar's cap.

Roz mamoora-i-duniyaa mein kharabi hai Zafar
Aisi basti se toh weeraana banaayaa hotaa[31]
There are many a defect, many a flaw, in this habitation
You had better turned this habitat into a wilderness.

Baat karni mujhey mushkil kabhee aisee to na thhee
Ab hai jaisee teri mehfil kabhi aisee to na thhee[32]
It was never so very hard to speak but now
Your assembly was never so bleak, but now.

Le gayaa chcheen ke yoon kaun tera sabr-o-qaraar
Beqaraari tujhey ai dil kabhi aisee to na thhee[33]
Who robbed you of your patience, my poor heart?
Never so restless and ever so meek, but now.

Zafar was not a major poet, but he certainly was a chronicler of the last days of an empire that had lost itself finally to the British. Similarly, his literary mentor Sheikh Muhammad Ibrahim Zauq (1789–1854), too, was a poet and eulogist of little consequence, but he enjoyed respect on account of being in his court, although its glory had already become a thing of the past. Zauq joined the young prince to train him in the art of writing poetry and was given four rupees a month for his services. Recognizing him for his skills as a wordsmith, Akbar Shah II gave him the title of *Khaqani-e-Hind* after the great Persain poet Khaqani (1106–1190) when he wrote a panegyric for him at the age of nineteen. When Zafar came to the throne, he appointed him as his mentor in 1808 and Poet Laureate in 1837. He also raised his stipend to rupees one hundred per month. Zauq lacked philosophical depth, but he had mastered the idiom. His capacity to exploit the splendour of the written word turned him into an important panegyrist, which won him favours from the emperor. Although he had little to contribute to form and style, he could distinguish himself for his verbal felicity:

Behtar to hai yehi ke na dunyaa se dil lagey
Per kya karein jo kaam na be dil lagi chaley[34]

Better not to be a prey to the world's magic
But what to do if not fall a prey to the world's magic.

In dinon garchey Deccan mein hai badi qadr-e sukhan
Kaun jaye Zauq per Dilli ki galiyan chhod kar[35]
Deccan values poets these days, I hear
But who will leave Delhi—I wouldn't ever.

In spite of his limitations, Zauq continued as Poet Laureate as long as he lived and was succeeded by Asadullah Khan Ghalib with whom he had a long-standing rivalry. Ghalib excelled Zauq in all respects as a poet and enjoyed no less respect in the court of Zafar. He was an exceptionally accomplished poet and a prose writer, an epistolarian and a diarist, a lexicographer and a polemist, a critic and a historian, but above all, an arbiter of taste. He was assigned the job of writing the Mughal history of which he completed the first part called *Mehr-e Neem Roz* that takes the period from Timur to Humayun into account. He had compiled his Urdu *divan* by the age of twenty-five. By this time, he had also developed a keener interest in Persian writing of which his Persian *divan* is a rich testimony, and he valued it much more than his Urdu *divan*, calling it colourless. He enriched the literary traditions of Urdu and Persian with his individual improvisations in form and technique. Ghalib's wit remains unparalleled, his diction refreshingly original, and his playfulness reminds one of the English metaphysical poet, John Donne. His letters included in *Aud-e Hindi* and *Urdu-i-Mualla*, and his diary called *Dustumbu*, detailing the events of 1857, distinguish him among all the poets and prose writers for the way he chronicled his time with the sensitivity of a literary artist. Ghalib remains, till this day, the most contemporaneous of all the literary masters in Urdu and Persian. In return for being Zafar's literary mentor, and in recognition of his multiple talents, he earned three coveted titles of *Najm-ud-daula*, *Dabir-ul-mulk*, and *Nizam Jung* from Zafar. He lived a life of want and longing and wrote poetry of great metaphysical depth. He received rupees fifty from the Mughal court and rupees one hundred from the court of

Rampur. He was a recipient of rupees seven hundred per annum as part of the family pension from the British to the heirs of his uncle who worked as a subedar at Agra. His getting close to the court of Zafar and later making peace with the British for the restoration of his pension, which had been stopped as he was suspected of inciting the events of 1857, underline his need and also his susceptibility to the centres of power. Ghalib witnessed the downfall of the Mughal Empire and the revolt of 1857 with pain. He recorded his despair in philosophical terms in his ghazals. He took both his vocation as a poet and his association with the emperor as a source of pride and acknowledged the same in clear terms:

Ghalib wazeefa khwar ho do Shah ko dua
Wo din gaye ke kehtey thhe naukar naheen hoon main[36]
You receive stipend Ghalib, bless the king
Gone are the days when you said: I'm nobody's servant.

Huzoor-e shah mein ahl-e sukhan ki aazmaayish hai
Chaman mein khush nawayaan-e chaman ki aazmaayish hai[37]
There's a trial in the king's court for who can compose the best of verse
It's a test indeed for all those who may compose the best of verse.

Hua hai shah ka musahib phirey hai itraata
Wagarna shehr mein Ghalib ki aabroo kya hai[38]
He's the king's attendant; so full of air
Else, what's his price, what's his value?

He developed a more serious view of his predicament, as he redefined himself and his context. In another set of verses, he reflected upon his personal predicament at a philosophical level that exuded his sense of confidence mixed with despondency:

Na sataaish ki tamanna na siley ki parwa
Gar naheen hain merey as'aar mein maani na sahi[39]
I don't desire a word of praise; I don't care for a return
If no meaning in my verse, let it be so, if it's so.

Yoon hi gar rota raha Ghalib to ai ahl-e jahan
Dekhna in bastiyon ko tum ke weeran ho gaien[40]
If Ghalib kept shedding tears like this, my friends
You would these abodes turn desolate one day.

Na gul-e naghma hoon na pada-i-saaz
Main hoon apni shikast ki aawaz[41]
Neither the blossom of a voice, nor the veil of being
I am indeed the echo of my own defeat.

Ghalib maintained a queer position as he subscribed to the given order of the day, yet remained confident about maintaining difference. Being the last of the court poets, he put a seal on the institution of patrons and poets and made way for poetry to survive in a secular world after him.

The Problematic of Patronage and Literary Writing

Considering these poets associated with courts, one comes across some questions that call for contemplation. Did these poets write because their association with the court could empower them socially, or did they write to earn financial favours by eulogizing their patrons? Another question underlines a political issue, that is, whether these poets maintained their individual stances even at the risk of losing their patronage, or whether they appropriated their skill as poets only to indulge into politicking with their patrons at the cost of a literary tradition? Yet another serious argument poses itself, that is, whether these poets played only a limited role towards promoting a larger literary culture, or whether they were more interested in constructing their personal myths? Finally, it is equally pertinent to ask whether these poets chose only to romanticize and create utopias, or whether they were broadly writing about their times while writing about themselves?

With reference to patrons like Quli Qutb Shah, Ali Adil Shah, Akbar, Jahangir, Shah Jahan, and Bahadur Shah Zafar, it might be posited that these patrons took pride in patronizing their poets, but all the poets they patronized did not necessarily submit themselves to their patrons at all costs. While Khusrau, who constitutes a class by himself, maintained his position and dignity, Sauda, Mir, and Insha remained proud and unyielding. Zauq and Ghalib are two different kinds of cases. Zauq took great pride in being the emperor's mentor and also in having too many disciples in his fold. Ghalib accommodated with his lot and made compromises, taking exceptional pride in his genius that he rightly thought was unsurpassed. It would be justifiable to posit that the poets who sought or got patronage from the courts wrote poetry of subterfuge quite often, but they mostly wrote a kind of poetry that was intensely their own. As such, when they wrote of themselves, they also wrote of their times and their patrons. Being in the court imparted them an identity and a strength of their own, which distinguished them on the one hand and earned them rivals on the other. They created sociocultural contexts for themselves and problematized their vocation in the process. In this respect, they obliterated the distinction between the court and the non-court poets, and took to sharpening their talent and refining their language to join and promote a great tradition of poetry and poetry writing. In this manner, they also redefined the form, rhetoric, and tools of poetic expression. While they wrote as poets, they also helped their patrons to write as poets and discover a language for themselves, as they could not have written in the language available to them as rulers and nobles. It may be posited further that though rulers and nobles might be patrons and that poets might be patronized, but only those poets survived who served poetry and not necessarily the patrons.

Ultimately, it was poetry that found a space for itself and, through that, the poets who constructed a genre of court poetry. In this process, the poet emerged as a chronicler and the patron as the chronicled. The relationship between literary writing and patronage has always been dichotomous. In medieval India, nobles and kings patronized poets and established their own identity as liberal promoters of arts; in modern times, there are several kinds of agencies that patronize authors. What the patrons did earlier, the academies of culture and literature, award-giving bodies, publishing houses, press, and centres of knowledge construction and dissemination are doing now. The significant feature of this patron–poet relationship is that it helped develop a literary culture of a certain kind. It also brought forth a readership that made way for this culture to grow and sustain. Without this critical and crucial readership, neither literary culture, nor canon, nor form, nor genre, not even the patrons and their poets could have survived beyond a time.

Endnotes

1. Reference may be made to the three major schools of poetry—Deccan, Delhi, and Lucknow—where poetry grew with individual marks and contributed broadly to the development of three different kinds of literary cultures.
2. Again, we may refer to Deccan, Delhi, and Lucknow, apart from other literary centres that developed in Azimabad and Rampur.
3. This refers to various forms of poetry, some of which include *ghazal, qasida, mathnawi*, and *marsiya*.
4. Some of these are *rubai, qita, musaddas, rekhti, wasokht, shahr-e ashob, hamd, naat, manqabat, and munajat.*
5. See, for example, Mir Taqi Mir's *Zikr-i Mir* (1999), Altaf Hussain Hali's *Yadgar-e Ghalib* (1897), Muhammad Husain Azad's *Aab-e hayat* (1880), Ram Babu Saxena's *Tareekh-e Adab Urdu* (1978), Jameel Jalibi's *Tareekh-e-Adab-e Urdu* (three volumes), and Saleem Akhtar's *Urdu Adab ki Mukhtasar Tareen Tareekh* (1984), among several others.
6. It is difficult to draw a line of clear distinction, yet Amir Khusrau's works can be classified with a certain amount of justification in terms of historical narratives and literary writings. Although he is known and celebrated primarily as a poet, his literary works also draw upon contemporary history and culture. Under the category of his literary works/poetry, one may put together *Tuhfat-us-Sighr* (1271), a collection of his early works; *Wasat-ul-Hayat* (1279), a collection of his maturing days; *Ghurrat-ul-Kamal* (1294) and *Nihayat-ul-Kamal* (1325), works representing his prime achievements; *Masnavi Duval Rani Khizr Khan* (1316), a narrative of love; *Khamsa* (1298), a collection of five romances; and *Aijaz-e-Khusrawi*, a compilation of other valuable writings. In the category of his historical narratives, one may put together *Qiran-us-Sadain* (1289), *Miftah-ul-Futuh* (1290), *Tughlaq Nama* (1320), *and Tarikh-i-Alai.*
7. Gopi Chand Narang, ed., *Amir Khusrau ka Hindavi Kalam* (Delhi: Educational Publishing House, 1992), p. 46.
8. This and all translations are by the author of this chapter.
9. See http://kavishala.in/amir-khusrow/ (accessed on 27 August 2018).
10. Narang, *Amir Khusrau ka Hindavi Kalam*, p. 43.

11. See https://allpoetry.com/Chaap-Tilak- (accessed on 27 August 2018).
12. See https://www.hindi-kavita.com/HindiDoheAmirKhusro.php (accessed on 27 August 2018).
13. See https://open.spotify.com/album/4jbwDS4XQXGEHjoR6UKa9i (accessed on 27 August 2018).
14. See https://blogs.harvard.edu/sulaymanibnqiddees/2015/03/20/the-path-to-the-well-is-rough/ (accessed on 27 August 2018).
15. Sayyada Jafar, ed., *Kulliyat-e Mohammad Quli Qutub Shah* (New Delhi: National Council for Promotion of Urdu Language, 1998), p. 297.
16. Ibid., p. 494.
17. The major poets from the late sixteenth century to the late nineteenth century who constituted parts of literary canon and remained outside the court include Wali Deccani (1667–1707), Mirza Mazhar Jaan-e-Janan (1699–1781), Siraj Aurangabadi (1715–1763), Khwaja Mir Dard (1721–1785), Ghulam Hamdani Mus'hafi (1750–1824), Imam Baksh Nasikh (1776–1838), Khwaja Haidar Ali Aatish (1777–1847), Momin Khan Momin (1800–1851), and Nawab Mirza Khan Dagh Dehlvi (1831–1905).
18. Rasheed Hasan Khan, ed., *Intekhab-e Sauda* (New Delhi: Maktaba Jamia Ltd., 2004), p. 355.
19. For a detailed discussion on the patronage that Mir received or did not receive, see C.M. Naim's 'Mir's Patrons' in *Zikr-i Mir*, pp. 85–95.
20. See https://www.rekhta.org/qita/kyaa-buud-o-baash-puuchho-ho-puurab-ke-saakino (accessed on 27 August 2018).
21. See https://www.rekhta.org/ghazals/mir-taqi-mir-ghazals-121 (accessed on 27 August 2018).
22. See https://www.rekhta.org/ghazals/jis-sar-ko-guruur-aaj-hai-yaan-taaj-varii-kaa-mir-taqi-mir-ghazals (accessed on 27 August 2018).
23. See https://www.rekhta.org/couplets/miir-saahib-zamaana-naazuk-hai-mir-taqi-mir-couplets (accessed on 27 August 2018).
24. See https://www.rekhta.org/couplets/shaam-se-kuchh-bujhaa-saa-rahtaa-huun-mir-taqi-mir-couplets?lang=hi (accessed on 27 August 2018).
25. See https://www.rekhta.org/ghazals/dekh-to-dil-ki-jaan-se-uthtaa-hai-mir-taqi-mir-ghazals?gclid=Cj0KCQjw-JvaBRDGARIsAFjqkkriGruJpqe_Gg4gdcCBiVTQcBwX5sE3lVsPGlwjr32kE5XKRz-XdFwaAjSUEALw_wcB (accessed on 27 August 2018).
26. See https://www.rekhta.org/ghazals/is-ahd-men-ilaahii-mohabbat-ko-kyaa-huaa-mir-taqi-mir-ghazals (accessed on 27 August 2018).
27. See https://rekhta.org/ghazals/kamar-baandhe-hue-chalne-ko-yaan-sab-yaar-baithe-hain-insha-allah-khan-insha-ghazals?lang=ur (accessed on 27 August 2018).

28. See https://rekhta.org/ghazals/kamar-baandhe-hue-chalne-ko-yaan-sab-yaar-baithe-hain-insha-allah-khan-insha-ghazals?lang=ur (accessed on 27 August 2018).
29. See https://www.rekhta.org/ghazals/kamar-baandhe-hue-chalne-ko-yaan-sab-yaar-baithe-hain-insha-allah-khan-insha-ghazals (accessed on 27 August 2018).
30. See https://www.rekhta.org/ghazals/yaa-mujhe-afsar-e-shaahaana-banaayaa-hotaa-bahadur-shah-zafar-ghazals (accessed on 27 August 2018).
31. Ibid.
32. See https://www.rekhta.org/ghazals/baat-karnii-mujhe-mushkil-kabhii-aisii-to-na-thii-bahadur-shah-zafar-ghazals (accessed on 27 August 2018).
33. Ibid.
34. See https://www.rekhta.org/couplets/behtar-to-hai-yahii-ki-na-duniyaa-se-dil-lage-sheikh-ibrahim-zauq-couplets-3 (accessed on 27 August 2018).
35. See https://www.rekhta.org/couplets/in-dinon-garche-dakan-men-hai-badii-qadr-e-sukhan-sheikh-ibrahim-zauq-couplets (accessed on 27 August 2018).
36. See https://www.rekhta.org/ghazals/daaim-padaa-huaa-tire-dar-par-nahiin-huun-main-mirza-ghalib-ghazals (accessed on 27 August 2018).
37. See https://www.rekhta.org/ghazals/huzuur-e-shaah-men-ahl-e-sukhan-kii-aazmaaish-hai-mirza-ghalib-ghazals (accessed on 27 August 2018).
38. See https://www.rekhta.org/couplets/huaa-hai-shah-kaa-musaahib-phire-hai-itraataa-mirza-ghalib-couplets (accessed on 27 August 2018).
39. See https://www.rekhta.org/couplets/na-sataaish-kii-tamannaa-na-sile-kii-parvaa-mirza-ghalib-couplets (accessed on 27 August 2018).
40. See https://www.rekhta.org/ghazals/sab-kahaan-kuchh-laala-o-gul-men-numaayaan-ho-gaiin-mirza-ghalib-ghazals (accessed on 27 August 2018).
41. See https://www.rekhta.org/ghazals/na-gul-e-nagma-huun-na-parda-e-saaz-mirza-ghalib-ghazals (accessed on 27 August 2018).

References

Naim, C.M. 1999. Translated, annotated, and with an Introduction to *Zikr-i Mir: The Autobiography of the Eighteenth Century Mughal Poet: Mir Muhammad Taqi 'Mir'* by Mir Taqi Mir. New Delhi: OUP.

Naim, C.M. 2004. *Urdu Texts and Contexts: The Selected Essays of C.M. Naim.* New Delhi: Permanent Black.

Language, Culture, Bombay/ Mumbai Cinema: Cinematic Representations of Muslims

Language, Culture, Cinema: A Prologue and Three Interrogations

If language is a medium of expression, and culture a mode of life, then creative representation may quite justifiably be read as their metaphor. The medium, the mode, and the metaphor are inseparable in all texts—verbal, visual, and written. They complement each other to grow into a form worthy of critical cognizance. In its ultimate configuration, this form becomes an index of a people's behaviour, their ways of communication, and, finally, their identity. Taking this as my point of initiation, I would posit that reading a filmic text is like reading a form in its verbal and visual manifestations that represent the major marks of a given culture.

All creative arts, including films, represent various stages in the development of this matrix of medium, mode, and metaphor. This becomes all the more significant in a multilingual, multicultural, multi-ethnic, and multireligious country like India, where various cultural clusters contribute towards the emergence of a broad Indian reality. When put on the screen, this reality is best appreciated in terms of arts and artefacts, myths and metaphors, social and political responses, and ritual and spiritual practices. As such, films create their own iconographies through their stock or experimental modes of representation.

A community or a group of people who constitute a part of the medium–mode–metaphor matrix and who configure a larger nationalist paradigm may be appropriately and broadly identified with reference to their cultural marks and linguistic behaviour. In the case of cinematic representation, however, this matrix needs to be problematized differently, as cinema acquires its strength from the plausibility and concrescence of visuals as reconstructed for the screen. Here, the spoken language broadens its frontier to incorporate both gesture and music in its fold. This theoretical basis may be applied to discuss the cinematic representation of the Muslims who have been prominently visible on the Indian screen, and have represented a certain cultural pattern and a certain linguistic taste. As the Bombay cinema carved a definite space for Muslim cultural marks and the language used by them, it also remained influenced, in turn, by these very marks. It remained so for several decades, especially till the emergence of a cinematic diction that drew its life from the linguistic habits of the masses, and which could not be assigned to any particular class or community of people. These issues may be appreciated in a critical perspective by interrogating at least three essentialist positions that have evolved over a period of time and have been reiterated incessantly. As these positions bear directly upon our reading of the cinematic representations of the Muslims, it would be proper to examine them and develop a paradigm to appreciate the issues involved.

First, is there anything called Hindi cinema? While one may understand what is meant by regional cinema, or even Hindustani or Indian cinema(s), one may not identify the so-called Hindi cinema with the same confidence. We are aware that the question of categorization is a problematic one in the Indian context, as it may be variously approached in terms of regions, languages, and cultures, apart from genres, forms, and techniques of representation. This constraint should not, however, help one language appropriate over other language(s), as it is quite liable to create a map of misreading. Developing an entirely objective view of the issue, I may posit that irrespective of the long-drawn and irreconcilable stances adopted regarding Urdu, Hindi, and Hindustani,[1] Hindi cinema is clearly a misnomer as it has subsumed several other linguistic and geographical spaces without ascertaining its own position in the larger imagination of the people. Unlike the regional cinemas which use given languages, the so-called Hindi cinema, which Yves Thoraval has discussed in great detail in the chapter 'The Supremacy of Hindi Cinema' in *The Cinemas of India: 1896–*

2000 (2000) to establish its 'supremacy', has unhesitatingly appropriated the benefits of hegemony that a national language is supposed to exercise over the entire length and breadth of a country, which Hindi does not obviously do. This cinema found its home in the Bombay of yesteryears and appropriated the space even of that cinema which was decidedly Urdu in its language, culture, and essential make-up.[2] In the years that followed, this cinema used a language that was commonly understood and negotiable, even though it was not so commonly or uniformly adopted or spoken.[3] Although Bombay emerged as the centre of this so-called Hindi cinema, it broadly produced the cinema *of* and *for* the northern part of India,[4] which is home to the Indo-Aryan group of languages. As northern India speaks in different languages, this cinema also absorbs and evolves its own language for different levels of reception. Today, this cinema speaks in Hindi now, now in Urdu, in Hindustani now, now in Hinglish, in Bombaiyya now, and now in an argot of a mixed variety, and all of these are passed under the broad identity of Hindi, with the final seal put over it by Central Board of Film Certification of the Ministry of Information and Broadcasting. This mixed linguistic baggage of Bombay cinema, as may be testified, creates a variety of impressions—serious, comic, and plebeian—either by turns, or even simultaneously, and constructs diverse Indian discourses in turn.

Second, what is Bollywood and what does it signify? To put it precisely, Bollywood is a queer construct, a fashionable pictogram, a bizarre hybrid that seeks its identity through a lingering hangover for Hollywood on the one hand, and our loyalty to the mythical Bombay of pre-Thackerite days on the other. It is a self-defeating exercise in carving a unique identity for one's own self. It is yet another misnomer, after Hindi cinema, which needs serious contestation. It relegates the major postcolonial questions reiterated ceaselessly regarding history, identity, indigeneity, and the contexts of power, language, and image. In spite of a host of filmic texts narrating the nation in distinctive terms, Bombay cinema has been unquestioningly and ubiquitously canonized as Bollywood cinema. With the silence of film critics and historians on this issue,[5] as also on the other issue of Hindi cinema, Bollywood stands authenticated as a term of reference for Bombay cinema, and it has become a part of the larger Indian imagination in spite of its being too priggish and self-conscious. Even if it is reincarnated in future as Mollywood cinema, in response to the compulsions of a segment of contemporary local politics, it would remain a portmanteau of Mumbai cinema. It would not be too remote to imagine that in spite of this, it would carry the burden of the canonized and overpowering Hollywood. It needs to be asserted that this is the very Bombay or Mumbai cinema[6] of our own make and mix that has remained the citadel of authentic cultural configurations of the larger part of north India of which Muslims, being the largest minority of India with a population of more than a hundred million, form a significant part.

Third, like the two problematic identifiers mentioned before, there is yet another identifier—Islamicate—that seems to have emerged as a category to discuss the representation of Muslim subjects in Bombay cinema ever since Marshall Hodgson, a historian of repute, used it to associate Muslims with Islam. Mukul Kesavan, Rachel Dwyer, Ira Bhaskar, and Allen Richard appropriated it for the same purpose in the context of films, and to designate all motifs and manners associated with Muslims as 'Islamicate'.[7] To put it in a perspective, I may ask as to what is Islamicate and how can this be possibly used as a category to study the representation of Muslims in Bombay cinema? I would put forward that like Hindi cinema and Bollywood, Islamicate is another misleading label that has not only gained currency in reading filmic texts with Muslims as their subject, but it has been presumably done with certain academic justification, although the justification does not hold well. All the pleas put together by a more informed set of critics, however, fail to erase one seminal line of distinction that a religious faith and a people who follow it do not necessarily and compulsively need to be taken as inevitable constituents of one or single formation. Like all religious faiths and their followers, Islam and Muslims are also linked, but all constructions relating to Muslims are not to be assessed in terms of their religious identity. The thesis advanced by those projecting the Islamicate category, thus, crumbles, as it fails to take note of a simple distinction that Islam is a faith while Muslims are the followers of that faith, and the two are not necessarily the one and the same for all possible reasons. Muslims are a people in a social matrix and live as simple or complex a life as anyone else to deserve a cinematic representation. While they profess one faith, they speak many languages and reflect many cultures. As such, equating a people only with their faith and not contextualizing them in a complex cultural formation is negating them legitimate space for larger participation in life's various manifestations. It would, thus, be grossly unjust to designate all of their actions and responses to history and society under the category of the Islamicate. It would be as unfair as equating the responses of Hindus with Hinduism, or of Christians with Christianity. As Muslims represented in the Bombay cinema are a part of the larger Indian reality, they have to be viewed as such rather than shown to be representing a separate category in conformity with their religious identity. Categorizing all subjects related with Muslim life and culture under the broad label of the Islamicate would be stereotyping and essentializing a people and their sociocultural identity of which religious faith is only a part and not the whole. I would, thus, assert that Islamicate may be used with great profit in areas where studies focus on faith, its history, religious practices, rituals, and other related manifestations, rather than social practices and cultural norms.

With this, I go back to my argument about cultural representations of a people. Now I pose yet another set of questions in relation to the representations of the Muslim culture. What are the signs of this culture, let me ask? Is it *mujra* or mushaira, ghazal or qawwali, or is it simply the skullcap or lungi (*tehmed*), or domes or minarets? Is it not civility and refinement that also distinguish this culture, or is it not a modest and modernist outlook that could identify these people as Muslims? One could also ask: are Muslims essentially decadent, or are they simply incapable of looking forward? Further, do they act and react, write and speak, and relate and respond differently from others? My contention is that the critical readings of filmic texts, conducted by some perceptive critics who have engaged with the idea of the Islamicate, have grossly overlooked the layers of implications carried in the three contestable categories—Hindi cinema, Bollywood, and the Islamicate—even though Bombay cinema has chosen to address the issue of Muslim representation in some of the most imaginative ways. Let me take you on a tour.

Bombay Cinema: A Tour

With the 1930s began the history of the Bombay sound film,[8] and it began with *Alam Ara* (1931), a Muslim cultural representation, which also happened to be a commercial success. The decade also saw on screen films of the same genre in *Lal-e-Yaman* (1933), *Char Darvesh* (1933), and *Pukar* (1939). Four out of the eight films related with Muslim subjects or Muslim representation—two neutral expressions I choose in preference to Islamicate—and produced during this significant colonial decade underlined the important thesis that the subject was considered worthy of attention, and that it had a respectable number of viewers in the market. The 1940s followed with five more of the type: *Najma* (1943), *Mumtaz Mahal* (1944), *Zeenat* (1945), *Shahjehan* (1946), and *Omar Khayyam* (1957). These five figured in a list of less than two dozen films produced during the decade. The dwindling number of Muslim representations in the 40s, as compared with the 30s, did not suggest anything against their reception except that this decade made way for the production of some of the most remarkable films like *Bandhan* (1940), *Anmol Ghadi* (1946), *Jugnu* (1947), *Nadiya Ke Paar* (1948), *Mela* (1948), *Barsaat* (1949), *Andaz* (1949), and *Mahal* (1949). In other words, the decade sought its character at a broader level of reception and a more holistic representation of the Indian society and culture, which the subsequent two decades sharpened further.

The 50s and the 60s could best be described as the golden period of Muslim representation on the celluloid. The 50s saw the production of approximately two dozen films that dealt with Muslim subjects, although it was *Mirza Ghalib* (1954) that stole the show. The 60s produced about three dozen Muslim subject films for an ever-growing number of viewers and it produced some of the classics like *Chaudhvin ka Chand* (1960), *Mughal-e-Azam* (1960), and *Sahib Bibi Aur Ghulam* (1962).[9] These films became a part of the collective memory of those who lived during this period, and indeed many of them grew with these films over the years. It would be significant to note that most of the films produced during this golden period were character-plot centric, and that they drew upon history and places, although they did not necessarily succeed at the so-called box office. A particular geographical location that engrossed the attention of the film-makers repeatedly and, by implication, of the viewers was Baghdad. The mythic and real characters that caught both their fancy and imagination included Ali Baba, Alif Laila, and Laila Majnun, among several others, on the one hand,[10] and Jehangir, Akbar, Anarkali, Mirza Ghalib, and many more of this type on the other.[11] All these showed a typical hangover for romantic themes, plots, characters, and situations. They seemed to have the potential to engage the viewers and hold them in spell for three hours of cinematic entertainment.

Bombay films started developing new genres, new modes, and new techniques in the 70s, which has continued with remarkable success ever since. While the thief of Baghdad and Ali Baba still held a limited space in the common imagination of the film-makers and viewers, the 70s showed a general decline in the representation of Muslim subjects. As the age of celebrating the regal splendour, kings, queens, and princesses had gone by, and as these subjects had also been fully exhausted, newer subjects caught the attention of film-makers. Films like *Lal Patthar* (1971), *Pakeezah* (1972), *Garm Hava* (1973), *Shatranj ke Khilari* (1977), and *Noorie* (1979) appeared as the new classics of the age, and they offered a new dimension to the classics of the golden period mentioned earlier. Among these, *Shatranj ke Khilari* and *Garm Hava* were new additions to the common imaginary of the Indian viewers, as these films spoke a new language and premiered new concerns. In the 80s, *Umrao Jaan* (1981), *Nikaah* (1982), *Tawaif* (1985), and *Salim Langde Pe Mat Ro* (1989) emerged as yet other modern classics, and extended the concern manifested in earlier films like *Pakeezah*. Films as varied in form and content as *Henna* (1991), *Sardari Begum* (1996), *Train to Pakistan* (1998), *Mission Kashmir* (2000), *Refugee* (2000), and *Fiza* (2000),[12] among others, in the first decade of the twenty-first century, problematized the scenario of Muslim representation still further.

This tour through the Bombay cinema affords me with a way to assess its essential nature and character. While I have gone on in a chronological order, underlining the hallmarks of this cinema through the eight decades of its development, I have refrained from offering neat classifications to trace the trajectory of this cinema. Classifications are tricky; they are limiting and lead to oversights and slippages. While some effort has been made to study Bombay cinema with this methodology by Ira Bhaskar and Richard Allen,[13] I would desist from doing so, as a number of remarkable films representing sociopolitical issues, ideological shifts, and rebuttal of stereotypes cannot be properly appreciated if they are viewed from fixed perspectives. Similarly, there are films that reconstruct Indian history with Muslims playing their part in it, as there are films on cross-cultural representations, resistance, fear, exploitation, and marginalization. Then there are films that engage with issues that concern religious faith and problematize gender, language, rural–urban divide, or, in other words, a cluster of motifs and icons spread over time and space. If needed, one could place these films in more secular and commonsensical categories like epicals, musicals, chronicles, romances, *courtesanate*s, *masal*s, melodramas, parallels, *mafiate*s, comedies, satires, thrillers, and religious etc., rather than put them under an unjustifiably fanciful, broad, and misconceived category of the Islamicate.

I would, therefore, suggest that more important than sticking to the neat categories of Bombay cinema and arriving at tidy conclusions are the issues concerning the very emergence and development of this cinema that may tell us about its types and stereotypes. This cinema has emerged out of the multiple influences of the Indian epics, the Sanskrit drama, the theatrical conventions and traditions of North India, the Parsi theatre, and, finally, the inescapable Hollywood. Early Bombay cinema went back to Parsi theatre for all its theatricality and its high-flown style of the Urdu verse. The reasons were obvious: Urdu could reach out to masses as it was a descendant of the Persian language, an heir apparent, so to say, that had been used as the language of literature and administration during the British rule. For at least four decades ever since the consequential 30s,

Bombay cinema has used Urdu as its prime language, even though it was popularly branded as Hindi cinema in almost all descriptions and entries on individual films. Let me also posit that the Bombay cinema of today is not worried about Urdu or Hindi or Hindustani as its language; it is concerned basically with an idiom that makes good sense to the common people who are composed of an extremely mixed variety of viewers. It is concerned, to a very great extent, with how this cinema may secure a safe place for itself in the market. This thesis finds further explanation through certain cinematic representations in terms of their dialogues and lyrics, which call for a closer look.

Language as Gesture

Language acquires a variety of forms in filmic texts. Apart from verbal appropriation, it is also used as a gesture or as a way of expressing a mood. Depending on its nature, every film discovers its own schema of expression. Even though Urdu has been stereotyped both as a language and a culture, it is in the films where it has acquired its remarkable strength. Although the grace of the Urdu language and the cultural legacy associated with it helped create an environment for the film, it was the strength of the given plot and the resilience of the characters that combined to make a dramatic impact on the viewers. Strong deliveries helped them become a part of the common memory, as it happened in the case of *Mughal-e-Azam*. It could be possible with the available talent who nurtured a linguistic culture and created a register that appealed to the literary and the popular imagination together. One could underline the strength imbued in some of the narratives and dialogues only to show that language performs many a role as a tool of expression, a gesture, or a mood. This could be well borne out by the kind of language appropriated in *Mughal-e-Azam* (1960), *Mere Mehboob* (1963), *Umrao Jaan* (1981), *Lal Patthar* (1971), *Pakeezah* (1972), and many other films like these. It was not only the language, however, that played the magic, but the right accent and intonation, the quality of speaker's baritone, and style of delivery as it came from masters like Prithviraj Kapoor, Dilip Kumar, Raj Kumar, and several others in a variety of films.[14]

In Bombay cinema, Urdu language could be used in many of its avatars—as the language of love, war, court, diplomacy, and of the common day-to-day interaction. It must also be noted that many Urdu writers, lyricists, producers, and directors of significance like Agha Hashar Kashmiri, A.R. Kardar, and K. Asif,[15] and many more who formed a league and practised their arts at that point of time, or joined them in subsequent years, were well aware of the rich and expressive conventions of the Urdu language. They worked from behind the scene to create an auditory and visual culture in a series of memorable films ever produced. They also helped create a condition for a broader reception by recharging the language and making it accessible. Beginning with the 1930s, Urdu stayed as the lingua franca of Bombay films for at least till the 70s, when other linguistic and dialectic traditions found their way and a new argot for the new filmic tradition was created. It only strengthened the idea further that Bombay films could well develop their own medium of expression, keeping in view the shifting paradigms of life and culture. Bombay could well realize, more than ever before, that language alone could not do the trick; it was the camera also that spoke a language of its own and the commercialization of the age that dictated the nature of language. The age of romantic exuberance was gone where language could be charged emotionally and made to sound romantic and husky; language was now a tool in hand to support the complex scheme of film-making.

This thesis may also be borne out by looking at the kind of titles that are chosen for the new films. Depending on the nature of the film, the titles were sometimes in Urdu like *Aashiqui* (1990)[16], *Shola Aur Shabnam* (1961), and *Hazaaron Khwaishein Aisi* (2005), and sometimes in Hindi like *Ankur* (1974), *Nishant* (1975), and *Swades* (2004).[17] At the third remove, there were titles that were neither Urdu nor Hindi, but simple Hindustani that could echo the heartbeats of the general viewers and reflect their simple joys of life, love, and romance. Here are some interesting examples with emphasis on *dil*, as in *Dil Hai Ke Manta Nahin* (1991), *Dilwale Dulhania Le Jayenge* (1995), *Dil to Pagal Hai* (1997),[18] and others with emphasis on *pyaar*, as in *Pyaar To Hona Hi Tha* (1998), *Hum Hain Rahi*

Pyar Ke (1993), and *Aur Pyaar Ho Gaya* (1997). The changing trends of communication have made good space for both English and Hinglish in the recent past. Some English titles that make practical sense and find ready appeal include *Luck by Chance* (2009), *Rock On!!* (2008), and *What's Your Raashee?* (2009).[19] Yet another variation on this liberal trend may be seen in the use of Hinglish, which is also equally and totally acceptable as a part of common parlance in India today. These include *Love Kaa Taddka* (2009), *Jab We Met* (2007), and *Pyaar Impossible!* (2010). These titles succeed like the success with the new groups of viewers, who book their seats on the Internet and watch the movies in multiplexes. This thesis may be extended and justified further, if one chooses to look closely at the language used by the characters and the general atmosphere created in the film to hold the attention of the viewers.

Language as Music

Bombay films present the richest possible variety of lyrics written in varied registers for an immensely varied audience. Like the titles that we have surveyed previously, there are lyrics that also come from various linguistic traditions and registers like Urdu, Hindi, Hindustani, Hinglish, and the common parlance of the day. These lyrics live their short and long lives, depending on how imaginatively they are composed and sung. They combine the linguistic traditions of Urdu and Hindi, with themes ranging from religious to secular and from secular to profane. Let us take, for example, some of the Urdu lyrics that are devotional in nature and also fall in a literary tradition. These include *Bekas Pe Karam Kijiye Sarkar-e Madina* (Have mercy on this poor soul, O, lord of Medina), *Aaqa Salim Chishti, Maula Salim Chishti* (O, my lord Salim Chishti, O, my saviour Salim Chishti), and *Khwaja Mere Khwaja* (Saviour, my saviour). It reflects the tradition of the religious/mystical poetry of the Perso-Arabic tradition, as carried over in the Urdu language. The same language, when used in a romantic context, evokes nostalgia, suffering, and pangs of love. We may note this in examples like *Mili Khaak Mein Mohabbat/ Jala Dil ka Aashiyana* (My love's ruined, my heart's abode lies tattered), *Jurm-e-Ulfat pe Humein Log Saza Dete Hain*

(The world punishes me for I loved my love), and *Rang Aur Noor ki Baraat Kise Pesh Karoon* (Whom shall I offer this grand gift of colours and light).[20] Both the kinds of lyrics—spiritual and romantic—have had their acceptance with huge clusters of audiences and have stayed in public memory ever since they were sung and enacted on the screen. Bombay films proved a major channel through which the worth of this tradition could be passed on to the common people, who could internalize them and hum at leisure to ameliorate the pains and pleasures of their life and living.

Another facet of audience–language negotiation may be seen in some of the Hindi lyrics that develop a different idiom. It harks back to the indigenous literary traditions of the most secular kind, which is completely different from the Perso-Arabic religious/mystical and romantic traditions mentioned earlier. This may be marked in lyrics like *Mohe Panghat pe Nandlal Chhed Gayo Re* (My love has teased my by the banks of the river), *Thare Rahiyo O Baanke Yaar* (Wait, o, my love, wait a while), and *Chandan Sa Badan, Chanchal Chitwan* (The body like sandalwood, the looks so wanton).[21] Yet another facet of an extremely popular variety of lyrics may be seen in romantic love songs. This is a novel variation that may, for the sake of convenience, be called Hindustani in its linguistic make-up. Examples of this kind may be marked in lyrics such as *Hawa Mein Udta Jaye Mera Lal Dupatta Malmal Ka* (My red muslin scarf waves in the wind), *Jane Kya Tune Kahi* (Don't know what you said), and *Chhod Do Aanchal Zamana Kya Kahega* (Please let off the end of my sari, what will the world think?).[22] Lyrics of this kind turn into pure romantic dramas in duets like *Aap Yun Hi Agar Humse Milte Rahe, Dekhiye Ek Din Pyaar Ho Jayega* (Look, I'll fall in love one day if you meet me like this so often). A fine illustration of this variety may be found in *Hum Aapki Aankhon Mein Iss Dil ko Basa Dein Toh?* (What if I settle this heart in your eyes?). Let us see how this delicate dialogue of love develops in dramatic terms:

Male: *Hum aapki aankhon mein iss dil ko basa dein toh?*
(What if I set up a home in your eyes?)

Female: *Hum moond ke palkon ko iss dil ko saza dein toh?*
(What if I shut my eyes and punish your heart?)

Male: *In zulfon mein gundhenge hum phool mohabbat ke*
(I will string the flowers of love in your tresses)
Female: *Zulfon ko jhatak ke hum yeh phool gira dein toh?*
(What if I jerk my tresses to drop your flowers?)

Male: *Hum aapko khwabon mein aa aa ke satayenge*
(I'll get into your dreams and tease you to no end)
Female: *Hum aapki aankhon se neendein hi uda dein toh?*
(What if I steal the sleep from your eyes?)

Male: *Hum aapke qadmon par gir jayenge ghash kha kar*
(I'll faint and fall at your feet, my love)
Female: *Is per bhi na hum apne aanchal ki hawa dein toh?*[23]
(What if I don't soothe and help you back to breath?)

This is a fine example of sheer romance, fun, and playfulness. These couplets of hardly any literary worth, sung on the screen decades ago, find an echo in the hearts of young lovers even today. What makes it so is the combined magic of language, music, voice, and tonal variations. This is a stock example of many such romantic lyrics that stay in our memory essentially because of their intense musicality and instant appeal to popular imagination. These lyrics came from a phase of popular romantic movies which were soon to be replaced by more earthy ones, written in the popular parlance of the market. The new age defied much of the rhyme and reason that characterized the earlier lyrics. Even though the new lyrics had shorter lives, they reflected the contemporary popular culture which was prone to changes at a much faster pace than ever before. These lyrics were funny, witty, dramatic, and purely entertaining, and were aimed at a larger audience of an extremely mixed variety. These qualities of the downright popular lyrics could be marked in *Khaike Paan Banaraswala* (Chewing the betel leaves of Benares), *Aati Kya Khandala?* (Aren't you coming to Khandala?), and *Chal Chhaiyan Chhaiyan* (Move in shade, the thick shade).[24] These lyrics take a whole lot of people to sing as if in a rote, without ever running the risk of being pooh-poohed. To bring this discussion on lyrics to an end, let me also refer to the Hinglish incarnation of the Bombay lyrics. There is nothing odd, nothing forbidden in this domain of the significant absurd. Listen to these, for example: *Love Kaa Taddka Re, Hotty Naughty Baby in Town*, and *Give Me Some Sunshine.*[25] This is the idiom of modern India, the lingo of the new nation carving its identity each day in yet another way, and revising it at a faster pace than ever before. Considering the immense variety of Bombay lyrics, I may propose further that they have been composed in diverse linguistic registers and sung in an amazing variety of tone and tenor, representing almost all the nine rasas. Most of them represent *shringar*, *hasya*, *veera*, *karuna*, and *shanta*, but they are not entirely devoid of *bhayanak*, *raudra*, *vibhatsya*, and *adbhuta*. The only occasions when lyrics or even dialogues fail to hold the popular imagination are those when they are unable to synchronize with the tone and tenor of the age for which they are composed. A stock example of this may be seen in the lyric that begins thus: *Priye Praneshwari! Yadi Aap Hamein Aadesh Karein To Prem Ka Hum Shri Ganesh Karein* (My dear, the breath of my heart! If you so order me, I will just begin to love you).

Let me bring my argument to an end with reference to a film called *Dil Dosti Etc.* (2007) that interrogates stereotypes and reflects iconoclastic aspirations of some young Indian boys and girls who constitute the major cast of this film. They are in search of their distinct individual identities and an idiom for themselves; they nurse their own aspirations and speak their own kinds of lingo. One of the characters, played by Imaaduddin Shah, speaks a pure and Sanskritized version of Hindi which only evokes laughter, although whatever he says deserves serious critical attention. The intention is not to pooh-pooh a language but to portray the character as a type, who is one of the many other types as well as a queer part of the whole. This film represents a way of life that the young generation in India prefers to live today. It reflects their predominant attitudes, their world view, and their special manners of speech. It stands as a major signpost of contemporary India, and it also accounts for the long distance covered in terms of India's emergence as a nation state, marked by severe odds and pleasant events since the production of *Alam Ara* (1931). During the eight decades between the two films—*Alam Ara* and *Dil Dosti Etc.*—Bombay cinema has configured and reconfigured itself again and again; it has created liberal space for scripting the histories of the nation, initiating significant sociopolitical discourses, negotiating with languages and cultures, and reinventing appropriate medium, mode, and metaphor.

On being asked once in an interview on what was more important—pure communication or expression of one's ideas—Shyam Benegal answered that the film was nothing else but only a communicative medium of ideas, and that the success of a film depended on the kind of language one chose to make it in. This brings me to mention a recent film called *Yeh Saali Zindagi* (2011) and to reflect on why this could not have been called *Yeh Saala Jeevan*. Even though the bare intents remain the same in both the titles, the impacts they create are decidedly different. More than a matter of language, or choice of words, *Yeh Saali Zindagi* hits the popular imagination instantly, which the other possible title could not have even touched.

As suggested earlier, the Bombay film today is not so much concerned with matters of linguistic chastity or choice as it is concerned with its commercial viability, which comes from making right thematic, linguistic, and stylistic preferences. Film-making is an industry today; it is a profit-making concern involving high stakes, and it faces threat from the small screen, new art forms, and international challenges in filming. One has been hearing of the demise of Urdu language and *tehzeeb* (etiquette) for long; one has already lamented that Uttar Pradesh, the so-called citadel of the growth and development of Urdu, has turned its back on this language, and one also knows that the younger generation in Uttar Pradesh fights shy of its complete ignorance of the Urdu alphabets. This may well be an appropriate story for a Bombay film, but even that film will have to speak in its own language and discover its own form. Films that sustain themselves do so through imaginative reconstructions of a given society and culture. They also do so by discovering a new medium of expression, which, in today's scenario, would neither be Urdu pure, nor Hindi absolute, not even

Bombaiyya pukka, but just a new verbal construct which is ever-ready to be revised with each turn of history, and with each imaginative leap that catches its reverberations.

Endnotes

1. Much has been written on this issue from social, political, literary, and linguistic angles, as also on the issue of script and its acceptability. Some of the works include: Christopher Shackle and Rupert Snell, *Hindi and Urdu Since 1800: A Common Reader* (London: School of Oriental and African Studies, 1990), Christopher King, *One Language, Two Scripts: The Hindi Movement in Nineteenth Century North India* (New Delhi: Oxford University Press, 1994), David Lelyveld, 'Zuban-e Urdu-e Mu'alla and the Idol of Linguistic Origins,' *Annual of Urdu Studies* 9 (2003); Alok Rai, *Hindi Nationalism* (Hyderabad: Orient Longman, 2001), Alok Rai, 'The Persistence of Hindustani,' *Annual of Urdu Studies* 20 (2005).
2. While Mukul Kesavan, a renowned historian and novelist, considers Urdu to be the 'bedrock' of Bombay cinema, Harish Trivedi, a former English professor at Delhi University, develops an opposite view in favour of Hindi. These opposite views may be seen in Mukul Kesavan, 'Urdu, Awadh, and the Tawaif: The Islamicate Roots of Hindi Cinema,' *The Ugliness of the Indian Male and Other Propositions* (New Delhi: Black Kite, 2008) and Harish Trivedi, 'All Kinds of Hindi: The Evolving Language of Hindi Cinema,' in Vinay Lal and Ashish Nandy, eds. *Fingerprinting Popular Culture: The Mythic and the Iconic in Indian Cinema* (Delhi: OUP, 2006).
3. Yves Thoraval presents a detailed account of the rise of the so-called Hindi cinema, beginning with a brief historical-cum-political survey from 1940 to 2000. He goes on to discuss other aspects like colour film, the commercial cinema, the golden age of Hindi cinema, and the star system, along with discussions on music, dance, producers, directors, actors, and some major films. See chapter 3 entitled 'The Supremacy of Hindi Cinema,' *The Cinemas of India: 1896–2000* (New Delhi: Macmillan, 2000).
4. The linguistic map of India is clearly divisible between the Indo-Aryan and Dravidian languages spoken in the northern and southern parts of India respectively. Even though North India comprises diverse linguistic states (Jammu and Kashmir, Himachal Pradesh, Punjab, Haryana, Uttarakhand, Uttar Pradesh, Rajasthan, Bihar, Jharkhand, Madhya Pradesh, Orissa, and West Bengal), the so-called Hindi is commonly understood, although it is not so commonly spoken except in the Hindi heartland. Even if it is spoken in other states, it is spoken in a way that it may not be designated as Hindi in a strict sense.

5. Bollywood has engaged the attention of a large number of writers, who accept this hybrid nomenclature without ever interrogating it. Taking it as it is, they have only reiterated the basic spirit of the colonial discourse even further. A quick glance at the title of some of the books published during the last one decade would bear it out quite amply that Bollywood has been unhesitatingly and unabashedly adopted as a favourite name for the Bombay filmdom, and there is no stopping or interrogating this phenomenon. The books that may be mentioned in this regard include: Vijay Mishra's *Bollywood Cinema: Temples of Desire* (2001), Jonathan Torgovnik and Nasreen Munni Kabir's *Bollywood Dreams* (2003), R. Dawar's *Bollywood: Yesterday, Today, and Tomorrow* (2006), Derek Bose's *Brand Bollywood: A New Global Entertainment* (2006), Robert James Elliott and Nicholas R. Bradley's *Bollywood: Behind the Scenes, Beyond the Stars* (2007), Mihir Bose's *Bollywood: A History* (2007), Anandam P. Kavoori and Aswin Punathambekar's *Global Bollywood* (2008), Rachel Dwyer's *100 Bollywood Films* (2008), Anwar Jamal and Saibal Chatterjee's *Hollywood Bollywood: The Politics of Crossover Films* (Hindi, 2008), Rajinder Dudrah and Jigna Desai's *The Bollywood Reader* (2008), Ajay Gehlawat's *Reframing Bollywood: Theories of Popular Hindi Cinema* (2010), and Anustup Basu's *Bollywood in the Age of New Media: The Geo-Televisual Aesthetic* (2010).
6. A brief note on why I call it Bombay cinema would be relevant and central to the argument that I am trying to build. I call it so because India is a complex site with two thousand dialects, eight hundred distinct languages, and twenty-four official languages. As far as films are concerned, we have regional cinemas in India (which cater to identified linguistic and regional groups) and, all of them taken together, can be considered to be the various faces of Indian cinema. Since Indian cinema is an amorphous body to me and signifies, at best, a broad spectrum, I consider it proper to designate it as Bombay or Mumbai cinema, which (in spite of also being the site of production of Marathi cinema) is traditionally associated with the so-called Hindi cinema that caters to larger number of people than other cinemas.
7. The expression 'Islamicate' was first used by a historian Marshall G.S. Hodgson in his book *The Venture of Islam: Conscience and History in a World Civilization* (1974). In the first volume titled as, *The Classical Age of Islam*, he uses it as a term to associate Muslims with Islam. The impact of this nomenclature proved infectious, as it was later overstretched by some others to discuss all Muslims subjects in the category of the 'Islamicate'.
8. The history of Indian cinema begins with *Raja Harishchandra*, a silent film by Dadasaheb Phalke in 1913. This paper does not, however, consider the era of silent films, although it may offer important clues towards the understanding of the Muslim cultural configurations.

9. The following may also be added: *Mere Mehboob* (1963), *Taj Mahal* (1963), *Ghazal* (1964), *Jahan Ara* (1964), *Qawwali Ki Raat* (1964), *Bahu Begum* (1967), and *Mere Huzoor* (1968).
10. More characters of this nature that grappled the imagination of film-makers included Char Dervesh, Alauddin, Sinbad, Hatim Tai, Gul Sanobar, Laila Majnun, and Rustom Sohrab.
11. Other historical figures chosen as subjects were Babur, Jehangir, Akbar, Shah Jahan, Anarkali, Noor Jehan, Mumtaz Mahal, Jahanara, Razia Sultan, and Nawab Siraj-ud-Daulah.
12. Some others in this category are *Gadar: Ek Prem Katha* (2001), *Zubeidaa* (2001), *Tehzeeb* (2003), *Veer-Zaara* (2004), *Maqbool* (2003), *Jodhaa Akbar* (2008), *Iqbal* (2005), *Shaurya* (2008), *Bombay* (1995), *Zakhm* (1998), *A Wednesday* (2008), *Fida* (2004), and *My Name is Khan* (2010).
13. See, for example, Ira Bhaskar and Richard Allen's, *Islamicate Cultures of Bombay Cinema* (2009). They study Muslim subject films under four neat categories: Muslim historical, Muslim courtesan films, Muslim socials, and new wave Muslim social and after. They discuss *Pukar* (1939), *Mirza Ghalib* (1954), *Mughal-e-Azam* (1960), and *Jodhaa Akbar* (2008) under Muslim historical; *Pakeezah* (1972), *Umrao Jaan* (1981), *Tawaif* (1985), *Sardari Begum* (1996), and *Umrao Jaan* (2006) under Muslim courtesan films; *Najma* (1943), *Chaudhvin ka Chand* (1960), and *Mere Mehboob* (1963) under classical Muslim socials; and *Garm Hava* (1973), *Salim Langde Pe Mat Ro* (1989), *Fiza* (2000) under new wave Muslim social and after. Another reference may be made to Rachel Dwyer, 'The Islamicate Film.'
14. There are other remarkable voices to be heard in Madhubala, Meena Kumari, Nargis, Nimmi, Noor Jehan, Waheeda Rehman, Rehman, and Iftekhar.
15. A number of talented literary figures to boost this tradition included Rajinder Singh Bedi, Saadat Hasan Manto, Khwaja Ahmad Abbas, Kamal Amrohi, Mehboob Khan, Abrar Alvi, Jan Nisar Akhtar, Sahir Ludhianvi, Akhtar ul Iman, Kaifi Azmi, Shakeel Badayuni, and Majrooh Sultanpuri.
16. Consider tiles like *Fanaa* (2006), *Bekhudi* (1992), *Gardish* (1993), *Jazbaat* (1994), *Tapish* (1999), *Aitraaz* (2004), *Qayamat* (1983), *Aks* (2001), *Fareb* (1996), *Elaan* (1994), *Jurm* (2005), *Nigehbaan: The Third Eye* (2005), *Kurbaan* (2009), and *Lamhe* (1992).
17. More in the category, like the following, may be mentioned: *Lakshya* (2004), *Abhay* (three different films in the years 1995, 2001, and 2009 were made with this title which show preference for a certain language), *Yuddh* (1985), *Aakrosh* (2010), *Drohi* (2010), *Mrityudand* (1997), *Yugandhar* (1993), *Shaurya* (2008), *Khalnayak* (1993), and *Mithya* (2008).

18. More films exploited the popularity of *dil*, as in, *Hum Dil De Chuke Sanam* (1999), *Diljale* (1996), *Dil Chahta Hai* (2001), *Dil Se..* (1998), and *Dil Dosti Etc* (2007).
19. Some more examples may be seen in *Karthik Calling Karthik* (2010), *Don* (2006), *LOC Kargil* (2003), *Gang* (2000), *Refugee* (2000), *1942: A Love Story* (1994), *1947: Earth* (1999), *Duplicate* (1998), *Yes Boss* (1997), *Singh Is Kinng* (2008), *My Name Is Khan* (2010), *3 Idiots* (2009), *Paa* (2009), *Family* (2006), *Race* (2008), *Krazzy 4* (2008), *All the Best* (2009), *Black Friday* (2007), *Welcome to Sajjanpur* (2008), *Well Done Abba* (2009), *Idiot Box* (1996), *Trump Card* (2009), *Hide and Seek* (2010), *Chance Pe Dance* (2010), *Life Partner* (2009), *Wanted* (2009), *Wake Up Sid* (2009), *The Warrior* (2001), and *Monsoon Wedding* (2001).
20. There is a huge number of memorable lyrics that have formed a part of the collective consciousness of the audiences. Some more of them are: *Waqt ne kiya kya haseen sitam* (How tyrannical has the time been), *Wo jab yaad aaye bahut yaad aaye* (My ruminations go endless, whenever I ruminate), *Phir wahi sham wahi gham wahi tanhai hai* (It's again the same evening, the same misery, the same loneliness), *Banda parwar, thaam lo jigar, ban ke pyar phir aaya hoon* (Love! Be happy, have heart, I'm here once again), *Ye kya jagah hai dosto, ye kaun sa dayar hai* (What place is this my friends, what abode), *Dil cheez kya hai aap meri jaan lijiye* (Not to mention my heart, I offer you my life), and many more, as the list is endless.
21. To add further to this category of lyrics, one could also mention *Ab ke baras bhej bhaiyya ko babul* (Send me my brother, I am all alone my father), *Kahe ko byahi bides* (Why did you marry me off to one in an alien, far-off land), *Bhaura bada nadaan re* (The bee is just too innocent), *Man re tu kahe na dheer dhare* (Why don't you have patience, my poor heart), *Piya to se naina lage re* (My love, my glances meet yours and, yours mine), *Poocho na kaise main ne rain bitayi* (Don't ask me how I spent the dark night), *Mere naina sawan bhadon* (My eyes are streams; they shower like rains), and *Tum bin jeevan kaisa jeevan* (What a life! What a life is this without you).
22. One naturally recalls to mind some more lyrics like *Pyar kiya to darna kya* (What fear, I have loved, and say so), *Teri zulfon se judai toh nahi mangi thi* (I hadn't asked for separation from your tresses), *Chura liya hai tum ne jo dil ko* (You have stolen my heart, my love), *Dekho rootha na karo* (Don't sulk, my love), *Abhi na jao chhod kar* (Don't leave me yet), *Tumko dekha to ye khayal aaya* (It occurred to me as I saw you), *Chehra hai ya chand khila hai* (Is that your face, or has the moon shown up), *Ek ladki ko dekha to aisa laga* (I saw a girl, I felt as if), and *Ghar se nikalte hi/kuch door chalte hi* (Stepping out of the house, walking a few steps ahead).

23. Quoted from the song 'Hum Aapki Aankhon Mein' from the movie *Pyaasa* (1957). Lyrics by Geeta Dutt and Mohammed Rafi.
24. These numbers may also be mentioned along this line: *Beedi jalai le* (Lit your beedi), *Yara sili sili* (O friend, sili sili), *Ibn-e Batuta bagal mein joota* (Ibn-e Batuta tucks his shoes by his side), and *Gum sum gum sum sum kyun ho tum* (Lost, all lost, why are you so lost?).
25. Comparable numbers of this kind are *Zoobi doobi zoobi doobi, Hu tu tu,* and *Tara rum pum* that sound like jingles.

References

Bhaskar, Ira and Richard Allen. 2009. *Islamicate Cultures of Bombay Cinema*. New Delhi: Tulika Books.

Dwyer, Rachel. 2006. *Filming the Gods: Religion and Indian Cinema*. New York: Routledge.

Hodgson, Marshall G.S. 1974. *The Venture of Islam: Conscience and History in a World Civilization*, vol. 1: 'The Classical Age of Islam'. Chicago: The University of Chicago Press.

Kesavan, Mukul. 2008. *The Ugliness of the Indian Male and Other Propositions*. Ranikhet, New Delhi: Black Kite.

Thoraval, Yves. 2000. *The Cinemas of India: 1896–2000.* New Delhi: Macmillan.

Filmography (only of the films referred to in the main text)

Aashiqui, 1990. Director: Mahesh Bhatt. Major Cast: Rahul Roy, Anu Aggarwal, Deepak Tijori, and Tom Alter.

Alam Ara, 1931. Director: Ardeshir Irani. Major Cast: Master Vithal, Zubeida, Jillo, J. Susheela, and Prithviraj Kapoor.

Andaz, 1949. Director: Mehboob Khan. Major Cast: Dilip Kumar, Raj Kapoor, Nargis, Murad, Cuckoo.

Ankur, 1974. Director: Shyam Benegal. Major Cast: Anant Nag, Priya Tendulkar, Shabana Azmi, Sadhu Meher, and Dilip Tahil.

Anmol Ghadi, 1946. Director: Mehboob Khan. Major Cast: Surendra, Suraiya, Noor Jehan, and Murad.

Aur Pyaar Ho Gaya, 1997. Director: Rahul Rawail. Major Cast: Bobby Deol, Anupam Kher, Aishwarya Rai, and Shammi Kapoor.

Barsaat, 1949. Director: Raj Kapoor. Major Cast: Raj Kapoor, Nargis, Prem Nath, and Nimmi.

Char Darvesh, 1933. Director: Prafulla Ghosh. Major Cast: Angurbala, Kanan Devi, and Benoy Goswami.

Chaudhvin ka Chand, 1960. Director: Mohammed Sadiq. Major Cast: Guru Dutt, Rehman, Waheeda Rehman, and Johnny Walker.

Dil Dosti Etc., 2007. Director: Manish Tiwari. Major Cast: Shreyas Talpade, Imaad Shah, Nikita Anand, Smriti Mishra, Ishita Sharma, and Dinesh Kumar.

Dil Hai ke Manta Nahin, 1991. Director: Mahesh Bhatt. Major Cast: Aamir Khan, Anupam Kher, Pooja Bhatt, and Tiku Taslania.

Dil To Pagal Hain, 1997. Director: Yash Chopra. Major Cast: Shahrukh Khan, Madhuri Dixit, Karisma Kapoor, Akshay Kumar, Deven Verma, and Farida Jalal.

Dilwale Dulhania Le Jayenge, 1995. Director: Aditya Chopra. Major Cast: Shahrukh Khan, Kajol, Amrish Puri, Farida Jalal, and Anupam Kher.

Fiza, 2000. Director: Khalid Mohammed. Major Cast: Karisma Kapoor, Hrithik Roshan, Bikram Saluja, Jaya Bachchan, and Sushmita Sen.

Garm Hava, 1973. Director: M.S. Sathyu. Major Cast: Balraj Sahni, Farooq Shaikh, A.K. Hangal, and Jalal Agha.

Hazaaron Khwaishein Aisi, 2005. Director: Sudhir Mishra. Major Cast: Kay Kay Menon, Chitrangada Singh, and Shiney Ahuja.

Henna, 1991. Director: Randhir Kapoor. Major Cast: Rishi Kapoor, Zeba Bakhtiyar, Ashwini Bhave, Saeed Jaffrey, and Farida Jalal.

Hum Hain Rahi Pyar Ke, 1993. Director: Mahesh Bhatt. Major Cast: Aamir Khan, Juhi Chawla, and Dalip Tahil.

Jab We Met, 2007. Director: Imtiaz Ali. Major Cast: Shahid Kapoor and Kareena Kapoor.

Jugnu, 1947. Director: Shaukat Hussain Rizvi. Major Cast: Noor Jehan, Dilip Kumar, Agha, and Shashikala.

Lal-e-Yaman, 1933. Director: J.B.H. Wadia. Major Cast: Jal Khambatta, Karimja, Padmadevi, and Feroze Dastur.

Lal Patthar, 1971. Director: Sushil Majumdar. Major Cast: Raaj Kumar, Hema Malini, Vinod Mehra, Raakhi, and Ajit.

Love Kaa Taddka, 2009. Director: Rajan Waghdhare. Major Cast: Nauheed Cyrusi, Sammir Dattani, Bakhtiyaar Irani, and Satish Kaushik.

Luck by Chance, 2009. Director: Zoya Akhtar. Major Cast: Rishi Kapoor, Dimple Kapadia, Juhi Chawla, Hrithik Roshan, and Isha Sharvani.

Mahal, 1949. Director: Kamal Amrohi. Major Cast: Ashok Kumar and Madhubala.

Mela, 1948. Director: S.U. Sunny. Major Cast: Dilip Kumar, Nargis, Jeevan, Rehman, and Noor Jehan (Three other films with similar title were produced in 1971, 1980, and 2000).

Mere Mehboob, 1963. Director: H.S. Rawail. Major Cast: Rajendra Kumar, Sadhana, Ashok Kumar, Nimmi, Pran, Johnny Walker, and Ameeta.

Mirza Ghalib, 1954. Director: Sohrab Modi. Major Cast: Bharat Bhushan and Suraiya.

Mission Kashmir, 2000. Director: Vidhu Vinod Chopra. Major Cast: Sanjay Dutt, Hrithik Roshan, Preity Zinta, and Jackie Shroff.

Mughal-e-Azam, 1960. Director: K. Asif. Major Cast: Prithviraj Kapoor, Dilip Kumar, Madhubala, Durga Khote, Ajit, and Murad.

Mumtaz Mahal, 1944. Director: Kidar Nath Sharma. Major Cast: Khursheed Bano, Madhubala, Chandra Mohan, and Yakub.

Najma, 1943. Director: Mehboob Khan. Major Cast: Ashok Kumar and Veena.

Nikaah, 1982. Director: B.R. Chopra. Major Cast: Raj Babbar, Deepak Parashar, and Salma Agha.

Nishant, 1975. Director: Shyam Benegal. Major Cast: Shabana Azmi, Naseeruddin Shah, Smita Patil, Anant Nag, Amrish Puri, Satyadev Dubey, and Kulbhushan Kharbanda.

Noorie, 1979. Director: Manmohan Krishna. Major Cast: Farooq Shaikh, Poonam Dhillon, Madan Puri, and Iftekhar.

Pakeezah, 1972. Director: Kamal Amrohi. Major Cast: Ashok Kumar, Meena Kumari, Raaj Kumar, Veena Sapru, and Nadira.

Pyaar Impossible!, 2010. Director: Jugal Hansraj. Major Cast: Uday Chopra, Priyanka Chopra, and Anupam Kher.

Pyaar To Hona Hi Tha, 1998. Director: Anees Bazmee. Major Cast: Ajay Devgn, Kajol, Om Puri.

Pukar, 1939. Director: Sohrab Modi. Major Cast: Chandra Mohan, Naseem Banu, and Sohrab Modi (Two other films with similar titles were produced in 1983 and 2000).

Refugee, 2000. Director: J.P. Dutta. Major Cast: Abhishek Bachchan, Kareena Kapoor, Sunil Shetty, and Jackie Shroff.

Rock On!!, 2008. Director: Abhishek Kapoor. Major Cast: Farhan Akhtar, Prachi Desai, Arjun Rampal, Luke Kenny, and Purab Kohli.

Sahib Bibi aur Ghulam, 1962. Director: Abrar Alvi. Major Cast: Guru Dutt, Meena Kumari, Rehman, and Waheeda Rehman.

Salim Langde Pe Mat Ro, 1989. Director: Saeed Akhtar Mirza. Major Cast: Pavan Malhotra, Makrand Deshpande, Neelima Azeem, and Ashutosh Gowariker.

Sardari Begum, 1996. Director: Shyam Benegal. Major Cast: Kiron Kher, Amrish Puri, Rajit Kapur, and Rajeshwari Sachdev.

Shahjehan, 1946. Director: A.R. Kardar. Major Cast: Rehman, P. Jairaj, K.L. Saigal, Nasreen, and Ragini.

Shatranj ke Khilari, 1977. Director: Satyajit Ray. Major Cast: Amjad Khan, Richard Attenborough, Sanjeev Kumar, Saeed Jaffrey, Shabana Azmi, Victor Banerjee, Farooq Shaikh, and Tom Alter.

Shola Aur Shabnam, 1961. Director: Ramesh Saigal. Major Cast: Dharmendra, Tarla Mehta, Abhi Bhattacharya, Vijayalakshmi, and M. Rajan (Another film with the same title was produced in 1992).

Swades, 2004. Director: Ashutosh Gowariker. Major Cast: Shahrukh Khan and Gayatri Joshi.

Tawaif, 1985. Director: B.R. Chopra. Major Cast: Rishi Kapoor, Poonam Dhillon, Rati Agnihotri, Ashok Kumar, and Kader Khan.

Train to Pakistan, 1998. Director: Pamela Rooks. Major Cast: Nirmal Pandey, Rajit Kapoor, Mohan Agashe, Smriti Mishra, and Divya Dutta.

Umrao Jaan, 1981. Director: Muzaffar Ali. Major Cast: Rekha, Farooq Shaikh, Naseeruddin Shah, and Raj Babbar.

Yeh Saali Zindagi, 2011. Director: Sudhir Mishra. Major Cast: Irrfan Khan, Arunoday Singh, Chitrangada Singh, Aditi Rao Hydari, Saurabh Shukla, and Sushant Singh.

Zeenat, 1945. Director: Shaukat Hussain Rizvi. Major Cast: Noor Jehan, Yakub, Bibboo, and Karan Dewan.

Discoursing Minority: Twentieth-Century Constructions of Indian Muslims

A Metaphor for an Argument

Dair naheen, haram naheen, dar naheen, aasataan naheen
Baithhey hain rahguzar pe hum, ghair hamein uthhai kyun

—Ghalib

I do not intend to translate this Urdu *sher* by Mirza Asadullah Khan Ghalib. I rather choose to engage with what he intends to state in as defiant a term as is characteristic of his poetry. Literally, he means that he neither has a temple nor a mosque, neither a threshold nor a shrine where he could presumably seek his solace. Since he has none of the four, he sits with pride on the pathway and daringly questions as to why anyone should remove him from there. Metaphorically, Ghalib is trying to suggest that it matters little even if those four sources of his sustenance are not available to him, as he has already claimed an open space for himself and feels better rewarded in a state of dispossession than in that of possession of the traditionally powerful sites of belonging. I allude to Ghalib not because he belonged to a community that is designated now as a 'minority', nor do I refer to him because he wrote in a language that is associated with the Muslim minority today, but more significantly for the fact that he constructs his 'self' in relation to the 'other' and inhabits a free space that may not be usurped. Instead of lamenting over his deprivations, he gathers courage and seeks a secular space as a site of his belonging. Ghalib could not have guessed how this stance could bear upon the larger minority discourse today, and how it could serve as a metaphor for a people oddly labelled as 'minority'. In his audacious step to secure a place on the pathway without blocking the passage for others, he underlines the need to carve a space and an identity for the dispossessed, as also the necessity to ensure their individual liberty and the power of self-determination. Drawing upon this metaphoric frame of reference that offers an occasion to examine the larger predicament of a people, I would like to engage with some issues relating to the Muslim minority that constitutes a major part of the modern Indian discourse on individual, society, culture, and politics.

Parameters

As a people and a community, Muslims have been a curious phenomenon of history. In India, they form the largest numerical minority today. They have presented themselves and have been represented by others in diverse ways. The racially conscious twentieth century has had a plethora of Indian intellectuals, littérateurs, historians, social thinkers, politicians, and others belonging to non-defined categories who have found it perennially obligatory to develop their loose or structured discourses on this hugely contested community of people. In the complex web of narratives developed on Muslims in relation to their faith, culture, education, economic status, social assimilation, and political affiliations, there are significant issues that concern their lives, their vulnerability, the broader conditions of their survival, and, more importantly, their individual, communal, and national identities. In the melee of widely different constructions, the Muslim community in a multi-religious and multicultural country like India is considered now a cultural boon, now a social bane; and now the nation's self, now the nation's other. While the points and counterpoints of reference have differed consistently, the community has been unwittingly projected in this process as an enigma, defying an easy definition or classification.

To put the argument in a context, I should like to divide the modern Indian discourse on Muslims into two broad categories and identify them as *exclusivist discourse* and *inclusivist discourse.* While the exclusivist discourse is too clearly marked by its tenacity, the inclusivist one is characterized by a liberal tone and tenor, emphasizing on resolution and reconciliation, understanding and indulgence. As the exclusivists and the inclusivists have represented two different mindsets, they have written two widely disparate texts, created two incompatible structures of meaning, and disseminated two irreconcilable kinds of messages. They might further be identified as creating the *discourse of divergence* and the *discourse of convergence* in their own rights. The exclusivists, representing the discourse of divergence, have projected the rightist understanding of society, while the inclusivists, representing the discourse of convergence, have configured the largely looming 'other', identified as minority, in a concurrent, sometimes even conflicting relationship with the majority. In sum, the two discourses have been distinguishable for their sharp differences with each other, even as they have negotiated and mediated with myriad sociopolitical realities and pursued their own commitments towards contextualizing and relocating their two-pronged projects of exclusion and inclusion with respect to the Muslims.

To expand on the argument further, I might posit that the champions of exclusivist discourse have marked the inherent discrepancies between the minority and the majority communities, and registered their disagreement with the Muslim minority in particular, more especially with reference to their religious faith and culture. They have insisted on their arrival in India as 'invaders' who encroached upon the space of the Hindu natives, and have made a case, therefore, that they must belong to this land only on their terms and conditions. They have evolved their own notions of cultural nationalism along the lines carved by the philosophy of Hindutva, and projected their own principles of universality, power, and dominance. As their perceptions turned into stubborn ideologies, they perceived religion as the foundation stone of the state and became the committed ideologues of Hindu revivalism, reiterating the supremacy of the Hindu race, Hindu nation, and Hindu nationalism with great obstinacy. These exclusivist ideas have been developed and disseminated by ideologues like B.S. Moonje, Bhai Parmanand, V.D. Savarkar, M.S. Golwalkar, K.B. Hedgewar, and their descendants like K.S. Sudarshan, Praveen Togadia, and Subramanian Swamy, to name only a few of them. Their ideologies have come to be implemented in practical terms in the succeeding generations by the Sangh Parivar, broadly constituted of Rashtriya Swayamsevak Sangh (RSS), Vishva Hindu Parishad (VHP), Bajrang Dal, Bharatiya Janata Party (BJP), and Shiv Sena, apart from a plethora of other social and political organizations. It might be quite possible to mark that while the spirit of intellectual engagement and restrained rhetoric declined after Savarkar, the activities of the political parties to realize the ideologies propounded earlier gathered greater momentum. All their efforts, in totality, have been political in nature and have been aimed at rewriting the nation, both in literal and metaphorical terms, by gaining political control at the centre.

It may be marked further that while the Hindutva ideologues have problematized the Muslim minority, they have made themselves susceptible to contestations in turn. In engaging with the Muslim issue, they have operated as agents of image-making who have developed their own instruments in terms of their own logic and language. While they have emerged as the defining agencies of the Muslim community, they have typified and characterized their own insular function rather unwittingly. They have contested their own cases, developed their own discourses of difference, and become, in turn, yet another site of contestation themselves. As they have problematized the minorities, they have also problematized the so-called 'majority', and the two, taken together, have projected a larger collection of people living in a complex social matrix. In this intricate process of marking the other, and being marked as a defining agency in consequence, these ideologues and their followers have reiterated a self-constructed gospel, namely that the Hindus alone have constituted the nation ever since, and shall do so ever after. This has amounted to denying space and identity to the Muslims, which could be given to them, as they argued, only if they relinquished their religious and cultural identity and joined the exclusivist bogey that defined nation, nationalism, and nationhood in insular terms.

As against this, the inclusivist discourse has negated the monolithic notion of a nation constituted of a people following a single faith and culture. Instead of limiting the nation and the people to a certain race and a religion, it has tried to delimit its boundaries to welcome multiplicities of all kinds—social, cultural, religious, and political. It has set aside the coercive principles of universality, and the rule of unilateral power and dominance. It has looked for points of convergence and has projected the eminent possibilities of union between the majority and the minority communities, as it has created space for cordiality, mutuality, and unity. This has been reflected in a rich variety of writings by statesmen and politicians, writers and historians, and social thinkers and commentators. There is, however, an interesting point to note that while the exclusivists have put forth their ideas as agenda, the inclusivists have left their ideas open to contestations even within themselves. Their varied stances might be seen in the works of writers and reformers like Sir Syed Ahmad Khan and Altaf Hussain Hali, iconic nationalists like M.K. Gandhi, Jawaharlal Nehru, and Abul Kalam Azad, proponents of Muslim cause like Muhammad Ali Jinnah and Muhammad Iqbal, historians like Mohammad Mujeeb, Ramachandra Guha, and Rajmohan Gandhi, social commentators like Rafiq Zakaria and Asghar Ali Engineer, liberals like Khushwant Singh and Kuldip Nayar, and a host of others representing various other shades of opinion. These diverse groups of inclusivist authors and intellectuals have represented the dynamics of a vibrant civil society, underlined its priorities, and made a case for the homogeneity of a people and the sanctity of their nation.

This is precisely the point where I should like to make a few propositions. *First,* while the exclusivists, in representing the types and stereotypes of the Muslim minority, have indirectly represented the articles of their religious faith and reflected upon their politics, the inclusivists have represented their notions of the secular and reflected upon themselves as secularists. *Second,* while the exclusivists have created a sacrosanct notion of the majority, necessarily representing the mainstay of power, the inclusivists have constructed a larger paradigm of the Indian people, constituted of the majority and the minority together. *Third,* while the exclusivists have been driven by their well-defined motives to exercise their sociopolitical control over the minorities, the inclusivists have not been necessarily moved by any condition of complete control. *Fourth,* while the exclusivists have constructed the Muslim minority as the silent recipients of their dispensations, the inclusivists have allowed them occasions to speak and take part in the larger scheme of the nation as a secular space. *Fifth*, the exclusivists have represented a narrow psychic condition nurtured over ages, while the inclusivists have represented broader mindsets nursed to negotiate with multiplicities of faith and culture. As both the exclusivists and the inclusivists have kept playing their given roles in relation to the Muslim minority, both have been engaged in image-making of distinct kinds. In understanding and problematizing the Muslim minority, both have pursued their well-defined policies. However, I would posit that it is in this persistent and divergent representation of the types and stereotypes of the Muslim minority that the parameters for the existence and survival of this community of people can be found.

Paradigms

Let us now look at some of the important paradigms that the exclusivist and inclusivist discourses have created during the twentieth century in India. Let us begin by examining the exclusivist stances evolved and reiterated by at least two major organizations—Akhil Bharatiya Hindu Mahasabha and Rashtriya Swayamsevak Sangh—which paved the way, in the coming decades, for the emergence of the Sangh Parivar, a conglomerate of like-minded right-wing parties and organizations. Apart from individual variations with respect to their subsidiary aims, all of them stood committed essentially to Hindu revivalism. This being their basic aim, they presupposed the exclusion of all other races, religions, and cultures from the domain of Hindu. The manner in which they constructed the Muslims can only be understood with the help of their essential predilections in which Muslims remained a constant obsession for them ever since the founding of the Hindu Mahasabha in 1914 and that of the RSS in 1925. B.S. Moonje and Bhai Parmanand, the two presidents of the Hindu Mahasabha and the two Hindu ideologues of the earlier days, adopted a stance against the policies of the Congress party, Gandhi's principle of non-violence, as well the Muslims who, they thought, were unduly favoured. Their ideologies found full flowering in V.D. Savarkar, an agnostic, a littérateur, an advocate of militarism, a critic of the Congress party, and a president of the Hindu Mahasabha, who emerged as the most influential figure towards propagating a religio-political philosophy, which he chose to call Hindutva. In his famous-infamous treatise called *Hindutva* (1923),[1] he engaged with some seminal issues that he projected as the keystone of his thesis. He defined 'Hindu' as one who considered Bharatvarsha, spread from the Indus to the seas, as his fatherland as well as his holy land, which also empowered him with a religious faith. Keeping close to this, he evolved the philosophy of Hindutva, which embraced the perceptions and aspirations of all the Hindus, and was different from 'Hinduism' in its reach and sweep. Further, he perceived the Hindus both as a nation and a race that had the blood of the Aryans, the Kolorians, and the Dravidians in them, and Sindhusthan, not Aryavarta, as their home. He obviously disparaged the Muslims and labelled them as invaders, an expression that has carried on ever since. Developing a larger picture of his people, their religious faith, and their land of belonging, he considered 'civilization' to be the cumulative heritage of the Hindu race spread over a vast span of time and space. Savarkar expressed his views as a creed, a credo, and a philosophy drawn basically upon history and religious faith. He influenced the like-minded Hindu nationalists and brought about a climactic change in favour of his philosophy which was well appreciated by his contemporary and subsequent followers. Savarkar's Hindutva denied space to the Muslim and Christian minorities, as he thought that taking them into the fold would amount to putting the Hindu majority to disadvantage. He was unable to reconcile with Muslim presence and believed that the Muslims could pose a danger to the nation because they still dreamt of re-establishing their rule in India. He turned naturally against the Congress, Gandhi, and Jinnah, and thought that all their acts, directed towards Muslims, were acts of appeasement. The two phrases—'Hindutva' and 'appeasement'—that have been at the core of recent Hindu discourse in India hark back to Savarkar's philosophy of exclusive Hindu *rashtra* (nation) with no space for the minorities of any origin.

Savarkar's legacy was ably carried forward by Hedgewar and Golwalkar, who exerted their personal conviction with official sanction given to them by RSS. Hedgewar was the founder and the first *sarasanghachalak*[2] (supreme head) of RSS. He kept the Muslim factor outside the domain of his consideration, criticized the Congress party for Muslim appeasement, and promoted Hindu nationalism along the lines laid out by Savarkar. Golwalkar succeeded Hedgewar as the second *sarasanghachalak* of RSS. He was opposed to the idea of a secular Indian state, as he drew upon the logic of exclusion whereby the non-Hindus could be taken into the fold only if they held the Hindu religion in reverence, embraced the Hindu culture, and became a part and parcel of the *rashtra* as a native rather than a foreigner. He was extremely vituperative against the Muslims and offered them too stringent a condition for living in this country.[3] He took his argument to the extreme right, which led the future commentators to call him and his followers the advocates of fascism and anti-Semitism. His plea for the maintenance of racial and cultural purity by drawing upon the German example with reference to the Jews gave him a unique logic to deal with the Muslim factor in India.[4] He thought that the Hindus, the Muslims, and the British were the three parties involved, and the Hindus had to fight and establish their power over them, more especially over the Muslims. *Rashtra*, according to him, was composed of five elements: a geographical area, a race, a religion, a culture, and language. India was 'the noblest in the world' as a *rashtra* in spite of its 'degenerating contact with the debased "civilization" of the Musalmans and the Europeans for the last ten centuries' (41). The descendants of Savarkar and Golwalkar carried these fundamental arguments further with individual variations. K.S. Sudarshan and his successor Mohan Bhagwat kept the logic alive with the same conviction after them.

With Bal Thackeray, the supreme commander of the Shiv Sena, a right-wing party with ethnocentric bias, a different note was struck. Like the earlier ideologues, he too equated Islam with violence and considered its followers as the perpetrators of the wrong. As such, he went in consonance with the exclusivists, but added yet another dimension to their argument by imparting a sectarian touch to it. Although it might appear a minor change of little consequence, but the renaming of Bombay as Mumbai was a symbolic pronouncement of a different kind which transformed the secular nature of the city in a palpable way. Similarly, the slogan of Mumbai for Mumbaikars was yet another step towards the same end of segregating a space in exclusive terms for its own people. These steps were both concrete and symbolic, as they placed premium on the local against the national. The logic of Hindu *rashtra,* thus, shrunk to the logic of a region for the regionalists. Shiv Sena's mouthpiece *Saamana*[5] struck the notes of dissidence rather strongly, which went in tune with the rhetoric of defiance developed after Savarkar. The Mumbai riots of 1992–93 gave him an opening to reiterate his stance against the Muslims with greater intensity. It also gave him an opportunity to strengthen his argument for the regional against the national. With these riots, another exclusivist Subramanian Swamy got an opportunity to appropriate the old logic of extreme disaffection and express himself in an idiom of hatred and with gestures of militancy. He set up a blatant agenda for dealing with the Muslim factor. He propagated terrorism in open terms and made a retrograde case by suggesting that Hindus should now do a serious soul-searching as they can no longer be killed in 'halal' fashion and bleed till the nation met its end. Like the propagators of hate, he blatantly asserted that every Hindu–Muslim riot in India since 1947 had been started by the Muslim fanatics. He echoed the stereotypical stance of the Hindu ideologues, especially Golwalkar, when he asserted that the Muslims will have to accept the Hindu religio-cultural legacy in order to be accepted as a part of the larger Hindu society. He came up with his suggestions, typical of his retrograde mindset, that the Hindus must develop a pure Hindu outlook. Rightly claiming that the Hindus must not bow down to terrorists' demands, he wrongly advised that they must retaliate at every terrorist attack, as if terrorism could be contained by terrorism. He came up with several strategies, which included the removal of Article 370, demolition of the mosque at Kashi Vishwanath along with three hundred such other mosques elsewhere, implementation of the Uniform Civil Code, and making the learning of Sanskrit and the singing of *Vande Mataram* compulsory. Echoing Golwalkar's extremism, he demanded that India be declared a Hindu *rashtra* where only those could have a voting right who acknowledged that their ancestors were Hindus. He further advocated for a law that allowed people from other faiths to convert to Hinduism, but he argued that this law must prohibit the Hindus to convert to other faiths. While he declared that caste could not be decided by birth, he also argued that land from Bangladesh could be annexed to make space for the migrants from there.[6] It would not take much effort to establish that Swamy was only falling in line with the hardcore exclusivists, as he shared his views with Savarkar and his rhetoric with Golwalkar. Swamy defied all sense of balance and proportion and spread the worst kind of hatred. He rode the exclusivist bogey and used a blasphemous diction only to reiterate an already defeated thesis. This mindset has often been reflected in inflammatory addresses of Pravin Togadia. Commenting on him, the politician and scholar Rafiq Zakaria wrote:

> The spokesman of Vishwa Hindu Parishad, Pravin Togadia, has publicly approved of the massacre of Muslims in Gujarat. He told *Time* magazine: 'Things will get more and more violent. You can impose a curfew in one place, but there will be an incident somewhere else. When you control that, there will be a third place.' Told about it, a Muslim woman in Ahmedabad said: 'I know we are all going to be killed. I will ask my sons to escape and be terrorists.' (344)

The stances of Swamy and Togadia have many a point of intersection in how they construct Muslims and how they create a case for an *akhanda* (indivisible) Bharat. The inability of one to live with the other was well diagnosed by M.N. Roy who said, 'Indeed, there is no other example of two communities living together in the same country for so many hundred years and yet having so little appreciation for each other's culture. No civilized group of people in the world is so ignorant of Islamic history and contemptuous of the Mohammedan religion as the Hindus.'[7]

Alongside the narrow and negative exclusivist constructions of the Muslims, the intellectually tempered and rationally justifiable inclusivist projections have always been making their way at the same pace. We have had a number of inclusivists to strongly interrogate the exclusivists and project a holistic view of Indian history and the Indian Muslims. One might begin this account with Sir Syed, a judicial officer in the British East India Company, who was the first philosopher, reformer, and educator to place Muslims in a modernist context. His anxiety regarding the status of his people and their coexistence with other communities led him to make a big case for their educational and political empowerment. It also led him to develop a holistic view of modern India and the modern Indian. His friend and biographer Hali, who distinguished himself as a littérateur and a reformer, carried forward his concern for the community in yet another direction. He got more concerned with the problem of social and moral degradation of his people in general, and the condition of women in particular. Both Syed and Hali shared their anxiety about the Muslim community, not as political leaders would do, but as intellectuals with acute social concern. Taking the discourse about the Muslims still further, one might also refer to Jinnah and Iqbal. Jinnah, who took the line of a nationalist and argued for Hindu–Muslim unity in the early phase of his political career, got disappointed with Congress and the growing Hindu communalism, and moved ultimately towards championing the Muslim cause exclusively. He grew from a nationalist to a sectarian, and from sectarian to a separatist during the hectic phase of his political career. He found in Muslim League a platform for championing his cause for Muslim representation and, ultimately, a separate land for them. This was clearly borne out by the passing of the Lahore resolution in March 1940, whereby the case for the Muslims to claim a nation found its way. This logic went in line with those of the Hindu nationalists, who too had been making a case for India as a Hindu *rashtra*. Iqbal, a philosopher-poet, not quite in tune with the Muslim leaders and the Congress party, also believed in the political empowerment of Muslims. He evolved a way to combine the social and the political with the religious, and tried to develop a modernist context for the survival of the Muslims. Both Jinnah and Iqbal came to flag the case of the Muslims—Jinnah with his demand for a Muslim state and Iqbal with his desire for a safe space for Muslims in the dominion of India. However, none of the two nursed views that could be called communal, although they expressed their dissatisfaction with the order of the day and sought their own ways of resolution.

The case of Gandhi and Nehru falls in an entirely different category. With 'truth' and 'non-violence' being the two cardinal principles of his philosophy, Gandhi evolved a completely different modus operandi to earn India's independence and keep it united. These principles also served him as the bases of his religious doctrine and political ideology to bring the Hindus and Muslims together. He firmly believed that both the communities had equal privileges to share, equal rights to exercise, and equal duties to perform. The fasts that he observed to stop the Hindu–Muslim riots, and the position he took to protect the Muslims stand testimony to his comparative understanding of religions, especially Hinduism and the Abrahamic religions. In bringing truth, politics, and religion to bear upon one another, he made an extremely catholic and philosophically charged comment on those who held bigoted views on these three and thought of the land as divided along narrow lines.[8] Keeping close to Gandhi's ideology, Nehru, who distinguished himself as a statesman, a liberal democrat, and an architect of modern India, developed a clinical view on the Hindu–Muslim issue. He was against communalism quite clearly, and he did not hesitate in identifying the communalists even if they belonged to the Congress. 'Many a Congressman was a communalist under his national cloak', (136) he wrote while assessing the worsening communal situation in the country. He held both the Muslim and the Hindu communalists responsible for inculcating an insular view of Indian nationalism.[9] Through their writings and speeches, both Gandhi and Nehru developed a perspective that was political in appearance but intellectual in reality. Both of them maintained their disapproval of the communalists, irrespective of their political affiliations and sociocultural upbringing. They could not have, thus, appreciated the stances of the likes of Bal Gangadhar Tilak, Sri Aurobindo Ghosh, and Lala Lajpat Rai who brought in religion to define the contour of the nation-to-be.

A larger discourse on Muslims was, however, best developed in Azad, who stood apart from Jinnah and Iqbal, and who combined the best qualities of a nationalist, a secularist, and a democrat. On the questions concerning nationalism, human brotherhood, minority, Hindu–Muslim/ Hinduism–Islam dichotomy, and a deep commitment to India as a nation,

Azad emerged as the most seminal of all the thinkers. As a committed nationalist, he shunned the Hindu–Muslim divide on religious and communal terms. In his Congress Address of 1923, he came out in quite clear terms: 'Instead of Swaraj and Khilafat, slogans of *Shuddhi* are being raised. "Save the Hindus from Muslims," says one group, "Save Islam from Hinduism," says another. When the order of the day is, "Protect Hindus" and "Protect Muslims", who cares about protecting the nation?' (145). Another facet of this very problem got manifested in yet another address about two decades later in 1940, when he expressed himself in much more biting terms and said,

> If there are any Hindus among us who desire to bring back the Hindu life of a thousand years ago and more, they are just dreaming and such dreams cannot become real. Likewise, if there are any Muslims who wish to revive their past civilization and culture, which they brought a thousand years ago from Iran and Central Asia, they too, dream and the sooner they wake up the better. (162)

Azad dug at both the Hindu and Muslim ideologues and defined nationalism in terms of 'man's collective consciousness and a notion of social order' (51). Clearly striking a note of difference as compared with Golwalkar, he identified race, country, colour, and language as the four major hindrances in the way of human brotherhood, and suggested that Islam rejected all the four in favour of healthy universalism. Significantly, therefore, Azad did not consider Muslims as a minority because numbers, he thought, did not decide a community's status as a minority or majority group of people. He rather believed in the validity of the shared heritage when he categorically proclaimed in his Congress Address of 1940: 'Our shared life of a thousand years has forged a common nationality. Such moulds cannot be artificially constructed. Nature's anvils shape them over the centuries. The mould has now been cast and destiny has set her seal upon it' (162). Azad did not consider Muslims a minority and foretold categorically that whatever be the constitution of India like in the future, it would surely be a democratic one, and that there should be no misgivings about the minority and the majority classification. As a great advocate of India's indivisibility, a great opponent of India's partition, and a great supporter of Hindu–Muslim unity, he said that he would like to go for their unity if he were to choose between swaraj and Hindu–Muslim unity.[10] He emphasized upon the claim of Hinduism on the Indian soil in the same measure as he emphasized upon the claim of Islam on this land.[11] This came out clearly in the way he exhorted the Muslims of Delhi against migrating to Pakistan in one of his most passionate speeches delivered from the ramparts of Jama Masjid. Azad was a liberal political visionary of the first order, who proposed a case diametrically opposed to those of the exclusivists.

One of Azad's close associates Humayun Kabir, a thinker and a politician in his own right, extended Azad's logic in yet another direction when he engaged with the question of the minority and argued that there could be no democracy without a minority, and that the minority communities were the 'problem' of the modern age only, as the earlier ages were essentially monarchic in nature and spirit. He defined this category of the minority in a more scientific manner five years after the death of Azad in his Srinivasa Sastri lecture at the University of Madras in 1963, by developing a psychological angle. He said,

> Every minority is in a sense a protestant group, a dissident group. Every minority is a heretical group when compared to the majority. It is not an exaggeration to say that the dissidents are the salt of the earth, provided that they remember that they are dissidents in terms of quality and not dissidents merely because of birth. (18)

He considered minorities to be a necessary part of a democratic set-up, who represented themselves as religious, economic, political, linguistic, tribal, racial, or linguistic groups. He considered Indian Muslims to be a part of the universal brotherhood and, more pertinently, as a part and parcel of the broader Indian sociopolitical complex. As such, he assigned them a place of parity with others.[12] Both Azad and Kabir seem to join hands on one essential point: it is the worth of a people that distinguishes them rather than their birth or numerical value, which are of no consequence. Kabir came up with an enlightened argument that an informed minority could be more powerful than the uninformed majority.

It should be in place to refer here to Mohammad Mujeeb, an eminent historian and author of *The Indian Muslims* (1967), who developed a detailed historical-cum-philosophical discourse on Indian Muslims. His single-line explanation that 'All human history is a complicated process of self-expression and self-realization' (555) holds good and makes an Indian Muslim retain oneself with remarkable confidence. As a historian who considered history to be a complicated process of self-realization and self-expression, he contextualized Indian Muslims in a larger perspective. He proposed that there can be no generalization about Indian Muslims, as it is likely to mislead and represent the truth only partially. He underlined the duality of Hindu–Muslim perception in an objective fashion by saying that: 'The Indian Muslims are judged by non-Muslims and, vice versa, the non-Muslims by the Muslims, as if the historical record of one party could be separated from the record of the other....' (555) Regarding how the Muslims have conducted themselves, Mujeeb developed a perspective which was as applicable to the reading of the past as it is to the reading of the present. He wrote:

> Indian Muslims lived their own life, according to their lights, that everything which might be considered as achievement was a part of the process of their self-expression and self-realization, and that the evils we see in their actions were, like all the evils we generally see in human actions and their results, due to diverse causes, of which the fact of their being Indian Muslims may or may not have been one. (556)

He separated popular bias from objective reality and suggested that personal choices and dispositions of individuals may not be taken for the testimonies of a community. While Mujeeb developed a theoretical and rationalistic perspective of Indian Muslims, there are others who approached this subject with entirely different tools in hand, which include the signs and symbols of the time, as also the facts and figures to substantiate their readings.

One might refer to one like Ramachandra Guha, who constructed the Hindus and Muslims in a sociopolitical framework and projected a point of view that combined the richness of personal observation, the rigour of research, and the power of drawing substantiated academic conclusions, even at the cost of being abused.[13] A succinct study of how Hindus and Muslims operated and interacted, and how some of the more prominent Muslims from the late nineteenth century to the mid twentieth century have constructed themselves and, in turn, constructed their community may be seen in Rajmohan Gandhi with great profit.[14]

It would also be in place to refer here to Rafiq Zakaria, whose concern with the plight of the Indian Muslims was expressed in the way he diagnosed and commented on their predicament in general. He mentioned ten notions prevalent among the Hindus regarding Muslims, namely: (a) Islam encourages destruction of idols, (b) The Quran permits destruction of places of worship, (c) Islam does not allow freedom of worship, (d) Islam believes only in Muslims instead of universal brotherhood, (e) Quran does not recognize the great savants born in India, (f) Islam does not encourage Muslims to be patriotic wherever they are in a numerical minority, (g) Islam treats Hindus as *kafirs*, (h) Quran asks for perpetual jihad (war) against *kafirs*, (i) Muslims and non-Muslims are not be treated equally by the state as per Islam, and, finally, (j) Islam permits polygamy (349). He was clearly diagnostic when he mentioned the following: If Indian Muslims have to preserve their identity, there are five factors they must concentrate on: (a) Education (b) Employment (c) Social adjustment with Hindus (d) Family planning and (e) Political realism (332). He referred to William Muir's defamatory book *Life of Mahomet* (1861), written in four volumes, and the writing of the blasphemous book *Rangila Rasul* (1927) by Pandit M.A. Chamupati, which resulted in Muslim fury and a Muslim fanatic killing the publisher (364). Zakaria's reading might further be related with the interpretation of history and historiography of communalism that has shown a phenomenal growth in our times and has been dealt with serious academic rigour for, at least, one simple reason that communalism has been a major threat to Indian democracy, which has called for detailed academic examination.[15] The concerns of journalists like Khushwant Singh and Kuldip Nayar, who shared many of Zakaria's comments in their own ways, are too well known to be discussed in any detail here. It would, however, be pertinent to bring this argument to a close by referring to a more recent intervention by a literary writer and academic like Tabish Khair, who has chosen to live abroad and yet remain connected with the land of his birth, as one who is born here remains connected. 'There is much I am proud of in India, and there is much I am ashamed of,' he wrote, and continued further: ' ... I am not a nationalist in the sense in which parties like the Shiv Sena define nation... (25–6). And so, I hang on to my passport. For I was born in India. If I were to relinquish my passport, I would do so in favour of a country that I found superior to India' (28). It may be posited that Khair's is the voice of the modern Indian Muslim who takes pride in being what he is, and does not either need to offer excuses for being so or defend himself against any charge made on the basis of subscribing to a religious faith or culture. The dichotomy between the two ways of approaching the Hindu–Muslim factor has resulted in some Hindus believing that the Muslims are a potential threat, they are terrorists, they owe allegiance to Pakistan, they cannot live at peace with others, and they do all that the Hindu society disapproves of. Similarly, there is a section among Muslims who believe that Hindus are the perpetrators of hatred, they are fascists, and that they would never accept Muslims as fellow countrymen. The number on both the sides is small, which is why such hideously diabolic perceptions have not yet succeeded in taking from India its deep faith in democratic principles of existence, although India has kept itself perennially engaged in negotiating with those forces to keep the existence of Muslims from hanging precariously.

Predicament

Moving away from the two diametrically opposed constructions of Muslims in India, let me now consider the broader Muslim predicament caught in the melee of opinions, arguments, and debates. While minorities may share certain common traits, they are also different in a variety of ways, not only from each other but even within themselves. If the members of a minority community are marked for sharing a history and a culture, for identifying with their community, and for sustaining stereotypical prejudices against themselves, the Muslims in India may not be necessarily judged as a minority with these traditional and constraining parameters. Indian Muslims embody multiple identities as a religious, cultural, linguistic, political, economic, and an educational minority. This gets all the more complicated when we consider the fact that as the largest minority in India, they have presented themselves as variously as they have been represented by the exclusivist, the inclusivist, and the intercessionist groups of scholars and activists. This also explains why Muslims as a minority have emerged as a non-negligible major in a country that rightly seeks its pride in taking its minorities—the Sikhs, the Christians, and the Parsis—together with the Hindus in a secular frame of survival.

Let me posit further that no study of Muslim minority in India may be possible in isolation without reference to history's consequential players, right from the seventh to the eighteenth century as traders, rulers, infamous invaders, and, finally, the Sufi saints. All of them, with their aims well defined, worked differently from each other. The traders worked for goodwill to earn their profits; the rulers ensured peace and stability to be in power; the invaders used aggression to subjugate and gain control; and the Sufi saints worked for the fusion of cultures to create a composite society. To this remarkable variety of approaches to the Indian land and the people, comprising essentially of Hindus and Muslims, may be added the examples of the dynasties like the Mamluks, the Khaljis, the Tughlaqs, the Syeds, the Lodhis, the Mughals, and the Surs, as also the regional Muslim kingdoms of the Qutb Shahis and the Adil Shahis who succeeded in their own ways by promoting local cultures and working for the local good. An entirely new sociopolitical dynamics emerged with the advent of the British, who were committed to finding roots for the British empire on the Indian soil and devising their policies accordingly. In fact, the plot of the British intervention thickened rather ominously, as they realized soon that their panacea lay in dividing the Muslims and the Hindus as two communities opposed to each other. It may be worthwhile to note that the post-partition phase saw yet another departure in this complex plot, when the Muslims came to be taken as a distinct minority, even though they had started showing fissures in their relationship with the Hindus during the independence movement itself.

The variegated patterns of the Hindu–Muslim relationship and the emergence of the Muslims as a minority project many questions deserving critical attention, both for a comprehensive understanding of the community as also of the nation. Thinking of Muslims as a minority in post-independent India, one needs to consider first, if Muslims, as a minority, can ever be fully and satisfactorily defined. The question as to who is a Muslim is as difficult to answer as it is to define who is an Indian, mainly because the idea of India and that of the Indian is too complicated and, therefore, too contested. Justifiably enough, it must evade even a workable answer. Even if one develops a view on their identity and their possible definition, one also needs to answer whether or not the nomenclature of the 'Indian Muslim' would be more appropriate than that of 'Muslim Indian'. Both these nomenclatures do not only carry different shades of meaning embodied in the prioritization of the 'Muslim' over 'Indian' and 'Indian' over 'Muslim'; they also define them distinctly and differently from each other with respect to their affiliations, motives, and manners. At yet another remove, there are more complicated questions to answer, which include questions like whether the Indian Muslims are a homogenous group of people, or whether they necessarily subscribe to the Quranic figure of the Muslim. Similarly, one may also ask if they could be taken as representing a certain cultural pattern symbolized by a worn-out *tehmad* and a soiled skullcap, or is it that their identity is to be determined mainly by their economic status marked by deprivation, or their political commitment characterized by adherence to a given political party. One also needs to answer whether they invariably venerate the space offered by the madrasa that has been much maligned in the recent past, or whether they keep themselves confined only to the holy precincts of the mosque. These images of the Muslim minority are projected more prominently than the ones where they are seen as highly educated, completely secular, culturally refined, remarkably affluent individuals and groups, representing the modern Indian milieu and taking part in realizing the nationalist aspirations.

It would appear from a closer analysis that Muslims live many lives in India. In each of the six domains of polity, economy, society, culture, education, and nation, they are distinguishable for the great variety they represent in their apprehension and action. In each of these domains, they project themselves both as retrograde and modern, fettered and liberated, economically deprived and remarkably affluent, and marginally educated and highly accomplished in modern knowledge. It is futile to look for any uniformity in the way they render themselves. It would be interesting to note that the heterogeneous nature of Muslim existence denies their stock image, even though it is the reiteration of stock images that has caught greater attention. These stock perceptions have been reiterated by diverse agencies of which the more important ones are the ideologues of the political parties, exclusivist forums, and a section of the press, which again is marked by regional, national, and linguistic differences. To counter the dominant discourse based on stereotyping of the community, it may be argued that the Muslim minority represents images of the grotesque and ironic, comic and tragic, and pathetic and pliable. Muslims in post-independent and postcolonial India are the non-negligible-major; they constitute a part of the main and stand for the whole.

It would also appear from a broader analysis of the present responses to the Muslims and the Muslim predicament that there are at least three banes that have contributed towards their stereotyping to a large extent. These include the three largely misconceived notions about jihad, *kufr*, and fundamentalism. Gandhi's notion of jihad as *dharma yudh* stands completely marginalized in comparison to jihad as an act of sheer militancy, just as *kufr* is totally misrepresented as blasphemy rather than a state of unbelief. Similarly, fundamentalism is taken as an attribute of the retrograde rather than a way to reach the spirit of the matter. In the same category of misrepresentation falls an expression like 'secularism', which is repeatedly used as a false refuge rather than a genuine way of life and living. Other incorrect notions reiterated over a long period of time include: Islam breeds destructive tendencies; it shuns other religions; it discourages patriotism; and it perpetuates polygamy. These are the misleading parts of the construction that challenge the exclusivist discourse. I should like to posit here that this huge map of misreading is made of scandalous readings of religion and sociocultural practices of the Muslims. As the truth lies on the other side of the argument, it must be said that there are significant cohesive forces that integrate and distinguish the people in the Indian subcontinent more than they do anywhere else, but they are not as easily marked as the outrageous constructions are. I would assert further that these texts, or metaphors of disaffection, are rooted in a historical moment of time in the Indian subcontinent, which is, ironically enough, the moment of India's freedom and also of its partition in terms of people and all their resources by which they lived. The year 1947, as I have argued elsewhere, is our 'intersection time'[16] that has shaped our consciousness and set us apart in many ways.

Conditions of belonging in a majority-minority state may not remain perennially stable. They cannot ever be so. Predicaments can only alter; history can only reconfigure itself. Life has to remain in a constant state of flux, now coursing well, now moving with jerks, now pacing precariously, but always confirming to what Ghalib had said:

Dil hi to hai, na sang-o-khisht, dard se bhar na aaye kyun
Roengey hum hazaar baar, koi hamein sataaye kyun[17]

For those who wish to connect, Ghalib says: 'What I have in my chest is a heart, not a piece of stone or brick; it must be moved by pain; and that I will weep a thousand times, but then why should anyone coerce me at all.'

Endnotes

1. *Hindutva: Who is a Hindu?* (1928) was originally published as *Essentials of Hindutva* in 1923. It is the first comprehensive treatise that made way for the future right-wing political parties, their votaries of various social and professional affiliations broadly called Hindu revivalists/nationalists. The book has a comprehensive thesis divided into thirty-one sections that develop discourses on a number of issues; some of the important ones being his discourses on Hindu, Hindutva, Hinduism, Hindu nation, Sindhusthan, Buddhism, Arya, Hindustani

language, foreign invaders, and civilization. Savarkar sounds scholarly, logical, and definitive in the way he builds his argument in favour of a people and their land.

2. A *sarasanghachalak* is the philosopher and guide of the organization and contributes towards character-building and maintaining order and discipline, which is the credo of the organization. The organization has had seven *sarasanghachalaks* so far who include: K.B. Hedgewar (1925–1930 and 1931–1940), M.S. Golwalkar (1940–1973), M.D. Deoras (1973–1994), Rajendra Singh (1994–2000), K.S. Sudarshan (2000–2009), and Mohan Bhagwat (2009–till date). Dr L.V. Paranjpe worked as the acting *sarasanghachalak* during 1930–1931 when Hedgewar was imprisoned on account of forest satyagraha.
3. Golwalkar's vituperation may be seen in what he had to say in such categorical terms: 'The foreign races in Hindustan…or may stay in the country, wholly subordinated to the Hindu nation, claiming nothing, deserving no privileges, far less any preferential treatment—not even citizen's rights.' (47–8)
4. Golwalkar wrote: 'To keep up the purity of the Race and its culture, Germany shocked the world by her purging the country of the Semitic races—the Jews. Race pride at its highest has been manifested here. Germany has also shown how well-nigh impossible it is for Races and cultures, having differences going to the root, to be assimilated into one united whole, a good lesson for us in Hindusthan to learn and profit by' (35).
5. Shiv Sena was founded by Bal Thackeray in 1966 and he launched his party's mouthpiece *Saamaṅa* in Marathi twenty-two years later in 1988. Its Hindi edition, intended for a larger readership beyond the Marathi, was metaphorically titled as *Dopahar ka Saamana*.
6. See his article Subramanian Swamy, 'How to Wipe Out Islamic Terror,' *DNA*, India, 16 July 2011.
7. Quoted by Rafiq Zakaria in *Indian Muslims: Where Have They Gone Wrong?* (Mumbai: Popular Prakashan and Bharatiya Vidya Bhavan, 2004), p. 365.
8. In the last chapter of his autobiography *The Story of My Experiments with Truth*, Gandhi made this point in quite clear and philosophical terms: 'To see the universal and all-pervading Spirit of Truth face to face one must be able to love the meanest of creation as oneself. And a man who aspires after that cannot afford to keep out of any field of life. That is why my devotion to Truth has drawn me into the field of politics; and I can say without the slightest hesitation, and yet in all humility, that those who say that religion has nothing to do with politics do not know what religion means.' (463)
9. In *An Autobiography*, Nehru wrote: 'Muslim communal leaders said the most amazing things and seemed to care not at all for Indian nationalism or Indian freedom. Hindu communal leaders, though always speaking apparently in the name of nationalism, had little to do with it in practice and, incapable of any

real action, sought to humble themselves before the Government, and did that too in vain...Muslim communal leaders said and did many things harmful to political and economic freedom, but as a group and individually they conducted themselves before the Government and the public with some dignity. That could hardly be said of the Hindu communal leaders.' (138)

10. While presiding over a special session of Congress in 1923, Azad made a truly unique assertion: 'Today, if an angel were to descend from the heaven and declare from the top of the Qutub Minar, that India will get swaraj within twenty-four hours, provided she relinquishes Hindu-Muslim unity, I will relinquish swaraj rather than give up Hindu-Muslim unity. Delay in the attainment of swaraj will be a loss to India, but if our unity is lost, it will be a loss for entire mankind.' (145)
11. Azad made this point quite confidently in his Congress address in 1940: 'Islam has now as valid a claim on this land as Hinduism. If Hinduism has been the religion of its people for several thousand years, Islam, too, has been its religion for a thousand years. Just as a Hindu can say with legitimate pride that he is an Indian and a follower of Hinduism, so can a Muslim proudly claim being an Indian and a follower of Islam.' (162)
12. Writing on Muslims, he expressed his views more liberally than many others who approached this subject. A Muslim, he said, ' ... is an Indian and he is an Indian not as a subject, not as a ruler but as part ruler and part subject.' (38)
13. See, for example, Ramachandra Guha, 'Minding the Minorities' and 'Riots' in *India After Gandhi: The History of the World's Largest Democracy* (India: Picador, 2007) and 'Hindutva Hate Mail' in ***Patriots and Partisans*** (New Delhi: Penguin, 2012).
14. See Rajmohan Gandhi, *Understanding the Muslim Mind* (New Delhi: Penguin, 2000). Gandhi presents a comprehensive account of Hindu–Muslim dichotomy and examines the stances of Syed Ahmad Khan, Muhammad Iqbal, Mohammad Ali Jauhar, Muhammad Ali Jinnah, A.K. Fazlul Huq, Abul Kalam Azad, Liaquat Ali Khan, and Zakir Husain.
15. See, for example, works by Romila Thapar, Harbans Mukhia, and Bipan Chandra, *Communalism and the Writing of Indian History* (1969); Asghar Ali Engineer and Moin Shakir, eds, *Communalism in India* (1985); Bipan Chandra and Khushwant Singh, *Many Faces of Communalism* (1985); K.N. Panikkar, ed., *Communalism in India: History, Politics and Culture* (1991); Mushirul Hasan, *Nationalism and Communal Politics in India: 1885–1930* (1991), Sudhir Kakar, ***The Colours of Violence*** (1995); Praful Bidwai, Harbans Mukhia, and Achin Vanaik, eds, *Religion, Religiosity and Communalism* (1996); M.J. Akbar, *Riot After Riot* (1988); Ram Puniyani, *Communal Politics: Facts Versus Myth* (2003); and Paul R. Brass, *The Production of Hindu–Muslim Violence in Contemporary India* (2011).

16. See Jasbir Jain, ed., 'Intersection Time: 1947,' *Reading Partition/Living Partition* (Jaipur: Rawat Publications, 2006).
17. See https://www.rekhta.org/ghazals/dil-hii-to-hai-na-sang-o-khisht-dard-se-bhar-na-aae-kyuun-mirza-ghalib-ghazals (accessed on 27 August 2018).

References

Azad, Abul Kalam. 1990. *India's Maulana*. Centenary Volume II, Selected Speeches and Writings. New Delhi: Indian Council for Cultural Relations in collaboration with Vikas Publishing House.

Gandhi, M.K. 1927. *An Autobiography or The Story of My Experiments With Truth*. Ahmedabad: Navajivan Publishing House.

Golwalkar, M.S. 1939. *We or Our Nationhood Defined*. Bombay: Asia Publishing House.

Kabir, Humayun. 1968. *Minorities in a Democracy*. Calcutta: Firma K.L. Mukhopadhyay.

Khair, Tabish. 2008. *Muslim Modernities*. New Delhi: Vitasta Publishing Pvt. Ltd.

Mujeeb, M. 2003. *The Indian Muslims*. New Delhi: Munshiram Manoharlal Publishers.

Nehru, Jawaharlal. 1962. *An Autobiography*. Bombay: Allied Publishers.

Zakaria, Rafiq. 2004. *Indian Muslims: Where Have They Gone Wrong?*. Mumbai: Popular Prakashan and Bharatiya Vidya Bhavan.

IMAGINARY LANDSCAPES

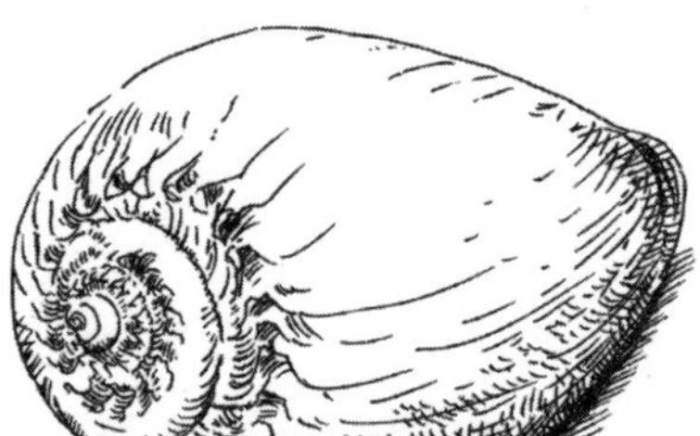

The Fall of the Romantic Ideal: Modernist Representations in Urdu Poetry

Prologue

Modernism in Urdu poetry that emerged with the fall of the romantic ideal is associated with the major marks of a historical period in turmoil, a political order in disarray, and a literary culture in making. While the pre-modernist Urdu poetry[1] nourished romantic idealism and cultivated chiselled rhetoric, the poetry since the 1930s acquired its strength in new modes of apprehension and expression. This new poetry, which is clearly traceable from the third decade of the last century, evolved along its highly individualistic lines and acquired its definite and organic identity during the following decades. Drawing upon the new-found poetics, the 40s and the 50s, which were terribly prone to happenings in the Indian subcontinent and elsewhere, spelt a new predicament for arts and ideas. The 60s sharpened the contours of modernism even further, and the following decades saw it firmly established as a tradition.

This chapter examines the context that made way for the expression of a new consciousness and a new poetics. Developing upon the sociopolitical significance of the 1930s in general, and India in particular, it goes on to examine the two modes of modernist representation in Urdu poetry. While the first one was manifested in the expression of social realism that the poets and writers associated with the Progressive Writers' Movement (Taraqqi Pasand Tehreek) chose for themselves to indulge, the second one was expressed in stylistic innovations made by the poets representing the Circle of Connoisseurs (Halqa-i-Arbab-e Zauq). Even while both the group of poets drew upon the sociopolitical conditions at home and beyond, they differed drastically in their understanding of reality and its expression in literary terms. In doing so, they projected a variety of stances in social, political, and literary domains. The chapter examines these two modes of poetic representation to posit that while one disengaged with the stereotypes of attitudes, the other resisted traditional poetics. As one contextualized life in the given time and site, the other discovered a language and a form to do so in a manner that was hitherto unknown in earlier phases of Urdu literary history. In identifying the major marks of the two groups of poets, an effort is made here to evaluate the significance of these poets who have come to acquire their historic and historical significance over a period of time.

Historical Context: 1930s

Identified with a number of major events in the domains of economy, polity, culture, and society in many parts of the world, the 1930s has influenced literary production in significant ways. Ever since the Great Depression following the Wall Street Crash in 1929, power brokers of the authoritarian kind took control of the major European countries,[2] while also casting dark shadows on smaller and weaker states of the world. The decade is marked by wars and conflicts,[3] rise of totalitarianism,[4] onslaughts of colonization,[5] and efforts at decolonization,[6] where the case of India deserves special mention for the manner it chose to gain its freedom from the British rule. The impact of the Great Depression on India was severe insofar as the British government devised an economic plan to suit its end, even though it adversely affected Indian economy which drew its sustenance from its agriculture, production, distribution, and other modes of sustenance.[7] It is no wonder, then, that various movements in arts and literature found their forte in social realism, as could be seen from the fact that a world conference of writers for the defence of culture was called in Paris in 1935. In keen response to the events all over, the Indian progressive writers, too, chose to openly denounce Mussolini's Ethiopian aggression, Japanese attack on China, and the British policies towards the suppression of press and civil liberties in India, which ultimately led them to develop a literary kinship for sociopolitical ends.

The significance of this consequential decade might further be noted with reference to some of the major developments in India that marked it too prominently. These included a series of crucial events, beginning with the call for Poorna Swaraj (complete independence) and Civil Disobedience initiated with Salt Satyagraha in 1930. Other events that left the people terribly shaken included the hanging of Bhagat Singh, Rajguru, and Sukhdev in 1931, the Hindu–Muslim riots in Bombay in 1932, and Gandhi's three-week hunger strike to protest against the maltreatment of the lower castes in 1933. As the crisis heightened and the political expediency demanded, the suspension of Civil Disobedience followed in 1934, which led further to the introduction of the Government of India Act in 1935. Gandhi's fast to protest against British autocracy, the formation of All India Forward Bloc (AIFB) by Subhas Chandra Bose in 1939, and several arrests and releases of Gandhi and other freedom fighters during the entire decade further underlined the predicament of a colonized site that was struggling to claim its liberation.

All these events of extreme political significance left their mark on the social and cultural lives of the people in general. Precisely, in the year of the Government of India Act, 1935, some Indian writers, in a sensitive response to the happenings all over the world, organized themselves into a group, which later came to be designated as Indian Progressive Writers' Association. The association aspired to champion the cause for a just sociopolitical order by producing a certain kind of literature,[8] which we would consider in the following section.

For Life's Sake: Progressive Writers' Movement

Progressive Writers' Movement has emerged like a constant refrain in almost all the studies of modernist Urdu poetry ever since the 1930s. It has been so in spite of the dual distinction it has earned as literally and metaphorically progressive on the one hand, and propagandist and hollow on the other. While it might be argued in one way that all writers (if they are real writers) and all their writings (if they are genuine writings) have to be essentially progressive, it might also be counter-argued in another that no writer and no writing could ever be real or genuine if they only followed the dictates of a given manifesto. Much that might be said to substantiate either of the positions might not hold well in our discussion here, as we are concerned with examining how these writers, who came to form a strong and cohesive group, made a historic mark in responding to their times and in evolving an appropriate idiom for the same. It would be instructive to see how this group came together and stayed on together to ponder over the possibility of evolving a voice and reinterpreting the times, which they considered to be oppressive and fit to be challenged. While discussing the policies and politics of Progressive Writers' Movement, along with highlighting the phenomenal support it received from a huge number of writers and politicians, Hafeez Malik in 'The Marxist Literary Movement in India and Pakistan' has added an interesting perspective by tracing this phenomenon back to Soviet affiliation: 'It is not merely a coincidence that only two years after the creation of the Union of Soviet Writers, Marxist intellectuals in India under the leadership of Sajjad Zaheer called the first All India Progressive Writers' Conference in Lucknow on April 10, 1936' (649). This clearly underlines one basic issue that the movement sought its inspiration from the Soviet writers and their ways of negotiating with the contemporary crisis, which gave it a clear political complexion, and for which it remained controversial ever after.

It has often been remembered with considerable pride that some Indian writers—Sajjad Zaheer (1905–1973), Muhammad Din Taseer (1902–1950), Mulk Raj Anand (1905–2004), and Ahmed Ali (1910–1994)[9], then living in London and concerned with the happenings at home, deliberated upon the need for a new sociopolitical order and a new literary culture. However, literary historians and critics have referred to more names than those mentioned earlier, even though the names do not always tally. While literary historian Ali Jawad Zaidi adds up the names of Kunwar Mohammad Ashraf Ali Khan, Abdul Aleem Khan, Akhtar Husain Raipuri, Rashid Jahan, and Mahmud-uz-Zafar (350) to the generally acknowledged list, Hafeez Malik, a literary critic, mentions further the names of Pramod Singh Gupta and Jyoti Ghosh, who contributed to the draft of the manifesto (651). While the number of persons and their affiliations could be a matter of historical record, it is important to consider that the group developed a manifesto[10] in 1935 for what came to be designated as the Progressive

Writers' Association. Essentially political in nature, and declamatory in tone and tenor, the manifesto made way for the emergence of a proper literary movement that shaped up in 1936 with a group of poets and fiction writers, subscribing to a given sociopolitical ideology.[11] Getting into public domain, it found sympathetic response insofar as the writer came to assume the role of more than a wordsmith and the text of more than a verbal construct. The fact that *Hans* (Allahabad) and *Left Review* (London) chose to publish the manifesto in October 1935 and February 1936, respectively, only testified its overpowering appeal and influence over popular imagination.

The manifesto that was no less than a radical statement against a decadent sensibility in life and literature gave a clarion call for reason against sentimentality, realism against romance, and freedom against subjugation. At the social level, it rejected feudal order and decadent morality; at the political level, it sought recourse to leftist ideology; and, in the domain of literature, it made an organized effort to refute and resist the centuries old romantic–spiritualist tradition, which it considered to be a way of escaping the stark realities of contemporary life. Aiming at sociopolitical rejuvenation, it called for the dismantling of all retrograde institutions surviving under the unchallenged authority of tradition and coercive power. Being anti-imperialist in nature, it fostered the spirit of decolonization, called for India's freedom, and brought people face-to-face with the general human condition characterized by poverty, backwardness, and oppression. It empowered them with a new mode of apprehension, a new idiom of assertion, and a new will to resist the historical legacies of overall subjugation. The literary writing of the new age had, thus, to disengage from clichés of all sorts and romantic exuberance of all kinds.

Even before the Progressive Writers' Movement became a reality, at least two literary events had already made way for its emergence. In 1932, the publication of *Angare* (Burning Coals),[12] a collection of ten short stories by some of the bolder realists like Sajjad Zaheer, Rashid Jahan, Ahmed Ali, and Mahmud-uz-Zafar, spelt out the possibility of writing on issues considered to be taboos. This collection with explicit sexual references and attack on the decadent moral order, represented by social, political, and religious institutions, had a liberating influence on moral politics. Taken as too radical in its make-up, the book had to be banned, but the stories had an impact as they were thematically interesting and technically innovative. The reader had suddenly become exposed to the worlds of Sigmund Freud, D.H. Lawrence, James Joyce, and Virginia Woolf. The movement called for shedding the age-old traditions, taking leave from stereotypes, and exploring a new world order. Following this collection of stories, there appeared in 1934 a critical work of radical nature called *Adab aur Inquilab*[13] (Literature and Revolution) by Akhtar Husain Raipuri, who, according to the reputed Urdu poet and scholar Ali Jawad Zaidi, also 'presented a manifesto at the Nagpur session of the Bharatiya Sahitya Parishad setting forth the aims and objects of the new Indian literature embodying the views of the London based Progressives in their manifesto earlier. The Nagpur manifesto was signed, among others by Jawaharlal Nehru and Acharya Narendra Dev, Premchand and Maulvi Abdul Haq' (350). In discarding the canonical poets like Mir Taqi Mir and Mirza Ghalib as degenerate representatives of a feudal culture, he pronounced the need for a new poetics empowered by Marxist ideology. This rejection was, however, based on extra-critical considerations, as he was more concerned with popularizing Marxist thought in literature than on appreciating the literary worth of writers and their texts.

It would be in place here to connect these manifestations with yet another literary event that further reiterated the need for a new literary dispensation. Premchand's (1880–1936) famous presidential address to the first conference of Progressive Writers' Association in Lucknow in 1936 was a much more precise call to relate literature to social reality. Since he believed that literature had a civilizing role to play, he called for revising the standards of beauty and emphasized upon the value of truth, freedom, and moral courage. Positing that human society was a court of justice, he emphasized that there had to be a balance between nature and society. He underlined the significance of a sound economic and political order, based on the principles of justice and egalitarianism, and went emphatically against capitalism, elitism, and militancy. He ended his address by emphasizing that good and healthy literature is required to be identified while carrying the quest for freedom, beauty, and realism.

The contours of new writing, thus, emerged with great clarity. Every progressive writer was a literary rebel, and every rebellion was for promoting a new poetics of resistance. Basically wedded to the idea of political and social revolution, these writers sought their inspiration in Marx. Major progressive poets, Makhdoom Mohiuddin (1908–1969), Faiz Ahmad Faiz (1911–1984), Ali Sardar Jafri (1913–2000), Jan Nisar Akhtar (1914–1976), Kaifi Azmi (1919–2002), and Sahir Ludhianvi (1921–1980), even though sharply unequal in literary merit, but charged equally by Marxist ideology, heralded a tradition of modernism, marked by dissent and resistance to age-old social, political, cultural, and literary establishments. Clubbed together as poets who subscribed to the ideology of the Progressive Writers' Association, they combined poetry with social activism and considered one as a supplement to the other. All these poets were passionate advocates of their ideas in poetry, and their poetry sometimes attained the status of impassioned speech, as many of their compositions on the stock themes concerning freedom, hunger, home, and hearth found a space in popular imagination. With a clear sociopolitical commitment, they developed their individual instances while seeking their inspiration from various quarters—indigenous and foreign, literary and extra-literary. They were prompted by their vision for a just sociopolitical order, as they aspired to construct the nation for its people. They wrote the poetry of their selves, but they reflected the hankerings of a whole generation of people at a particular point in the history of the subcontinent.

Among all the progressive poets mentioned before, one poet who has been most widely read and discussed is Faiz Ahmad Faiz, precisely because he has been singularly successful in striking a balance between arts and ideas. Even though he aligned with the group of poets who raised slogans more than they raised poetry on an artistic ground, Faiz did not indulge in creating sentimental catchwords in verse. Critically aware of the poetic traditions in Persian, Urdu, and English languages, he devised a technique and evolved a tone that sounded like soft notes of expostulation. He was inspired more by the spirit of liberation than by slogans. Even while strongly subscribing to an ideology, he could artfully transcend it to create a poem of great contemporary and personal appeal and relevance.

Faiz had a variegated career as an editor of *Lotus*, an international leftist magazine for many years, a teacher of English, a lieutenant colonel of the British Indian Army during World War II, a recipient of MBE for his wartime services, a broadcaster, and a political activist. His exile in Paris, London, Moscow, and Beirut, and his readings in Western literature helped him view his individual and social predicament with great confidence and clarity. With this unusual career, and with the kind of poetry he wrote to resist the structures of power, Faiz attracted the attention of a larger section of the general and informed readers, and also those who were socially and politically concerned. While he nourished his sensibility by drawing upon the contemporary history of colonial and capitalist oppression in many parts of the world, particularly our subcontinent, Faiz emerged as a dissenter. He was a dissenter, but of the most sophisticated sort; he exuded anger, but with control and culture; he opposed tyrannies of all kinds, but in a manner that made one and all hear him patiently. As such, in his role as a dissenter, he sought, in fact, to act as a negotiator rather than remain a victim of polarities. He, thus, composed his unique poetic oeuvre with great finesse, where he placed his central metaphors of freedom against slavery, justice against oppression, gloom against light, hope against despair, friend against foe, and union against separation.

In explaining his poetic credo, Faiz has very appropriately remarked: 'To me the old and the new, the traditional and the contemporary fall in their proper places in the larger composite tradition of literature. The great advantage—or miracle—of the ghazal form, for example, is that you can use it to render themes in traditional diction and still be in tune with contemporary reality' (ix). Appropriately enough, in drawing upon the ghazal tradition, Faiz found space for the more pathetic moments of life, which he represented with greater empathy than other progressive poets. This also leads one to posit that he was the last romantic who appropriated the best elements of the romantic tradition in Urdu poetry to configure and represent the vicissitudes of history, politics, and personal dilemmas. His poems like

'Bol' (Speak) 'Subh-e Azadi' (Freedom's Dawn), 'Tarana' (Anthem), 'Irani Talaba Ke Naam' (In the Name of Iranian Students), 'Aa Jao Africa' (Come Back Africa), 'Intisaab' (Dedication), 'Sipahi ka Marsiya' (Elegy for a Soldier), 'Dua' (Prayer), and 'Falasteen ke Liye' (For Palestine) bear ample testimony to his commitment and vision. These poems make sense as appeals, entreaties, complaints, and as songs of resistance and testimonies of faith. Two poems—'Speak' and 'Prayer'—that represent his will to take cudgels on the one hand and implore softly on the other are quoted here in full:

Speak, your lips are free,
speak, your tongue is still yours,
your slim body is yours alone,
speak, this life is yours, still yours.

See in the blacksmith's forge
flames leap up, iron glows red,
padlocks have started opening up
and every chain is softening its knot.

Speak this short while is long enough
before the demise of body and tongue.
Speak, the truth is alive still,
speak, what you wish to speak.

(*FAR*, 43)

We, who have forgotten how to pray,
we who have forgotten our idols, our gods,
we, who only remember our sears of love—
let's come together, let's too lift our hands to pray.

Let's pray that life, our beloved,
may pour tomorrow's honey in today's poison;
let's pray their nights and days
may turn smooth, who find them tough;

let's pray their dark nights
may lit up bright, who cannot see the dawn's face;
let's pray that they
may find their ways who have none;
let's pray that those who practice deceit and hypocrisy
may get courage to deny, resolution to believe;
let's pray that those whose heads wait for swords of tyranny
may have the nerve to fend off the assassin's hands.
Let's make a covenant today with our fevered souls,
the subterranean secret of love,
let's slake its fever.
Let's own the word of Truth
which pricks the heart like a thorn.
Let's end our anguish.

(*FAR*, 49)

Reading Faiz is experiencing the human predicament at large and appreciating the true meaning of suffering and glory. Faiz was an artist of ideas and most popular of the poets in both the literary and extra-literary circles. Ten collections of his poetry, published from 1941 to 1984, have represented issues that are private, public, contemporary, and historical. In spite of all their personal merit, sometimes poets acquire and establish their significance in a group rather than individually. From this perspective, Faiz could turn out to be a poet of larger relevance if read along with the Turkish poet Nazim Hikmet (1902–1963), the Chilean poet Pablo Neruda (1904–1973), and the Palestinian poet Mahmoud Darwish (1942–2008), who together constituted a tradition of resistance in their poetry which has now come to acquire a significant space in modern literary studies.

For Art's Sake: Circle of Connoisseurs

The name Circle of Connoisseurs is amply suggestive.[14] The poets who came together to form this circle were clearly different in their orientation and outlook compared to the progressive poets. They had no slogans to raise, no political ideology to follow; they only had the poem to engage with as an artefact. They were more preoccupied with form and language—the poem as a technically proficient work of art that stood for its own testimony. A poem for them was an attempt at redefining the poem itself that was typically modernist in tone, tenor, and style.

The circle comprised N.M. Rashed (1910–1975), Meeraji (1912–1949), Gopal Mittal (1906–1993), Yusuf Zafar (1914–1972), Qayyum Nazar (1914–1989), and Zia Jalandhari (1923–2012), even though it also had Muhammad Din Taseer and Patras Bokhari as the unacknowledged votaries. The group posited a poetics, different from the one championed by the progressive poets. It did not proclaim any political intentions, nor declare affiliations to any given ideology—social, political, or literary. Rather, it chose for a liberal approach towards the conditions of being that defied a logical or chronological sequence. The poets of this group yearned to apprehend life's mysteries and ambiguities which constituted its core and called for a liberal negotiation. It acknowledged the presence of baser and finer instincts in human beings, and dealt with them with greater catholicity than constraint. These poets chose to liberalize the form itself and make way for blank and free verse that could bear the burden of their experience. Quite naturally, a substantial body of their poetry turned out to be obscure and needed effort on the part of the reader to decipher the codes, as has been the case with the understanding of much of the modernist poetry written in English, French, and other languages with whom their association may be justifiably established.

N.M. Rashed's poetry was not instantly acceptable to a larger readership at the first instance,[15] but once he found certain acceptability, it grew upon his readers steadily. On a more critical note, it might be argued that his reputation as a poet kept pace with the appearance of the four collections of his poetry—*Mavara* (Beyond), *Iran Main Ajnabi* (Stranger in Iran), *La Insan* (No Man), and *Guman ka Mumkin* (Possible Conjecture), published between 1941 and 1977. While his first collection challenged the popular taste, it slowly and painfully worked towards creating a readership that could accept his poetic output which was drastically different, both in experience and technique. With each one of his collections, he gained greater ground till he came to be accepted as one of the three major vices of modernist Urdu poetry, the other two being Faiz Ahmad Faiz and Meeraji.

Rashed chose to face history, nature, and human instinct in his poetry and listen to unheard voices hidden in remote quarters. While rejecting age-old moral values, he initiated himself into life's essential spirit by joining it uninhibitedly. Poems in *Iran Mein Ajnabi* show how he sought meaning in alternating between past and present, as he did between the immediately perceptible and the remotely present. This brought him closer to hope and faith and to an understanding of existential vitality, which came out in his later poems with greater confidence. Lines from 'Ye Khala Pur Na Hua' (The Void Was Not Filled) and 'Mujhe Wida Kar' (Bid Me Farewell) represent his preoccupation:

> It does not matter if we have failed
> and all our efforts are laid waste.
> We who have not reached our goals and have suffered grief,
> like a beatific mendicant napping on some threshold,
> why shouldn't we fill this void with image of a minaret,
> or the din of colours,
> or the fragrance of dreams?
> So that death may stay away—far away from us.
>
> (*FAR*, 21)

> Bid me farewell,
> It's late, too late, perhaps much too late—
> the twentieth-century night has already struck the clock.
> Trees and stones, beasts and tired birds
> have all been engaged in parlance
> for a thousand years upon this earth.
> Just think what shall they feel
> that I, like gods,
> the eternally insincere,
> have again broken my sacred oath.
>
> (*FAR*, 27)

Rashed made bolder experiments in form than others. With his rhymed and unrhymed verse and with his vocabulary shorn of conventional sound and meaning, he drew upon the myriad facets of life lived in privacy and in community, and a faith practised in public and the one in seclusion or solitude. He drew upon shifting cultural motifs, melting geographical boundaries, quibbles of politics, failures of governance, and human values relegated to die in a limbo. In his poetic apprehension and rendition, Rashed went closer to Western modernists with whom he may be read with great profit. M.A.R. Habib, an American academic and translator of repute, has made a point with reference to his kinship with T.S. Eliot. 'Like Eliot's verse,' he posits, 'Rashed's poetry is obscure, allusive and questions the very nature of language. And, as with Eliot's work, these qualities conspire to deny it any "popular" appeal. Those who respect and enjoy Rashed are primarily intellectuals prepared to welcome novelty and difficulty' (52). He further says: 'The formal techniques of Rashed's poems are similar to those used by Eliot. And what is at stake in his individualism also is the complex phenomenon of secularization' (64).

In comparison with Rashed, Meeraji's attitude towards life was that of a total bohemian, but Meeraji's approach to poetry and poetic expression was rather regulated and well-considered. He subscribed to a non-conformist, sometimes even unpredictable, form and idiom to write his lines that went to explore the inner recesses of human psyche. Meeraji had little regard for conservative value system and showed as much in his eclectic and, quite often, wayward youthfulness. His free associations with objects of attention might be traced in Freudian psychoanalysis, as he was naturally drawn towards exploring the mysteries of the subconscious. This made him sensational at times, but he struck at the very root of the complex psychic functioning. His resorting to sources and inspirations as diverse as Hindu mythology, Sigmund Freud, Mirabai, Omar Khayyam, Amaru, Damodaragupta, Edgar Allan Poe, Charles Baudelaire, and La Corbière defined the nature of his poetry that was characterized primarily by a rich fusion of literary and extra-literary sources. His amazing range of references and his ways of drawing upon them in idiosyncratic ways underlined his typically modernist expression. Two extracts from 'Samundar Ka Bulaawa' (Sea Call) and 'Raas ki Anokhi Lehrein' (Strange Waves of Ecstasy) might be considered here:

> There's no desert now, no mountain, no garden,
> no motion in my eyes, no smile on my face, no gesture,
> only a strange voice is heard—
> 'Come on, come on, for years I've been calling ... calling ...
> I'm deeply tired in heart and soul ... '
> None has ever tired calling, nor shall ever tire.
>
> This voice is now a mirror to me.
> Only I've tired calling someone.
>
> (trans. by Rahman, 53)

> I wish the world's eye go on looking at me, so closely looking at me
> As one looks at the tender branch of a tree,
> Looks at the swinging, tender branch of a tree,
> But I wish the burden of leaves, like cast off robes should lie in a heap
> By the bed of roses.
> I wish the gush of wind should go on embracing me—
> Thrilling, tingling, saying something laughingly,
> Tottering, tarrying with the burden of shame
> in the colourful whispers of ecstasy.
> I wish to fare forward—now walking, now running,
> As the wind touching the waves of a river, rushes swiftly ahead,
> Does not pause.
>
> (trans. by Rahman, 59)

Greatly esoteric and experimental in nature, Meeraji reflected in his poetry over the nature of the word and the structure of the poem, which defied a given pattern as life itself often did. This could be borne out by the poems that followed a formal structure as in his songs, or the regular poems that often broke a rhythm to resume it again, or even the prose poems that went on and on without a stop and did not allow the reader a break of breath. His poems collected in *Kulliyat-e Meeraji* (Complete Poems) in 1988 represent the great depth and variety of his work. Geeta Patel, a reputed academic and scholar, in her chapter on 'Miraji's Response to the Progressives' has attempted an incisive reading of Meeraji's poetry to mark his aesthetic principles:

> *His* definition of new poetry is poetry that blends feeling and thought to completely express what goes on inside the person—'a feeling-thought or desire'—and suits form and language to the issue at hand. Such a poet, rather than resorting to the conventionality of the formal to assess his affiliations to newness and thus to the measures of value, turns form to his own use. (133)

'A feeling-thought or desire' is typically a Meeraji expression.

Rashed and Meeraji were poets of tough intellectual mould, who drew upon a rich variety of eastern and western, literary and non-literary sources. In resorting to indigenous, spiritual, and cultural sources, they turned them relevant. That was their way of imparting a philosophical halo to their poetry. The way they discovered their metaphors and symbols, their language and ideology, and their form and technique, Rashed and Meeraji might best be appreciated as *avant-garde* poets, closely comparable to their Western counterparts. As such, their significance could be traced in the fact that they established a robust tradition of modernism in Urdu poetry, and that the poets who wrote after them closely drew upon them to strengthen their tradition by substantiating, validating, and diversifying it.

Epilogue

Progressive Writers' Association and Circle of Connoisseurs were not opposed to each other; they viewed the conditions and expressed themselves differently. A major modernist poet, Akhtarul Iman has made a dispassionate assessment of the merits of both the groups in his autobiography: 'The basic difference lay in their perspective or attitude. To the progressive writers, writings that did not represent leftist angle were not valuable. It did not matter if that literature had little or no literary merit. I do not want to make any comments as to how far that literature was leftist, and as to how far propagandist' (104). He has further written about the poets of the Circle of Connoisseurs: 'The Circle of Connoisseurs did not have any slogan of that kind. They only said that all literary writing must be literary first, or should come under the category of good writing. It is only secondary whether they also have a slogan' (113).[16]

Developing another perspective, I might add that on account of the great emotional appeal of his ideas and the rhythmic nature of his lines, Faiz has enamoured alike the philanthropist and the philanderer, the pious and the profane, the music makers and the dreamers of dreams, but Rashed and Meeraji, arguably greater poets than Faiz, have little to offer to the popular readers or listeners of Urdu poetry, and have consequently made sense only to a select readership. The word, the matter, and the form were sensuous bodies for Faiz to play on; they were elusive substances for Rashed and Meeraji to experiment with. While Faiz exploited the romance of realism, Rashid and Meeraji fantasized the real and concretized the fantastic. Emerging as a myth in his own lifetime, Faiz has been evaluated and translated abundantly in English,[17] while Rashed and Meeraji have received only limited attention in spite of their remarkable literary merit. The three poets worked in their own ways, each distinct from the other; but considered cumulatively, it must be conceded that the trio broke fresh grounds and spearheaded the modernist movement in Urdu poetry.

Let me bring the discussion to a close by referring to an objective assessment of the entire phenomenon with reference to the two movements represented basically by three poets. I would refer here to the *Mahfil* interview of N.M. Rashed, who recorded as follows:

> This new spirit in Urdu poetry was inevitable, as much as it was inevitable in the poetry of any other language. It simultaneously threw up three poets, who in their different ways, sought to interpret modern life. Miraji made bold experiments with form, brought the language of poetry closer to everyday speech, and unraveled some of the mysteries of the subconscious in the light of the new psychoanalytical discoveries; Faiz using most of the traditional clichés, symbols and myths, even as Iqbal had done, evinced a new emotional response to

> current human problems in line with the socialist doctrine; and I, in my small way, experimenting with new rhyme arrangements, tried to stress some of the current problems, the foremost among them for me being the alien rule, religious dogmatism, moral repression etc. which had continuously dwarfed the Asian soul; and to achieve this, I drew upon my personal experience alone, rather than the experience of others or any ulterior doctrine. (2)

Modern poetry in Urdu has moved in several directions since the three poets wrote, but these poets have stayed on as canonical figures to whom the practising poets have turned again and again. Their contemporary relevance could be located in the resistance they have offered in apprehending and representing the stereotypes of life and art, which the post Faiz–Rashed–Meeraji poets ultimately chose to draw upon.

Endnotes

1. Altaf Hussain Hali (1837–1914) and Muhammad Husain Azad (1830–1910) initiated a new tradition in Urdu poetry that would shun sheer romanticism in thought and expression. Hali wrote his *musaddas Maddo-Jazar-e Islam* (The Rise and Fall of Islam) that highlighted sociocultural concerns. In 1867, he and Azad, under the auspices of Anjuman-e Punjab, Lahore, stressed on disengaging from romantic ideals and expressing new realities. Azad reiterated this concern in an address in 1874. Before the poets owed their allegiance to the Progressive Writers' Movement, poets like Iqbal (1877–1938) and Josh Malihabadi (1898–1982) wrote poetry of religio-philosophical vision and nationalistic and political fervour. Other poets like Firaq Gorakhpuri (1896–1982), Shad Azimabadi (1846–1927), Hasrat Mohani (1875–1951), and Yagana Changezi (1884–1956) wrote a kind of poetry that followed the ghazal tradition of Urdu poetry, which underwent a major transformation with the coming of the poets since the 1930s.
2. Two dictators, Adolf Hitler in Germany and Benito Mussolini in Italy, persisted with their policies of territorial expansion, which was one of the reasons for the outbreak of World War II in 1939.
3. Colombia–Peru War (1932–1933), Chaco War (1932–1935), Second Sino-Japanese War (1937–1945), World War II (1939–1945), Spanish Civil War (1936–1939) and Castellammarese War (1929–1931).
4. It swayed several countries like Japan, Spain, Russia, Italy, and Germany. The coming to power of Nazi party in Germany, for example, in 1933 by employing

coercive methods was an open declaration of fascist policies that led to the repudiation of the Treaty of Versailles, indulgence in persecution of Jews, territorial expansion, and sharp opposition to socialism.

5. Following the Japanese capture of Manchuria in 1931, Italy invaded Ethiopia during the Second Italo–Abyssinian War of 1935–36.
6. The Indian freedom struggle led by Mahatama Gandhi by employing non-violent means and by resorting to Satyagraha and the famous Dandi March in 1930 is a major example that goes diametrically against the authoritarian governance that was tearing the world apart.
7. This may be testified by the price decline that took place during 1929–31, whereby it was estimated to be 36 per cent compared to 27 per cent in UK and 26 per cent in US. [K.A. Manikumar, *A Colonial Economy in the Great Depression: Madras (1929–1937)* (Hyderabad: Orient Blackswan, 2003), p. 9.]
8. Literary history bears out quite amply that writers from all times and sites have always responded to political events and interpreted them in literary terms in their own ways. Written during the 30s, the poetry of W.H. Auden and other poets of his group may be quoted as a suitable example to illustrate this point. Reference may also be made to some fictional works from the English-speaking world written during this decade, which include F. Scott Fitzgerald's *Tender Is the Night* (1934), J.R.R. Tolkien's *The Hobbit* (1937), Aldous Huxley's *Brave New World* (1932), John Steinbeck's *Grapes of Wrath* (1939) and *Of Mice and Men* (1937), Ernest Hemingway's *To Have and Have Not* (1937), John Dos Passos's *U.S.A Trilogy* (3 volumes in 1930, 1932, and 1936), William Faulkner's *As I Lay Dying* (1930) and *Absalom, Absalom!* (1936), John O'Hara's *Appointment in Samarra* (1934), and *BUtterfield 8* (1935).
9. For Ahmed Ali's association with Progressive Writers Movement, see Zeno, 'Professor Ahmed Ali and the Progressive Writers' Movement,' *Annual of Urdu Studies* 9 (1994): 39–43.
10. The manifesto reads as:

    Radical changes are taking place in Indian society. Fixed ideas and old beliefs, social and political institutions are being challenged. Out of the present turmoil and conflict a new society is emerging. The spirit of reaction however, though moribund and doomed to ultimate decay, is still operative and is making desperate efforts to prolong itself.

    'It is the duty of Indian writers to give expression to the changes taking place in Indian life and to assist in the spirit of progress in the country. Indian literature, since the breakdown of classical literature, has had the fatal tendency to escape from the actualities of life. It has tried to find a refuge from reality in spiritualism and idealism. The result has been that it has produced a rigid formalism and a banal and perverse ideology.

'Witness the mystical devotional obsession of our literature, its furtive and sentimental attitude towards sex, its emotional exhibitionism and its almost total lack of rationality. Such literature was produced particularly during the past two centuries, one of the most unfortunate periods of our history, a period of disintegrating feudalism and of acute misery and degradation for the Indian people as a whole.

'It is the object of our association to rescue literature and other arts from the priestly, academic and decadent classes in whose hands they have degenerated so long; to bring the arts into the closest touch with the people; and to make them the vital organs which will register the actualities of life, as well as lead us to the future.

'While claiming to be the inheritors of the best traditions of Indian civilisation, we shall criticise ruthlessly, in its political, economic and cultural aspects, the spirit of reaction in our country and we shall foster through interpretive and creative work (with both native and foreign resources) everything that will lead our country to the new life for which it is striving. We believe that the new literature of India must deal with the basic problems of our existence today—the problems of hunger and poverty, social backwardness and political subjugation, so that it may help us to understand these problems and through such understanding help us to act.

'With the above aims in view, the following resolutions have been adopted:

- The establishment of organizations of writers to correspond to the various linguistic zones of India; the co-ordinations of these organizations by holding conferences, publishing of magazines, pamphlets, etc.
- To cooperate with those literary organizations whose aims do not conflict with the basic aims of the association.
- To produce and translate literature of a progressive nature and of a high technical standard; to fight cultural reaction; and in this way, to further the cause of Indian freedom and social regeneration.
- To strive for the acceptance of a common language (Hindustani) and a common script (Indo-Roman) for India. [This demand was later dropped in appreciation of the India's multilingual structure.]
- To protect the interests of authors; to help authors who require and deserve assistance for the publication of their works.
- To fight for the right of free expression of thought and opinion.'

[Quoted in Ali Husain Mir and Raza Mir, *Anthems of Resistance: A Celebration of Progressive Urdu Poetry* (New Delhi: Roli Books, 2006).]

11. Important writers associated with the movement included Sajjad Zaheer, Ahmed Ali, Rashid Jahan, Saadat Hasan Manto, Muhammad Din Taseer, Faiz Ahmad Faiz, Vijaydan Detha, Khagendra Thakur, Bhisham Sahni, Krishan Chander, Ismat Chughtai, Rajinder Singh Bedi, Premchand, Amrita Pritam, Sahir Ludhianvi, Majrooh Sultanpuri, Ghulam Rabbani Taban, and Jan Nisar Akhtar.

12. For a detailed discussion of this publication, see Shabana Mahmud, 'Angāre and the Founding of Progressive Writers' Association,' *Modern Asian Studies* 30 (2) (2008): 39–43.
13. Raịpuri had first written an article entitled 'Adab aur Zindagi' (Literature and Life) to illustrate at length what Sajjad Zaheer had laid out as the aim of the Progressive Writers' Association. It was published both in Urdu and Hindi to reach to a larger readership.
14. See *Mahfil* interview of Rashed, where he speaks at length about Halqa-e-Arbab-e Zauq (Circle of Connoisseurs) [Rashed, *Mahfil* 7 (spring–summer 1971): 1–2].
15. Responses to his first anthology *Mawara*, which created almost a stir for the new literary methods that Rashed had employed, were unduly harsh. A good account of his unacceptability at the beginning of his career may be seen in his *Mahfil* interview [Rashed, *Mahfil* 7 (spring–summer 1971): 1–2].
16. Translated by the author of this chapter.
17. Some of these include V.G. Kiernan, *Poems by Faiz* (London: George Allen and Unwin, 1971); Daud Kamal, trans., *Selected Poems of Faiz in English* (Karachi: Pakistan Publishing House, 1984); *Faiz A Faiz: The Living World* (Tunis: Lotus Books, 1987). Mouin Beseisso and Alex la Guma, *A Black Rainbow Over My Homeland: A Commemorative Volume on Faiz Ahmed Faiz*, ed. Kalpana Sahni (New Delhi: Afro-Asian Writers' Association, n.d.); Naomi Lazard, trans., *The True Subject* (Princeton: Princeton University Press, 1989); Agha Shahid Ali, trans., *The Rebel's Silhouette* (Delhi: OUP, 1992), Shiv K. Kumar, trans., *Selected Poems of Faiz Ahmed Faiz* (New Delhi: Penguin Books, 1995); Sarvat Rahman, trans., *100 Poems by Faiz Ahmed Faiz* (New Delhi: Abhinav Publications, Hind Pocket Books, 2002, 2009); Salima Hashmi and Shoaib Hashmi, *A Song for This Day: 52 Poems by Faiz Ahmed Faiz* (Lahore: Sang-e Meel Publications, 2009).

References

Iman, Akhtarul. 1996. *Is Aabaad Kharaabe Mein*. Delhi: Urdu Academy.

Malik, Hafeez. 'The Marxist Literary Movement in India and Pakistan.' *The Journal of Asian Studies* 26 (4) (1967): 649–64.

Patel, Geeta. 2002. 'Miraji's Response to the Progressives.' In *Lyrical Moments, Historical Hauntings: On Gender, Colonialism, and Desire in Miraji's Urdu Poetry.* Stanford: Stanford University Press.

Rahman, Anisur, trans. and ed. 1995. *Fire and the Rose: An Anthology of Modern Urdu Poetry*. New Delhi: Rupa & Co.

Zaidi, Ali Jawad. 2006. *A History of Urdu Literature.* New Delhi: Sahitya Akademi.

The Problematic of Impact and Response: The Case of Faiz Ahmad Faiz

Internalization: Two Paradigms

Let me begin by posing some interrelated questions concerning internalization. Let me ask, to lay the ground, as to what is internalization, what does it signify, how does it work, what does it entail, how does it matter, and what does it offer in a limited or a broader context?

Let me try and offer some interrelated answers to the questions posed earlier. Internalization is an act of personalizing or subjectivizing a phenomenon or a condition. It signifies the acquisition of a state of being and a way of enrichment, and works through discovering kindred kinds, both consciously and unconsciously. It entails the cultivation of a liberal attitude that helps discover and imbibe ideal figures or values, and finally contributes towards the attainment of a state of mind that serves as a basic condition for comprehensive human development. Precisely, it is a way of interiorizing a condition by acquiring and incorporating chosen marks and icons. At a more intricate level, it is a psychological process of inclusive growth which involves a critical method of rejecting and selecting modes and motifs to develop an inclusive identity.

I would like to put forward a thesis. In the literary context, the process of internalization works at two different levels, which may be identified as the primary and secondary levels of internalization. The primary level of internalization is rather natural, unilateral, and homebound. At this level, informed people from a cultural site operate within the very confines of their own area and respond to their authors and texts as naturally as they do to their cultural logos. As literary capital, accumulated over long periods of time, becomes a part and parcel of their collective consciousness, it gets interiorized or internalized in the normal course of their personal development. In this process of growth, people develop a natural affinity with their authors and texts for which no conscious effort at internalization is required to be made. This implies that Shakespeare, for example, is as easily and naturally internalized by an English reader, as Ghalib is by an Urdu reader. As such, this primary level of internalization relates with the framework of a given literary tradition, where words, images, metaphors, symbols, and myths—independently or cumulatively—constitute the integral part(s) of the common literary imagination of a people.

As opposed to the primary type, the secondary type of internalization is bilateral or even multilateral, and makes serious demands upon the readers belonging to a different cultural site. It concerns an alien context, where people from one cultural domain are required to develop a level of familiarity with a different set of emblems, values, linguistic habits, and literary forms and styles belonging to another cultural domain. As the texts and authors are unfamiliar in the new cultural site, and as the literary manners and motifs are alien, a conscious effort is required to be made to appreciate the value of those literary formations. Only after those formations strike the imagination of this new set of readers, the question of their acceptance and subsequent internalization may arise. It implies, therefore, that an English reader will have to make a deliberate attempt at internalizing Ghalib, for example, as an Urdu reader would have to do in the case of Shakespeare. It would, thus, appear that while internalization is a natural, rather a biological process, in the first case, it is a deliberate and a demanding one in the other. However, both the processes of internalization help the people grow both unilaterally and multilaterally, and they contribute towards the comprehensive development of literary readership.

More important than the primary type of internalization, however, is the secondary type, where authors and texts find space in the literary imagination of the other people characterized by different sets of sociocultural identifiers. It is in the secondary domain of internalization that a reader sets out to negotiate with a kind of text which is different in its essential make-up, compared with the text in one's own language. This thesis may well be examined, for example, in the context of the English readership and its engagement with the literatures of India. With reference to the Indian context, it may be justifiably posited that the English readers have been picking on the classical Indian authors and texts rather traditionally, ever since the eighth decade of the eighteenth century. This engagement with India and the Indian religious and secular literatures continued through the next two centuries, which resulted in imparting a stereotypical identity both to India and its literatures. This choice of reading the Indian literatures was not so much for the purpose of internalizing Indian literatures, as it was for discovering the mystique of India and for incorporating India in the larger framework of the world literature for academic reasons. This approach underwent a change, however, in the later part of the twentieth century with the postcolonial need for a more catholic exploration of the new areas of writing. It also underlined, in the process, the larger relevance of these literatures in the liberal spaces of the modern world, as also the significance of the new sensibility that these literatures represented. Today, the growing acceptance of Indian literatures in the English-speaking world may be read as a due acknowledgment of the contemporary need to afford space to authors and literatures of new affiliations from the major literary sites of the world, especially the erstwhile colonies. These new authors and literatures are now placed face-to-face with those from the typical English stock, leading to the birth of a new literary condition. With the breaking up of the long-preserved citadels of the British literary culture, a different scenario is emerging with respectable space for literary expressions representing complex social configurations, minority discourse, political resistance, and stylistic variations. The modern literary horizon is, thus, remarkably widening with the dissemination of literatures from other languages, which has been possible largely because of the respectable translations of these literatures in the English language. This has also happened in the case of Urdu literature, which has, so far, been supposed to be a curious and romantic language even in its homeland. No longer being a curio of a language and literature, select Urdu texts are now finding their new habitats in English literary capitals, far beyond the confines of India and Pakistan.

By extending the two paradigms of primary and secondary internalization, that is, one within a given literary culture and another beyond it, we may find a way to understand and contextualize one of the most popular Urdu poets—Faiz Ahmad Faiz—in a fresh and larger perspective. To make my point, I may posit that Faiz stands already internalized at the primary level among those who write and speak the language Faiz himself spoke and wrote in. At this level of internalization, he has already become a part of the cultural heritage of Urdu and its related linguistic clusters. What distinguishes Faiz further is that he stands internalized not only in various linguistic and literary circles of India and Pakistan, but also among the common people who see their aspirations reflected in him and their tones of voice echoed in his rhythmic renditions. By this logic, Faiz is not only a poet but a popular icon who has been read, researched, sung, and celebrated more than any other modern Urdu poet, and turned into a myth in his own lifetime. This process of internalization in the case of Faiz relates, in fact, with a larger literary phenomenon of impact and response. As one of the canonical figures in modern Urdu poetry, Faiz made a remarkable impact on the common man, the literary reader, the political establishment, and the literary canon. As such, he has been received much more liberally than any other literary figure in and outside his own geographical and literary boundaries. While his reception in the Indian subcontinent for his multiple merits is one aspect of his worth, his reception in the larger English-reading circles is yet another facet of his literary and political significance. The following section makes an effort to examine how he is remarkably relevant to a larger world, and how he may find his appeal among the English readers in an age characteristically marked by increasing political upheavals and continuous social flux, irrespective of the place and the modes of governance.

Faiz and the English Language Reader

Of the several collections of English translations exclusively devoted to Faiz,[1] I would like to examine only three done by V.G. Kiernan, Naomi Lazard, and Agha Shahid Ali. They help me take my argument further regarding how this poet may possibly be internalized by a readership completely unaware of his poetry and poetics, his sociopolitical baggage, and his larger relevance in the contemporary world. Translating Faiz has not only been a curious literary engagement for these translators; it has rather been a matter of making a space for a virile voice that deserves to be heard like those of Pablo Neruda, Nâzim Hikmet, and Mahmoud Darwish in the complex sociopolitical scenario of the modern world.

Kiernan, Lazard, and Ali, the three major translators of Faiz, offer substantial material for us to study as to how this poet sounds and appeals in the English language, and whether their translations may possibly help those readers internalize Faiz who do not know either the Urdu language or its literary baggage. Let us examine their intentions behind translating this poet, their commonalities and differences, and, finally, their end products that they handed over to the readers in the English language. All three of them come from three different backgrounds: Kiernan is a historian of British origin known for his Marxist readings of history, his works on imperialism, Shakespeare, and his translations of Iqbal and Faiz; Lazard is a poet of American origin whose poems have appeared in major American journals apart from her own collections; and Ali, who identified himself as a Kashmiri-Indian-American, is an English poet, an American academic, and a multicultural being. English was the medium of expression for all of them, and all of them took up Faiz as a major project with their individual aesthetic principles in place. They respected Faiz for his world view and his poetry, and they evidently wanted him to transcend his language and location. All of them had personal access to Faiz and, through him, to his individual poems, as none of them knew the language that Faiz wrote in. Lazard and Ali, being poets, produced their versions of Faiz quite differently from the one that Kiernan produced. Kiernan identified with Faiz on an ideological level and approached him to validate his own way of looking at history and human predicament; Ali identified with him on a cultural level and wished to find a space for him in a larger world that knew little, or sometimes even nothing, of the Eastern literary figures deserving attention; and Lazard saw in him a poet who would bring a new way of apprehending the broader realities of life to the American readership. The three ways of approaching Faiz are, in fact, the three possible efforts to help an alien reader internalize this poet, whose impact on the Urdu readership had been rather phenomenal ever since the publications of his first collection of poems *Naqsh-e-Faryadi* in 1941, and who had enough potential to attract the English reader for all his poetic and sociopolitical worth.

While choosing to translate Faiz way back in 1945, putting his work in print in 1958, and making further revisions in 1971,[2] V.G. Kiernan did not only make a significant attempt at bringing him to serious readership in the English language, he actually ushered what may be called a Faiz translation industry. Kiernan's *Poems by Faiz* (1971) is a pioneering work in many respects. He provides the Urdu text, along with its English transliteration, and the literal prose renderings before he offers his translation. He also supplements his translations with brief notes to the poems, as required. As a translator, his intentions are clearly laid out, as he wished to cater to a larger readership—the Western students of the Urdu language, the East Pakistanis, and the Indians who might like to read Urdu literature of West Pakistan.[3] Kiernan's is the first serious attempt at translating Faiz with a well laid-out scheme and methodology. While his 'Preface' lays out the principles of translation and makes comments on the Urdu text and the transliteration, his detailed 'Introduction' offers observations on Faiz, his life and times, historical context, and literary traditions, which help us contextualize him in a larger framework of time and place. Kiernan's work may be marked as an academic exercise that follows a proper methodology in order to present a poet before a new readership that may be unaware of the language in which the poems were originally written. By selecting poems from different anthologies in order of their appearance, he creates a sense of the poet's development in terms of themes and style. He approaches Faiz first by paraphrasing the poems and then rendering them into verse translations. Each poem is faithfully and diligently rendered, with notes wherever required. He balances the English linguistic devices and bridges the hiatus between two different cultural conditions. Even though Kiernan has a certain group of readership in mind, his work caters more liberally to anyone who may like to approach Faiz in the English language. In this respect, Kiernan is quite objective and neutral in reading and rendering Faiz, and his work eminently qualifies for a larger readership.

Naomi Lazard's bilingual edition entitled *The True Subject* (1987) is a fine example of one poet translating another poet. As one who had no access to the source language, Lazard's engagement with the poetry of Faiz is an extremely demanding kind,[4] which is duly met in her association with Faiz who helped her apprehend the poems by offering the literal translations of his poems to her. Lazard identifies her problems in precise terms, which relate with appreciating the role and nature of a particular word or a phrase, an image or a metaphor. She is also conscious of the problems that arise while negotiating with cultural differences and the subsequent loss of meaning that might occur if she failed to strike a proper negotiation. She is further concerned about rightly appreciating the grammatical constructs, charging her diction, identifying her images, strengthening her verbs, discounting adverbs and adjectives, and finding a way to recreate a poem in English with the same spirit, feeling, tone, and music, which Faiz might possibly have in mind. Her other major problems relate with discovering an active rather than a passive and elusive way of expression, and evolving a distinct form for the poem.

Lazard addresses her problems by discovering a methodology of her own. She chooses to render many poems exactly as they were in words, images, and form in the source language, while in some others she chooses to be creative and liberal. She seems to confirm a truism rather insistently that, translating a word for a word, or an image for an image, would make little sense to the English readership. She, thus, imbibes the spirit of the source text and tries to recast it in a way that may suit the genius of the English language and the English reader. Lazard's is an act of striking a delicate balance between a text that exists in the source language and the one that might configure through the process of translational negotiation in the target language. As such, she prefers to interpret the poem on her own by finding her own image or cultural identifier to replace the ones executed by Faiz. She even discovers her own stanza pattern and her own titles, which she considers to be more communicative and relevant to the English reader. She even dispenses with many of the words used in the source text, and reconstitutes a poem either fully or partially for her readers. In spite of following such a revisionist methodology, Lazard does not impair the cumulative impact of the poem in terms of content and the essential style of the poet. She aims at the organic growth of her poem in translation with its own individual structure and poetics. Lazard's poems are for the American readership, translated with an intention to help them access and internalize Faiz. Her translations are a poet's translations, a way of complementing a fellow poet, and to own him/her for oneself, as for one's own people.[5] Her essential aim was to recreate a poetic text, plausible in English, both as a poem and as a work of translation.

Agha Shahid Ali's translated volume *The Rebel's Silhouette* (1992) is a remarkable example of his passionate engagement with Faiz. He had an impelling and significant cultural reason to translate Faiz. He took it as 'a terrible insult to a very significant element'[6] of his culture that Faiz should not be known to the Western readership, even though Nâzim Hikmet and Pablo Neruda enjoyed their space there. Translating Faiz was, thus, an act of cultural recuperation for Ali, which might justifiably lead the English readers to internalize Faiz. His decision to translate Faiz led him, first, to identify the problems he might have to face in engaging with this poet, and in meeting his professed intention of translating him. One of his major concerns was how he would be able to negotiate with the English language to embody a new aesthetic order. The issue of his own bilingual and bicultural obligations, and absorbing the music of the original text also posed another set of problems to him.

Identifying the issues in translating Faiz was, however, easier for Ali than finding a method to resolve them.[7] He internalized Faiz for himself in an unusual way, that is, not by reading him, but by listening to his poems in the voice of Begum Akhtar,[8] the iconic singer of India. Ali's sharp auditory imagination gave him a feel of the Faiz poem and its internal rhythm, which he apprehended as an orchestration of a culture. The image and the music proved, in fact, to be the two essential elements that brought Ali in tune with Faiz. Just as the raga and the poem coalesce in Begum Akhtar, the image and the music blend in Ali and they help him recreate Faiz in the English language. Ali made an attempt to recompose a Faiz poem without any irritable reaching after the theory of translation, as he saw each poem as an independent unit of expression. Translating Faiz has been for him a process of discovering his other self, a process in which his potential to belong and to transcend, to adhere and to disengage is at test again and again, and it is ultimately the poet, rather than the translator, in Ali who claims the other half.

Ali's translation *The Rebel's Silhouette*, however, calls for some close scrutiny. His calling Faiz a 'rebel' does not seem quite convincing. His explanation that Faiz is a rebel because he defies man-made courts and considers man to be only a plaintiff in the courts of the universe does not really hold good.[9] He says he is a 'plaintiff', and a plaintiff like him would hardly ever choose to be a rebel. Faiz does not raise loud slogans; he only utters soft notes of expostulation and is impelled by his spirit of liberation. His Marxist view of history, his association with the Progressive Writers' Movement and the Afro-Asian Writers' Association, his exiles and imprisonments—his whole life—so to say, do not make him a rebel, just as W.B. Yeats is not a rebel in spite of all his commitment to the Irish cause. Ali's own choice of poems from the collections of Faiz in a chronological order expresses the innate sensibility of Faiz, which is not that of a rebel but of a liberator. Far from being a rebel, Faiz was more of an explorer, a romantic, with an acute sensuous and metaphoric apprehension. He has accepted, in particular, the impact of Hafiz, Sauda, and Iqbal, and evolved a way different from what Ali considered to be the way of a rebel. He imparted a new meaning to the concept of the Orient, and his poetry is alive with a tone and tenor which is at once soft yet brave.

While attempting to translate the ghazals of Faiz, Ali acknowledged the impossibility of doing it, but did not consider it as an excuse to spare the effort. An attempt at translating the Urdu ghazal into English, or any other European language for that matter, is an attempt at initiating the curious reader into an alien zone of strange mysteries and rare delights. The ghazal, in fact, does not merely reflect the varied facets of a culture; it has its own culture as well, which is decidedly rich. It has, moreover, no model either in English or any of the European languages, and it is, therefore, difficult for the translator to help the reader comprehend this form and its delicate nuances. Ali did not adhere to the couplet form and the rhyme scheme, but took each couplet as a unit and enlarged it into a stanza consisting of several lines.[10] As Ali's translations are not for the purist, as he tells us in his 'Preface', his method of translating the ghazal may not be acceptable easily. But more important than this is whether Ali has succeeded in communicating the idea, the mood, and the rhythm so very special to ghazal. Even though Ali did not succeed here, he chose to reconcile by finding a mode of reincarnating the ghazal in a new form. Ali turned each couplet into a stanza, and however well the stanzas might read, they do not create any impression of the source text for any of its qualities.

Considering all the three translations, one may conclude that the works of Lazard and Ali closely compliment each other and offer many points of comparison and contrast. Both approach Faiz in their individual ways as poets, and both recompose the experience of the original poem and its aesthetic design, yet they create different impacts. Lazard, in order to compensate for her ignorance of the Urdu language, pays greater attention to the meaning and architectonics of the poem, while Ali, who can see the poem as an image, hear it as music, and identify with the essential experience, approaches it with obvious advantages. In spite of following their own methodologies, both of them act like natural translators, and both offer inspired translations. Considering some of the common poems they have chosen to translate, one may notice their personal choice of phrases, their interpretations, additions, deletions, oddities, and also their remarkable finesse in translating Faiz. The three works by Kiernan, Lazard, and Ali are capable enough to take Faiz beyond the confines of the Indian subcontinent and seek space for him in a language and culture so far characterized by a unilateral play of power. This culture of the so-called centre, which reiterated the personal as universal, is now finding its ways to apprehend the new realities of life in this postcolonial world. It is in this context that poets and writers like Faiz may help the erstwhile centre to redefine the human condition in a broader context.

An Argument Concerning Impact and Response

The problematic of impact and response relates directly with the question of power that a culture embodies in its three major constituents—the people, their history, and their language. It is the language and, in turn, the literature written in a language that qualifies a people and their culture for all their worth. As such, power resides in words that join together to create a text, and the text, subsequently, exercises that power on the readers who read that text. The stronger of the cultures overpower the weaker ones and condition their responses till new centres of power emerge to discover a new language and to create a new text. As such, the creation of the new text is as much a reconfiguration of a new culture as it is of history.

The new postcolonial condition has projected questions that relate with cultural identity, which, in turn, concern the construction of the new text and the new readership. It also puts forward the question of new canonical formations and of extending the boundaries of the text by incorporating the lesser known languages and their literatures, and filling them with a new power of difference. As the hegemony of given languages and literatures have been largely questioned, more than one language from more than one site have come together to constitute a confederacy of cultures and cultural productions. This richly unambiguous confederacy works through translations from a variety of languages into English, a language which stays in place not as the carrier of the earlier unilateral power, but as one of the new multilateral power structures of cultures, peoples, histories, and languages.

It is this phenomenon that makes the case of a poet like Faiz relevant to us, as he richly qualifies to reach out to a larger audience and be a part of their consciousness through the English language. The translations of Faiz posit him with a new power that is different from the one he had in the Urdu language. While the Urdu reader could internalize him as a part of his primary response to the poet, the English reader would do so, but only consciously and with concerted effort. This difference would lie in acclimatizing and interiorizing a condition of being different from the one the English reader hails from. Although demanding in its nature, this mode of internalization imparted certain richness to the reader's intellectual make-up.

With translations like those discussed before, Faiz may now be in a position to communicate his sociopolitical aspirations with a curious complex of readership representing a different culture, history, and language. The power that Faiz, and others like him, may exercise would rework the problematic of impact and response in a fresh perspective. It is the text of power that has the capacity to create an impact and invoke responses. It could be a poet like Faiz, in this context, who could create that impact on the English readership and cause response that might contribute towards the making of a new text, the new reader, and the new canon.

To put the aforesaid argument in a perspective, let it be asserted that since the modern English reader is no longer confined to the purist literary heritage in the English language, one could be a willing participant towards discovering new structures of power. As one may cast aside one's long preserved insularity, he/she may enrich himself/herself by reading across a variety of literary texts from diverse non-Western languages made available in English translation. As one may negotiate with new literary cultures and cultural codes, one may acquire fresh apprehensions of time, place, form, and meaning. This also goes to make a significant point that a postcolonial text does not exist unilaterally today, nor is this text self-regulatory or even self-determining. As the world around keeps negotiating with new sociopolitical matrix, a text can longer be autonomous and claim a canon in isolation. Even otherwise, texts hark back and forth in time and space as they connect with other texts in a larger process of enriching a tradition. It is in this process of striking new familiarities that an author from one language finds a space with the readers in another language, as Faiz may do with remarkable dividends to himself and to his readers.

It takes me to posit, finally, that the issue of approaching and internalizing a text from a different sociocultural and linguistic domain has acquired greater proportions in our times than it did in the past. With the obliteration of boundaries and the issues of postcolonial identities and histories assuming greater proportions, a modern literary text like that of Faiz may assume a greater power of relevance and appeal than the earlier hegemonic texts representing colonialist power structures. This new text may now connect multilaterally with languages and cultures at a broader level. This text may acquire its place in a larger canonical formation, defying distinctions among supposedly outlandish languages and cultures. What accounts for this great shift in the domains of writing and reception in our age is the emergence of a cultural condition that effaces rigid structures of literary form and value, and creates instead a respectable space for catholic tendencies, resulting in larger assimilation of alternative modes of perception and expression of reality.

Endnotes

1. Some of these include: V.G. Kiernan, *Poems by Faiz* (1971); Daud Kamal (trans.), *Selected Poems of Faiz* (1984) and *Faiz A. Faiz: The Living World* (1987); Mouin Besseiso and Alex la Guma, *A Black Rainbow Over My Homeland: A Commemorative Volume on Faiz Ahmed Faiz* (n.d.); Naomi Lazard, *The True Subject* (1989); Agha Shahid Ali, *The Rebel's Silhouette* (1992); Shiv K. Kumar, *Selected Poems of Faiz Ahmad Faiz* (1995); Sarvat Rahman (trans.), *100 Poems by Faiz Ahmed Faiz* (2002), Salima Hashmi and Shoaib Hashmi, *A Song for This Day: 52 Poems by Faiz Ahmed Faiz* (2009).
2. See Kiernan's 'Foreword' in *Poems by Faiz*. He writes:

   > This volume is an expansion of a set of verse translations from Faiz which were begun in a forest rest-house on the banks of Woolar Lake in Kashmir in the summer of 1945, continued at intervals over the next dozen years, and published in 1958 in Delhi (later reprinted at Lahore). These translations have now been revised throughout, and also brought into line with the latest editions of the originals... (9).
3. See Kiernan, 'Foreword', *Poems by Faiz*, p. 9.
4. See Lazard, 'Translating Faiz', *The True Subject*, pp. xi–xviii. Lazard speaks at length about the questions that engaged her attention and how she occupied herself with the poetry of Faiz and its translation in the English language. She writes:

   > From the beginning this work of translation has been a process of discovery for me. I have learned what my own language can do and cannot do. I have also learned that I have infinite patience for translation, the same patience I have for my own poems. I have learned that it doesn't matter how long it takes, how many transformations a poem must be brought through, until the English version works in the same way that I have written myself works. It must be faithful to the meaning Faiz has given it. It must move in its own spirit, with the same feeling and tone. It must have the same music, the same direction, and, above all, it must mean the same thing in English that it means in Urdu. (xii)
5. Lazard acknowledges the significance of Faiz as one of 'the few great poets whose stance and influence have altered the consciousness of the world'. [Ibid., p. xi.]
6. Agha Shahid Ali, 'The Rebel's Silhouette: Translating Faiz Ahmad Faiz' (paper presented at the workshop on 'Language, Culture and Translation', India International Centre, New Delhi, 31 October–1 November 1992), p. 3.
7. Ali wrote,

> My particular problem was how to 'pretend' that I was not burdened by a dual loyalty, to ignore that I was negotiating the demands of two cultures, both of which I felt in my bones that I was responding to the sounds of two languages simultaneously...I finally attacked the poem with no theoretical inhibition, letting each dictate its own agenda. I could always hear the music of the original, and that has been fruitful.... [Ibid., pp. 8–9.]

8. See Agha Shahid Ali, 'These Matters of Desire', *The Sunday Times of India Review*, New Delhi, 22 March 1992. Ali speaks at length about how he began to internalize Faiz with Begum Akhtar's magical voice and how his two loyalties to Urdu and English lent themselves to each other. He also tells why and how he chose to translate Faiz in English. He ends on an important note, saying: 'For me translating Faiz has led to its own—caressing—backlash, in which, somehow, my meaning as translator lies.'
9. See Ali, 'About the Title', *The Rebel's Silhouette*.
10. After writing ghazals in the form of stanzas rather than couplets, Ali came to compose his ghazals in couplet form in the subsequent phase of his career. This is so well exemplified in his anthology *Ravishing DisUnities: Real Ghazals in English*, where he puts together a large number of ghazals written in English by diverse hands, and all of them follow the strict metrical pattern of ghazal writing.

References

Ali, Agha Shahid. 1992. *The Rebel's Silhouette*. Delhi: OUP.

Besseiso, Mouin and Alex la Guma. n.d. *A Black Rainbow over My Homeland*. Ed. Kalpana Sahni. New Delhi: Afro-Asian Writers' Association.

Hashmi, Salima and Shoaib Hashmi, trans. 2009. *A Song for This Day: 52 Poems by Faiz Ahmed Faiz*. Lahore: Sang-e Meel Publications.

Kamal, Daud, trans. *Selected Poems of Faiz*. 1984. Karachi: Pakistan Publishing House.

———. 1987. *Faiz A. Faiz: The Living World*. Tunis: Lotus Books.

Kiernan, V.G., trans. with an introduction and notes. 1971. *Poems by Faiz*. London: George Allen and Unwin.

Kumar, Shiv K. 1995. *Selected Poems* of *Faiz Ahmed Faiz*. New Delhi: Penguin Books.

Lazard, Naomi. 1989. *The True Subject*. Princeton: Princeton University Press.

Rahman, Sarvat. 2002. *100 Poems by Faiz Ahmed Faiz*. New Delhi: Abhinav Publications.

On the Edge of Animation: Women Poets from Pakistan

Desired Existence: A Dot on the Canvas

> Even the most unemotional get excited.
> So here I am, on the edge of animation,
> A dream, a dance, a fantastic construction
>
> Moniza Alvi
>
> 'I Would Like to be a Dot in a Painting by Miro' (*The Country at my Shoulder*, *ADITS*: 403)

In quoting the aforementioned lines from Moniza Alvi, a poet born in Pakistan, raised in Britain, and now working and writing there, I wish to underline the remarkable sense of confidence she exudes in constructing and celebrating her identity. Born of a Pakistani father and English mother, she inherited both the elements of the native and the non-native, weighed and balanced the two together, and found a voice of her own that is lyrical, mnemonic, eerie, and yet so very certain about itself. With her poems contained in curiously titled anthologies like—*The Country at My Shoulder* (1993) and *A Bowl of Warm Air* (1996)—she repositions herself in a plethora of spatial, temporal, and cultural/multicultural references. Her lines quoted earlier may be read as her credo, which strengthens her position in being a dot, 'barely distinguishable from other dots' ('I Would Like to be a Dot in a Painting by Miro', *ADITS*: 403). It is only real, and affords her a chance to survey the linescape and reflect on her placement in relation to the other concrete images. Placed otherwise, she would not have the joy of realizing her own significance. She is happier further on not being a perfect circle, for it holds no curiosity; and not being so makes her more interesting. The poem is an address of belonging, a certain way of apprehending herself in relation to her time and place. It would become all the more significant if one remembered that the Spanish surrealist painter and sculptor Joan Miro (1893–1983) acquired his meaning by shifting focus to the open space rather than the concrete image, which has its relevance only in relation to the space left seemingly open and unused. Thus, being a dot in Miro's painting is being important for the poet in her new spatial context. Swinging back and forth in time and space, she collects a variety of images to compose a larger canvas of peculiar contradictions drawing close to reconciliation. In yet another poem ('Presents From My Aunts in Pakistan', *ADITS*: 404–406), salwar kameez, embossed slippers, candy-stripped glass bangles, silver-bordered, and an apple green saree received as presents from the aunts in Pakistan find a place in this half-English girl's home, alongside her denim and corduroy. The aunts from Pakistan, sending the countrymade presents abroad, request for themselves foreign-made cardigans from Marks & Spencer. The offshore presents, however, do not impress her school friends, and she continues living her life by striking a reconciliation and seeking an identity of 'no fixed nationality'. She remains at ease with the changing dynamics of the world around, its remarkable intermixing, and with her place in it. Thus, in yet another poem ('The Double City', *ADITS*: 406–407), she does not find it inconvenient to reach out to Indus, Trafalgar Square, Southall, Kiranjit Ahluwalia, Lord & Taylor, Ramayana, Ram, and Sita with ease, and strikes an affinity with them in her effort to create and recreate an imaginative and real space of belonging for herself. In this process, several identities of her being a Pakistani-British, an Asian-British, a half-Muslim, and a half-English, apart from many others possible, merge in her being quite naturally. As such, she does not appear to be anxious about establishing her identity; it comes out without making a conscious effort.

Moniza Alvi, however, is only one case in point. There are several other women poets like her living in or outside Pakistan, for whom identity is not a nagging cause or a source of crisis, and who do not work deliberately towards creating one or labour hard to acquire a voice.[1] It would appear from a general survey that the second-and third-generation writers[2] living outside Pakistan seem to have completely resolved and finally forgotten the issues of why they have chosen to write in English and acquire a new 'address'. They have been able to answer the questions posed by history, memory, location, and their individual lives. In the case of those at home, it would appear that in spite of the efforts made, they are not marginalized on account of their gender, region, or ideology; they have constructed, claimed, preserved, and celebrated their selves, their identities. An attempt is made here to read some examples of this new literary manifestation in some of the more prominent women poets of Pakistan writing in English and other languages, and to see how they problematize their new and shared history and configure their society and culture.

Pakistan: A Site of Contestations

The Pakistani nation state is a historical phenomenon, a curious combination of disparate elements. English is its modern medium of expression, Urdu its adopted national linguistic identity, while Punjabi, Saraiki, Sindhi, Pashto, and Balochi are its regional languages. All these languages have established themselves as the medium of literary expression in Pakistan. As they have also brought with them their own cultural baggage, they have emerged as the language of power for the creative writers and the people. Written in various linguistic literary registers, these literatures in Pakistan remain at best an expression of the essentialist concerns of the land.

Two more important points must be added here. First, there is a significant literary tradition of Urdu writing in India, which is shared by most of those writing in Urdu, and which helps them develop their own modes of expression. Second, English has been the common colonial heritage of all these writers, and this language has shaped their sensibilities to a very great extent. Since poetry constructs a more indirect narrative, and the poets in question represent a variety of cultural and linguistic backgrounds bearing curiously upon each other, it would be interesting to read them together to identify an underlying principle of coherence and continuity. This should not, however, create an impression that all Pakistani literatures constitute a single whole; in fact, each one of them has an identity of its own, but, taken together, they seem to represent the aspirations of a nation in more general terms. One may, for the sake of illustration, say that several of the contemporary Pakistani poets and writers writing in English and other languages are quite concerned about the experience of migration as such, but it does not hold the same meaning for all of them. Those based in Pakistan, and belonging especially to the first generation of migrants, are concerned with the consequences of migration following the partition of India. This great event changed the course of life and times in the subcontinent, while those writing in English outside Pakistan are more concerned with their new experience of migration to greener pastures. Both create their own diasporas and their own tensions. One could call the former 'primary' and the later 'secondary' migration, which the people of the same nation experienced during a brief period of history. In the same manner, it may also be said that those writing in English outside Pakistan are more concerned with the multicultural motifs, while those at home have their own myths to explore/create in their own sociopolitical set-up. Both, however, seek a condition of harmony with the world around, rather than be at conflict with the custodians of power and politics. Both seek their identities and, for both of them, it is a relative condition. It shifts too frequently at given points of time from a mother to a wife, to a colleague, to a citizen, and so on, in a single day of their lives. In the process of acquiring this identity/self, the poets and writers fill the gaps created by time and place to produce a semblance of continuous existence. And finally, it must also be added that the poets writing in English and those writing in other languages have two distinct literary hinterlands to draw upon. While one group cannot disengage from the English and the European sources, the other group has a vast and rich subcontinental heritage to fall back upon. In spite of this, the poets have frequently drawn upon each other's resources. Further, most of the poets have been extremely mobile, refurbishing themselves to think and write modern. An appropriate case has been made, though not along these lines, for the vitality of Pakistani literature by some Pakistani writers and critics. They refer to the quality of its cross-pollination, its non-self-conscious character,[3] and its emergence to power over a period of the last fifty years,[4] which are surely some of the other important factors concerning Pakistani literature in English to be taken into consideration.

So, poetry written by women poets like Moniza Alvi is only one facet of this rich phenomenon. There are several other important women poets in Pakistan, who deserve serious attention for a variety of reasons. These poets, writing both in English and other languages of Pakistan, have certainly created a space for themselves. They have explored new contexts for their survival by challenging the mechanics of power and patriarchy, and making a hole in the principalities of dominance. A critical study of their preoccupations would reveal that these poets are essentially concerned with the issues of female bondage/confinement, political injustice, their status as women, impatience with their current predicament, desire for independence, and the vast sprawling multicultural world around. A remarkable group of women poets in English has made its way by discovering a certain idiom and an identity for itself. Works by Maki Kureishi, Hina Faisal Imam, Farida Faizullah, Gulzar Bano, Mona Hasan, Perveen Pasha, Shahbano Bilgrami, Soofia Ishaque, and Zeba Hasan Hafeez bear it out quite well. Urdu poets like Zehra Nigah, Kishwar Naheed, Fahmida Riaz, Nasreen Anjum Bhatti, Sara Shagufta, Azra Abbas, Shaista Habib, Ishrat Afreen, Saeeda Gazdar, Neelma Sarwar, Mansoora Ahmad, and Noshi Gilani are remarkable for their heavy and compelling presence, their strong commitment to feminist issues, and for their view of literature as a by-product of their lives and times. Another literary tradition, represented by Sindhi women poets like Razia Khokhar, Pushpa Vallabh, Attiya Dawood, Sultana Waqasi, Tasneem Yaqoob, Munawar Sultana, and Sehar Imdad is of no less consequence, as is the tradition represented by Punjabi women poets like Bushra Ejaz, Sarwat Mohyuddin, and Afzal Tauseef.

No Exit: The Experience of Confinement/Bondage

A remarkable number of women poets based in Pakistan have made some of the most powerful expressions concerning female confinement/

bondage, as the problem concerned them much more directly than others. The consequential 70s, which brought forth the issues of Islamization and curtailment of democracy, had a far-reaching impact on the sociopolitical complexion of the land. The segregation of women from all visible sites (literature, art, painting, media, etc.) by going hoarse for *chadur* and *char diwari*, the promulgation of the Hudood Ordinance, and its implementation by the Federal Shariat Courts[5] led to severe controversy and large-scale opposition. Women organizations,[6] poets, and other creative artists raised voice against this repression. The Urdu poet Zehra Nigah's poem 'Hudood Ordinance', dedicated to the girls suffering imprisonment under the ordinance, may be read in this context:

> In this tiny cell
> I am both fettered and free.
> There is a tiny window
> Almost as high as the ceiling.
> When the sun is about to set
> it passes just above it
> a handful of rays beam through the window
> they form a kind of path
> for me to tread on
> so I can go home. (*PL*: 222)

This sense of imprisonment and the desire to seek a release is further aggravated as the victim girl innocently remembers her baba, ma, *apa*, and bhai, all of whom do their bit for her. The poem takes a grim turn at the end, when the mother picks pebbles, talks to the birds, and thinks the birds understand her message. The message here lies in a Quranic allusion,[7] where birds, with pebbles in their beaks, ravaged the oppressors on the earth, which the mother thinks the birds will do now as well. The poem ends pathetically, underlying a woman's helplessness and in her seeking God's intervention. Another poem 'Chadur and Char-diwari' by Fahmida Riaz may also be referred to in this context. The poem begins on a note of questioning and surprise: 'Sire! What use is this black *chadur* to me?/A thousand mercies, why do you reward me with this?' As it progresses, it denudes the sire who deserves the veil himself and ends on a note of great confidence:

> These four walls, this *chadur* I wish upon the rotting carcass.
> In the open air, her sails flapping, races ahead my ship.
> I am the companion of the New Adam
> Who has earned my self-assured love. (*PL*: 228)

There are many poignant, extremely angry, and devastating poems, centred around the problem of male order/hegemony, social constraints, and political superstructuring that one may read in the Urdu and Sindhi women poets. Some examples may be seen here: 'I sat down naked behind the sun/Both my feet were in one shoe/And both my arms in one bracelet' (Nasreen Anjum Bhatti, 'Banishment', *PL:* 248), 'How merciful and sympathetic are those who kill,/They avoid killing in each other's presence/After all, they observe propriety' (Shaista Habib, 'No Exit', *PL*: 254), 'If my hands are freed/ then I will blacken/the walls of this earth.../ and place this world/on the palm of my hand/and crush it' (Azra Abbas, 'If My Hands Are Freed', *PL*: 259), 'Every daughter of Eve/Who steps into this world/Must be made to wear/Shoes of iron' (Mansoora Ahmad, 'Centuries Back in Time', *PL*: 268), 'Whatever the season/Be it of confinement or oppression,/Of wastelands or forests,/This prisoners breathes' (Noshin Gilani, 'This Prisoner Breathes', *PL*: 274), 'Where can I go/This way or that/ To find freedom?' (Munawara Ahmad [Sindhi], 'In Captivity', *PL*: 283), 'That you love me, there is no doubt/But don't turn that love into a slave ring around me' (Attiya Dawood [Sindhi], 'The Boundaries of Love', *PL*: 288). The extracts quoted here represent a body language, a gesture of disapproval, supported by strong verbal expressions. They underline the poets' need to speak up. They are the internal mechanism of their self-defence, unreserved expressions of their anger, and proclamations of their self-confidence. The spirit of utter rejection enlivens them. Nowhere do we have a sense of fear, despair, or self-pity. They are ruthlessly ironic; they put forth a challenge and make a claim. This is a condition which unites them together, irrespective of linguistic or regional barriers. Languages and regions, insofar as they represent people, invite them to get together and construct an identity, which these examples amply demonstrate.

Buy My Flag: The Fall of Political Imperialism

Another aspect of this anger may be marked in poems with a clear political intent. Enraged at political injustice and efforts made to marginalize them, the women poets register their protest in clear terms. This protest has the elements of irritation, resentment, bitterness, and deep irony in varying degrees. Tired of ruthless subjection, Shahbano Bilgrami ironically represents a stark picture of the fourteenth of August, an important day in Pakistani history. The speaker on this day ironically seeks her personal freedom, as she calls for selling her flag:

> Buy my flag! Buy my flag
> So that I can pull myself out of
> Searing flames of engine heat
> And hellish, gnawing need,
> So I can cool my face,
> Hide from the heavy weight
> Of the immovable sun,
> Retreat into some silent,
> Full-stomached sleep
> In a country of my own. (*AA*: 88)

The green and white star-studded flag of her land, fluttering on that day, is no better for her than the meaningless market wares. It makes no promise, offers no pride, and it seems too insignificant before a real ten-rupee note. The poem has an important subtext of disaffection, and it has a history behind it which presents itself rather murkily even without any verbal expression by the speaker. In another poem, dramatically constructed with voices, questions, and answers, Gulzar Bano brings out the pathos of rape that women have been subjected to in all times and places, in spite of the regulatory social order, legal deterrents, and religious injunction. In her poem entitled 'The Rape of Macharanwali', the place represents all places where such crimes are committed, and the women stand for all women who have suffered this ignominy in all ages. The poem employs stark images of *chadur, char-diwari, adalat, kafan, bichuanwali, and sappanwali* to create a condition of insufferable pain. It begins on an extremely depressing note; yet, a very confident female voice throws a challenge:

> Land of my fathers and their mothers
> Clothed with proud Begs and silk scented Begums
> Broadcasting grand Commissions, Forums, Ministries
> We are the daughters of a naked land
> Bring us the ashes of our garments from Macharanwali. (*AA*: 30)

This part of the poem called 'Death Cry' is followed by 'Consolation', and a 'Second Cry', and subsequently 'Questions' and 'Answers'. The dramatic structure of pain and suffering is brought to an end with a 'Passive Confession', 'Third Cry', and 'Active Response', where the poet offers 'individual collective shame' and expresses faith in 'tomorrow' that may reverse their fate. It is a typically multiple text, reflecting sadly on the personal and the social, the cultural and the political. The poem can also be approached as a stock response to a predicament, irrespective of time and place, even though it particularizes the crime in relation to a given time and a place.

Various other poems may be quoted to show the deep concern of the women poets with their society, and the historical process of the configuration of a nation as a good, bad, or indifferent space. Some examples should illustrate the point: 'In those times when the camera could not freeze tyranny forever/only until those times/should you have written/that history/which describes tyranny as valor' (Kishwar Naheed' 'Censorship', *WSW*: 51), 'This law is a rag/Worthy of the dust/Off the rebels' feet/Dictatorship is a curse/This government of/Ordinances/We shall shred/in a public square' (Fahmida Riaz, 'The Interrogator', *WSW*: 83), 'You snatch from me the status of a human being./I refuse to give birth to you' (Saeeda Gazdar, 'Twelfth of February 1983', *PL*: 246), 'The thesis for the search of affiliations/Is in the last showcase of the museum,/So that future generations may go through it/And prepare notes on history' (Shaista Habib, 'Do Not Question', *PL*: 257), 'A greater punishment than hanging is to bear a borrowed life/the ace of spades does not prolong the game; it finishes it/it finishes all claims' (Nasreen Anjum Bhatti, 'Ace of Spades', *FAR*: 286), and 'We shall search the globe/to find a New homeland./We shall hold the right to look anew' (Hina Faisal Imam, 'The New World Order', *PL*: 302). As these poems reject the existing order, they also dream of establishing a new one. They nurture the hope for a new community of reconcilable beings, which may not be an ideal one, but the inhabitants may share respect amongst themselves. It may be a small island of survival, and not a jungle for perishing.

I Cannot be Sublime: The Status of Women

The status of women is an issue essentially relative in nature, but a major one by any standards. The poets have related to it at a personal level, as also at the social, political, and cultural levels. The poems in this category have the elements of anguish more than of ease, as the poets are quite conscious of their present status and have little hope for amelioration. This comes out quite clearly in Shaista Habib's 'I Cannot be Sublime'

> Lady Caroline Lamb was really brave,
> She thought life was in Byron's shoes
> And in waiting drenched in rain'
> She was well versed in living death
> But she was blamed even then
> For she could not be sublime
> Lady Caro!
> Smoke and chew betels,
> No, no, all intoxicants are alike—
> I am drunk on the love of my being
> And I adore my existence
> In which is dissolved the alcohol of tears.
> Come, let's clink our beings and drink this cup

In the name of all lovers
Who cannot be sublime. (*FAR*: 328–29)

The sense of independence the poem expresses has a streak of pride as also of helplessness. It is a queer feeling for them to be a woman in the given context, marked by uncertainties and fears. Expressions of confident womanhood may be heard in the poets we have been discussing. Kishwar Naheed's self-confessed 'We Sinful Women' is, in fact, a declaration of this womanhood characterized by a rare conviction. Ironically called 'sinful', these women do not sell their lives, bow their heads, or fold their hands; on the contrary, they warn the hands from raising the demolished wall. Her other poems, 'A Palace of Wax', 'Who Am I?', and 'Nightmare' (*WSW*: 37/43/47), have similar notes of faith and courage. The essential question of a woman's identity emerges in different ways in different poets: 'She is a woman impure/imprisoned by her flowing blood/in a cycle of months and years' (Fahmida Riaz, 'She is Woman Impure', *WSW*: 97), 'In my very first breaths it stirred/the bitter poison of defeat as I heard/'Oh, it's a girl!'/A girl!' (Ishrat Aafreen, 'The First Prayer of My Elders', *WSW*: 151), 'My man you are an infant/Fresh from your mother's womb/What do you know what a woman is' (Mona Hasan, 'My Foster God', *AA*: 56), 'Ever since I opened my eyes, I was taught:/'Society is a jungle and the home a shelter/Man is the owner/And woman its tenant/Who pays the rent/By obedience, by fidelity' (Attiya Dawood, 'Autobiography', *PL*: 286). These poems represent a variety of irreconcilable moods, as the women are sometimes impatient with life, and sometimes in love with it, in spite of all the attendant contradictions around. They proclaim independence and express their innermost desires as human beings. They represent themselves as beloveds, mothers, daughters, and citizens. Scared of the inevitability of pain in a woman's fate, Sara Shagufta advises her daughter: 'Whenever anyone causes you sorrow/name that sorrow—daughter' ('For Sheli, My Daughter', *PL*: 264), but Ishrat Aafreen chooses to be too expressive in her defiance when she says in 'The First Prayer of My Elders': 'She belongs to the tribe of Ego/This ruthless girl/And lives way beyond/

The bounds of your territory'. In yet another short poem, she maintains that gesture when she proclaims: 'I grew/Taller than my father/And my mother won' ('Dedication', *WSW*: 143/141). The poems may have notes of protest, rebellion, and negation, but they do not, by any means, create a sense of nihilistic pleasure or negative enjoyment. They are strongly reminiscent of many of the Western feminist and confessional texts. They, however, do not represent those conditions, but they certainly recreate the essentialist concerns of women and women writers as such. They need to disengage themselves from the fetters of conditioned response in their own respects, and acquire a self, a personality, and an individual independence while being a part of the system. They represent a condition of a desired existence, and project themselves as intellectually alive and socially engaged human beings.

A Note for Conclusion

The women poets discussed earlier are easily distinguishable for their iconoclasm and an independent feminist stance in the apprehension of their lives and their conditions. They neither necessarily blow out the traditional norms of a society, nor violate the conventional poetics or flaunt their offbeat stances. They try to achieve a precarious balance with the existing norm, but they do not give up when it betrays them. In writing themselves, they write a new social and literary order. They extend the possibilities of language as they speak in an entirely new idiom, while drawing upon the tradition and making radical improvisations upon them without valorizing themselves. This owes much to their mobility and their ways of intermixing the real with the mythic. Several of these poets have had an eventful career of taking bold stances, speaking without fear, and getting punished. What sustains them, however, is the genuineness of their experience and the honesty of their expression. The women poets of Pakistan are remarkable for the unique difference they make in their apprehension and expression and the new canon they create. It is a rare group of literary artists and social activists, the likes of whom are not to be found anywhere in South Asia.

Endnotes

1. Women poets have been discussed in the subsequent parts of this chapter. One may, however, like to look at the male composition. Among the male poets writing outside Pakistan, mention may be made of Zulfikar Ghose, Adrian A. Husain, Shuja Nawaz, Waqas Ahmad Khwaja, Tariq Latif, and Sheryar Singha. Among those at home, Alamgir Hashmi, M. Athar Tahir, Abbas Husain, Moeen Faruqi, Ghulam Fariduddin Riaz, and Masood Amjad Ali are more mentionable.
2. Consider, for example, this illustrious familial line of descent: Attiya Hussain>Muneeza Shamsie>Kamila Shamsie. While the grand-aunt Attia Hosain (author of *Sunlight on a Broken Column*) chose to migrate to England, Muneeza Shamsie (author of the short story 'Shahrazad's Golden Leopard') stayed mostly in Pakistan, and her daughter Kamila Shamsie (author of *In the City by the Sea, Salt and Saffron, and Kartography*), born in Pakistan, is based in US. Like the locations, their attitudes and sensibilities are remarkably different. There are many other third-generation writers who have found a home away from the ancestral home and have become a part of the new socio-cultural-literary order. It must also be added that opinions regarding their degree of adaptability vary, as there is a belief that even the second- and third-generation writers have not been able to identify themselves with their locations fully. This is, however, a debatable point.
3. See Huma Ibrahim, 'Transnational Migrations and the Debate of English Writing in/of Pakistan,' *Ariel* 29(1) (1998): 33-48.
4. See 'Introduction' to Shamsie Muniza, ed., *A Dragonfly in the Sun: An Anthology of Pakistani Writing in English* (Karachi: OUP, 1988).
5. Hudood Ordinances were promulgated on 10 February 1979. They were directed towards imposing maximum punishment (as per the *hadh* or limitation) on the acts of offence like theft, drunkenness, bearing false witness, and adultery/rape. Federal Shariat Courts (FSCs) were established to see their implementation. Since it gave an open license, there was fear of its being used indiscriminately, which several cases proved true at later dates. The case of a couple, Fahmida and Allah Bux, is one in point that shook the women organizations around and brought them together.
6. Shirkat Gah (site of participation), an important pressure group, brought several organizations together. Women's Action Forum (WAF) was established in Karachi, then in Lahore, Islamabad, Rawalpindi, and Peshawar. All Pakistan Women's Association (APWA), the generic organization, endorsed the actions of WAF.
7. See the Holy Qur'an, Surah CV (Fil) 1–5. Introduction and summary to the Surah reads as follows:

> This early Meccan Sura refers to an event that happened in the year of the birth of our holy Prophet, say about 570 A.D. Yemen was then under the rule of the Abyssinians (Christians) who had driven out the Jewish Himyar rulers. Abraha Ashram was the Abyssinian Governor or Viceroy. Intoxicated with power and fired by religious fanaticism, he led a big expedition against Mecca, intending to destroy the Kaba. He had an elephant or elephants in his train. But his sacrilegious intentions were defeated by a miracle. No defence was offered by the custodians of the kaba as the army was too strong for them, but it was believed that a shower of stones, thrown by flocks of birds, destroyed the invading army almost to a man. The stones produced sores and pustules on the skin, which spread like a pestilence.

Abdullah Yusuf Ali, trans. and ed., *The Meaning of the Glorious Qur'an*, Vol. 2 (Cairo and Beirut: Dar Al-Kitab Al-Masri and Dar Al-Kitab Allubnani, n.d.), p. 1791.

References

Ahmad, Rukhsana, trans. and ed. 1994. *We Sinful Women*. New Delhi: Rupa and Co. (referred to as *WSW*).

An Anthology. Karachi: OUP, 1997 (referred to as *AA*).

Pakistani Literature 3 (2) (1994). Special issue on Women's Writing (referred to as *PL*).

Rahman, Anisur, trans. and ed. 1995. *Fire and the Rose: An Anthology of Modern Urdu Poetry*. New Delhi: Rupa and Co. (referred to as *FAR*).

Shamsie Muniza, ed. 1988. *A Dragonfly in the Sun: An Anthology of Pakistani Writing in English*. Karachi: OUP (referred to as *ADITS*).

Counterposing Exotica and Stereotype: Sarojini Naidu's Text and Context

The Question of Identity

In order to find a context for the reading of Sarojini Naidu (1879–1949), let me first raise the question of her identity. I should like to begin by making a reference to *Mehir Muneer: A Poem in Three Cantos* (1893), generally mentioned in passing and neglected as 'juvenilia.' The poem embodies many meanings: it shows how Naidu set out acquiring her individual identity by deliberately concealing it and assigning the authorship of this poem first to 'a Brahmin girl,' and subsequently to 'a Hindu lady.'[1] The poem represents the love story of Mehir Muneer and Badar Muneer in adolescent terms. Even though the poem has lots of emphasis on rhyme and makes appeal to emotions, there is an effort to reconstruct a story, portray characters, create an atmosphere, and represent all these in an interesting framework of a romance.

Although Naidu herself identified Sir Walter Scott's 'Lady of the Lake' as a model for this poem, one of Sir Edwin Arnold's stories has also been considered to be the source of this romance.[2] It is important for us to note here that more than any other contrived source, Naidu's poem is quite clearly based on a homespun romance by Meer Ghulam Hasan 'Hasan' Dehlavi's Urdu *mathnawi* called *Sehr-ul-Bayan* (The Magic of Narration), published at Fort William College in 1805.[3] This fact has, however, remained unnoticed so far. Naidu criticism does not mention anywhere that she drew closely upon Meer Hasan, followed the same storyline, invoked the same atmosphere, and appropriated the same characters, except for a few minor changes she made to suit her narration. First, she changed the name of the lover from Benazir (The Peerless One) to Mehir Muneer (The Radiant Sun), but she chose to retain the name of the beloved as Badar Muneer (The Radiant Moon). Appropriately enough, the sun represents the male love in Naidu while the moon represents the female love. Second, the story in Naidu's poem is based in Persia, although in Meer Hasan, the story does not refer to any particular city or king. Third, while Naidu preferred to condense her story in three cantos of 1,022 lines, dispensing with several details from the beginning, middle, and end of the story, Meer Hasan's narrative is spread over thirty-four cantos of 2,200 couplets. Apart from the fact that Naidu adopted everything else from Meer Hasan's narrative, there is a great similarity in what the two poems brought to their poets. While Meer Hasan gained favours from the court of Nawab Asaf-ud-Daula of Lucknow by writing his *Sehr-ul-Bayan*, Naidu gained her passage to England from His Exalted Highness, the Nizam of Hyderabad, by writing her *Mehir Muneer*, which changed the course of her literary life drastically and helped her acquire a new identity in the years that followed. Read either in isolation or along with Meer Hasan's romance, Naidu's romance establishes quite clearly her ability to critically draw upon a source and construct her own narrative with a great sense of discrimination in yet another language.

Naidu's strategy in writing this poem raises certain important questions, which I would like to relate to the basic question of her identity being discussed here. Why did Naidu conceal the source of her poem? Why did she conceal the authorship and assign it to 'a Brahmin girl'? Why did she change the name of the lover from Benazir to Mehir Muneer? And why did she improvise upon the correct form of 'Mehr-e-Muneer' and 'Badr-e-Muneer' to the incorrect ones 'Mehir Muneer' and 'Badar Muneer'? Naidu knew her Urdu well enough to have followed the right constructions, but did not choose to do. She was a proud beneficiary of the old Hyderabadi culture that had its root in the Indo-Persian tradition. She knew several contemporary Urdu poets and was praised by them for her literary ingenuity, and had ample reasons and opportunities to draw upon the Urdu and Persian sources to enrich her poetic corpus.

Several answers can be given to the questions raised. Although Naidu did not live a cloistered life, she was made to observe discipline and lead a well-regulated and supervised kind of a life. She loved nursing dreams and writing poems in English, in spite of the fact that she had resisted learning this language initially. She seems to have negated this language in a strange psychological fit of dispossessing the other, before getting to accept it as her own. She realized in time the impending need of finding a medium of expression. Thus, she broke free of this psychological state and chose a better medium, which was English in her case rather than Telugu, Urdu, or Bangla, in which she neither chose to test her proficiency for creative purposes nor wished to do so. Considering her Muslim-Hyderabadi connection and her proximity with the Urdu literary figures and sources, it is only proper to suggest that she appropriated the fascinating story narrated by Meer Hasan in her own way to write a poem in her chosen language. It must have been a novel effort on her part to represent an Eastern story in a Western language, and to see for herself as to how a native experience and an alien language could bear upon one another. It is, thus, quite unlikely that she shunned her native languages and chose to write in English only to gain proximity with her Western sources and mentors, and that she wrote it mainly to wrest a passage to England from the nizam for whom she wrote an 'ode' to be presented at the Ramzan durbar. She neither wrote it to enthrall a Western audience, nor to seek her pastures elsewhere. She was obviously not aware of the issues involved in Orientalist constructions, which later emerged as the major issues in literary theory and criticism. In fact, writing in English at that point of time without a tradition, a readership, and sources of dissemination was in itself an act of unusual courage and conviction in her creative life, just as it was to change from a Chattopadhyay to a Naidu in her personal life. She chose to address her fellow Indians and the empire in the English language, for this was the language that had to matter in the ultimate analysis. Given this context, it seems a little far-fetched and unlikely that she pretended to assume a secular posture in rolling the two stock identities of a 'Brahmin' and a 'girl' into one, and lending it the authorship of an obviously Indo-Persian text. No less significant is the fact that even, in the context of her times, she did not allow her gender to stop her from fulfilling her aspirations. Passing through a phase of learning and unlearning, she ultimately chose to be explicit about her future references to the broader life of her land and the sources of its essential vitality. Instead of rejecting the poem as pure juvenilia and its author as a false entity, I would suggest that we may better take them more seriously as Naidu's ways of testing her poetic talent and acquiring an unusually bold identity, which she developed much more firmly in the subsequent years.

In spite of the fact that Naidu's sensibility was forming steadily on surer grounds, it is quite a difficult proposition to attribute a certain identity to her. Problems in Naidu criticism have arisen largely because we have tried to do this in a definitive manner. Her admirers in London had called her 'the little Indian princess' in the 1890s.[4] Gandhi called her 'Mirabai', 'singer', 'Bulbul', and 'Bulbul-e-Hind'.[5] Her eventful life passed through a series of climaxes. Having started her poetic career at the early age of eleven in 1890, by writing a poem instead of doing an algebra sum, she exposed herself to an extremely hectic life marked by acts of remarkable courage and rare conviction. Love outside her caste, a wisely planned trip to England for the double purpose of receiving education and also getting rid of the love bug, meeting with her much-talked-about masters Edmund Gosse and Arthur Symons, a marriage of choice solemnized under Indian Special Marriage Act of 1872, despite stiff resistance, and the building up of a rather swift reputation as the poetess of India broadly account for the making of Naidu's identity in the early years of her life. She was then seeking and finding a definite direction among a maze of influences and medley of alluring images. Subsequently, her entering into a life of active politics, discovering the spirit of religions, trying hard to bring about Hindu–Muslim unity, joining issues with the powers that granted the rights of franchise to women and education, forceful public speaking in and outside the country, and accepting the high public office of the governor of a state gave her a variety of identities in the later years.[6] Soon, she acquired the status of a cult figure in the minds of all Indians and those outside the country who had watched her all along become a political and literary icon. The magic of her multiple identities, quite frequently jostling against one another, has been carried down from generation to generation through the acts of reiteration. It is not baffling, however, to find a binding thread running through her extremely consequential career of promises, commitments, and remarkable accomplishments. It is an example of the life of spirit entering into the life of matter and vice versa, as well as realizing the significance and relationship between the means and the ends. Her poetry drew heavily upon all these sources to create what I would like to call her composite identity. All her ideas and issues, characters and situations, and modes and manners can be eminently read in the context of her immediate and remote references.

Let me end this argument by making reference to a later-day speech of Naidu. Fifty-five years after the publication of the so-called juvenilia *Mehir Muneer*, Naidu addressed the second All-India Writers' Conference at Varanasi in 1948. Having passed through all seasons of life and art, and having become a cult figure, she tried to make an aesthetically sound case for writers' choice of language ('of the human heart and spirit'), their mastery over it, and for keeping truth alive in literature. She did not speak, as she could not have spoken, given her literary and historical context, of the untruths, falsities, and lies of the land. We cannot, and should not, therefore, blame her for not apprehending the poetics of the future years, and for speaking in a characteristically romantic mode of her own choice and preference.

Naidu shared her concern for 'language' and 'truth' in a congregation of writers more than three decades after she had stopped writing poetry, and hardly a year before she died. By then, she had already made her contribution to the nationalist movement for freedom and had emerged as a politico-literary icon. In her plea to the writers, we may also clearly perceive a nationalist agenda apart from a literary one. Remarkably enough, in giving the writers a choice, she also acknowledged the virile linguistic variety of the land and the great potential it had to bear the truth. Truth, for her, was a huge national responsibility to define and establish. It meant certain kinds of truth that related to life in general and the contemporary history of India in particular. This truth had room for complexities, yet it did not get lost in the rigmarole of abstract thoughts and abstruse contestations.

In order to explore this truth, Naidu had to develop that essential human vitality which could sustain her through life. She acquired this vitality by grooming herself and developing an intriguing identity of her own kind. In the last line of the poem 'A Challenge to Fate' (134–35), she spelt out her gradual acquisition of power from a 'frail' creature to a 'serene' being, and ultimately to an 'indomitable' entity. It gave her the courage to challenge a 'foolish fate' and ask questions:

> Say, can you rob my memory's great dominion...? (134)
> Say, shall my scatheless spirit cease to hear...? (134)
> Say, shall my heart lack its familiar language...? (135)
> Shall my impassioned heart forget to sing...? (135)
> How will you daunt my free, far-journeying fancy...? (135)
> How will you tether my triumphant mind...? (135)

Naidu derived this strength and identity from nature and the human spirit, which imparted her literary and sociopolitical concerns an acute relevance in and beyond her time. While thinking of 'memory', 'spirit', 'language', 'hear, 'fancy', and 'mind', she was rethinking the basic philosophical questions that have always given human beings a conviction to live by and make life meaningful. Her indomitable self sought its expression by posing and answering these questions in the context of her times, and in a language that could sustain her literary aspirations. Quite justifiably, Naidu's literary career may be appreciated as a testament of faith in poetry and politics, in the impassioned word and courageous action.

Her life is a revolving dream
'The Pardah Nashin', The Sceptred Flute

Ideas and Issues

The public and the private domains meet so closely in Naidu that they ultimately turn inseparable. In fact, while making an effort at separating them, we run the risk of getting only a partial view of that 'revolving dream' (53) which she considered her life to be. Yet, for the sake of a comprehensive understanding, I would like to propose that her public domain had all space for issues like franchise for women, Hindu–Muslim unity, non-cooperation, civil disobedience, and Khilafat movement, and a plethora of other concerns that marked the sociopolitical map of India. Her participation in these matters was spread over a long period of time from 1901 to independence of

India, and even during the short period she lived after that. The other domain that I would, for convenience, call her private domain broadly included her vision of a culturally and politically united India, unity of religious faiths, mysticism, historical conditions, personages, and nature. To put the thesis broadly, while she was preoccupied with the philosophical questions of love, life, and death, and people, predicament, and landscape, she also had her equally important sociopolitical concerns weighing side by side.

A close chronological study of her engagements would suggest that she had joined public life even before the publication of *The Golden Threshold* in 1905. Her participation in public domain got much more fervid in the subsequent years, which also saw the publication of *The Bird of Time* in 1912 and *The Broken Wing: Songs of Love, Death and the Spring* in 1917. *The Sceptred Flute*, which had no new poems and was only a collection of poems from her previous three anthologies, appeared in 1928. *The Feather of Dawn*, her last collection, which had poems written during July–August 1927, appeared posthumously in 1961. If we look at the publication dates of her first three collections, it would appear that she pursued the vocation of writing poetry till 1917, and resumed it only in 1927 for a short spell after a gap of ten years. This means that she kept herself involved in the public domain for seventeen years, while also pursuing her purely personal interest of writing poetry. Her disappearance from the literary scene took place only after 1917, which means that she did not write during the last three decades of her life except for a brief spell in 1927. The question as to why she stopped writing poetry crops up in the minds of her readers rather naturally, and they wonder if she ceased to exist as a poet or if the public domain claimed the personal domain which used to afford the literary material. Poetry represented only one aspect of her personality, and that she found ways to extend the frontiers of her own self through her other writings and speeches which are as poetic as her poetic texts. More importantly, as suggested earlier, the two domains are so well intertwined in Naidu that any effort at separating them would lead us to making mere conjectures rather than arriving at convincing conclusions. In other words, Naidu internalized the public domain with the same ease as she externalized the private domain. It is in this respect that we do not have another author to compare or contrast her with for the kind of poetry she wrote and the life she lived. Moreover, we read an author by what she delivers rather than by what she could have if she had continued further.

Historical and other material in terms of documents, addresses, essays, and letters that have come down to us from Naidu suggest it only too well that her participation in the public domain was both gusty and effective. All of them bear her sociopolitical concerns and may be read as literary texts rather than pure verbal exercises in opinion-making. They show how words could be used as similes and metaphors, and how literary devices could be invoked to create impact. Her letters to Gandhi, her addresses like 'Women's Education and the Unity of India', 'Ideals of Islam', 'Indian Women and the Franchise', and writings like 'The Soul of India' (1917), 'Mah Rukh Begum: A Romance of Fate' (1897), and 'Nilambuja: The Fantasy of a Poet's Mood' (1993) are some of the examples that may be approached from a fresh perspective. While *Nilumbuja* is an exercise in imaginative fulfillment, it is like a poem in prose that may be read as another manifestation of her creativity. Similarly, the story of Mah Rukh Begum may also be taken as a prose rendition of what Naidu had to say about women, their dreams and desires, and fears and aspirations in several of her poems and addresses concerning their education, the observance of purdah, their rights and responsibilities, and their status as a whole. 'The Soul of India' and 'Ideals of Islam' are yet other expressions of her faith in the spirit of the land and its essential vitality that has sustained her through the ages. A big number of her poems may be rightly considered to be her imaginative reconstructions of the concrete experiences she had in actual life. Her folk songs, as also her songs of love, death, life, springtime, and spiritual urges, appropriately reinforce her ideals for which she sought space in her prose writings and addresses. All these creative expressions broadly represent her philosophical mind. Naidu wished to underscore the spirit of the land that might fill life with meaning in the larger context of a given society. She looked forward to construct a future on the foundations of a past. In doing this, she defined the value of a democratic tradition, human toleration, and reposed faith in the unity of beings. Naidu's creativity in her prose and poetry was directed towards the construction of a social space characterized essentially by sound humane, spiritual, and political values. These values, she considered, might make both the present and the future meaningful.

Naidu practised her proclamations, on the other hand, through protests, marches, delegations, campaigns, and going to jails for the issues at stake. Participations in war efforts with Gandhi after the outbreak of the First World War (1914), campaigning for the abolition of indentured labour (1917), leading a women's delegation to Lord Chelmsford and E.S. Montagu for educational, social, and political rights for women (1917), leading the Salt Satyagraha at the Dharasana Salt Works after the arrest of Gandhi (1930), going to jail (1932 and 1942), and joining the individual satyagraha movement against the enforced participation of India in the Second World War (1939) are some of the examples that may be quoted in this regard. They establish only too clearly that being a poet for her meant to be socially and politically committed. It also implied a liberal broadening of a self that negated all kinds of cloistering and efforts at fixing an identity in a given frame. Naidu's status as a poet may be defined in its entirety only in consideration of her composite personality that had space for a variety of expressions through words and action.

All these ideas and issues, and all these efforts to express them through various modes, as mentioned previously, have an intrinsic unity in them. On the surface, they might appear to be the manifestations of different urges and desires of an individual, but they are all united at the very core. Naidu's art is not limited to her poetry and prose writings alone, or even to her addresses and actions; it is located beyond the given and traditional confines of expression. She embraced and expressed the spirit of a larger world and proposed a larger definition of the relationship between art and life.

I ask thee no reward

'Devotion,' The Feather of the Dawn

Critical Reception: East and West

A modern researcher initiating his/her work on Naidu today would not take long to develop a preliminary bibliography that would have at least a dozen and half books and monographs on her. One would find it difficult to enlist all the articles and reviews in books and journals, for they are just too many and quite a few of them are not even traceable today. Assessing one's bibliography, he/she would be dismayed to find that Naidu criticism has generally been ambivalent towards her during all these fifty years or so. Before wondering over the causes for such ambivalence for long, one would soon discover that Naidu is one of those very few Indian English poets who has attracted greater attention than others in spite of all the ambivalences shown towards her. This would give the researcher good reason to move forward and find if there are possibilities of reading her afresh, and with profit.

The critics who have found blemishes in her poetry have also been quick to notice merits in her.[7] There are only a few who have accepted or rejected her fully. Fewer still are those who have looked at the limitations of Naidu and conditioned their responses accordingly. Looking at her blemishes, they have said time and again that Naidu's poetry does not have a sound intellectual basis; it is vague, sloppy, flamboyant, and romantic. They have argued that it is inflated in style and sugary in sentiment. They have further said that her poetry is made of adolescent material and that it does not show any signs of progression. They have added that Naidu had no traces of modernism in her, and she revelled only in metrical variation, embellished images, and lilting cadences. She has been charged of subscribing to feudal aesthetics, following a repetitive and formulaic structure, and choosing the conventional, ephemeral, and personal material for writing her poetry. More recently, with the coming in of the fashionable postcolonial readings of texts and authors, she has been criticized for appropriating the Orientalist project, for constructing an exotic East, which the West fancied, and for writing about an India that was too artificial. Further, she has been disapproved for constructing the essentialist kinds of feminity and masculinity. It has been added that although she was a rebel in her personal life, she did not have a feminist's courage, nor did she have any original thoughts on the issue. The critics have also declared her patriotism to be irrelevant for contemporary India, and asserted that her poetry does not have the strength and experience to hold the interest of the modern reader.

Most of these critics have also marked the qualities that sustain her poetry and make her a subject for our study today. They have taken note of the British romantic influences on her poetry, and considered her to be one who was singularly successful in visualizing a poem as a lyric. They have praised her very individual tone and tenor, saying that it was only appropriate for the kind of material she chose to write on. They have noted that Naidu has recreated the opulence and charm of the traditional Indian life and brought prestige to Indian writing before Tagore. She has been praised for recognizing the native urges and for representing them truthfully. The critics have posited that she was an idealist like the aesthetes, and she could sense beauty, colour, fragrance, song, and movement. As such, she has been able to write at least a few poems that have stood the test of time and retained their value.

We may put the Western response in a different category altogether, as it has developed along a different line of argument and constructs a Naidu that is different from our construction. The publication of *The Golden Threshold* brought her to the notice of the West more prominently. Early reviews of the book show that the critics were more patronizing than critical and were delighted to note that an Indian, more especially a woman, could write poetry with such flourish. They mentioned that Naidu had the ability to find space for thoughts and emotions in a lyrical mode, which was not an easy mode to practice with success. They also noted that her poems were songs essentially, and that these songs had something very fundamental about them that obliterated the distinction between the East and the West. *The Bird of Time* also received equally positive reviews and was praised for profusion of beauty and, more importantly, for enriching the language of the West, and for letting the West know the spirit of the East.[8]

In more recent years, response from the West has created an entirely different perspective. The new postcolonial critics have taken a serious note of the advice Naidu received from Edmund Gosse, as some of our own critics have done, and have said that his intervention was of a coercive nature; it made Naidu work docilely to represent the East as desired by the Western masters, who were Gosse and Symons in her case. In spite of that, she failed in yet another way and created a different kind of pastiche. This pastiche, it has been asserted, was once again a Western invention. It resulted in double colonial mimicry of a poetics that had its roots in the

West. It has taken note of the East–West dichotomy and has made use of the tools of colonial discourse theory. There has been a reiteration in the way the elements of biography, body and writing, have been appropriated to suit the Orientalist project and in creating the image of a perfumed, feminized, and lyrical orient.[9] In yet another response, this reading is taken further and claiming that attempts at objectification, infantilization, and exoticization have always been made in the criticism of Naidu, and it has been carried down to the reading of even Arundhati Roy. References to an essentialized past, ethnic and gender stereotypes, and creation of an odd linguistic register have also been made to give emphasis to the point.[10]

An assessment of the Naidu criticism produced during the early phase would establish that there was a definite effort to construct an exotic Naidu, who was a lyricist and a nationalist essentially. Many of the later critics reiterated such readings and added yet another aspect to it by referring to her blemishes in more prominent terms. As such, Naidu emerged as one who was neither fully rejected nor fully accepted. By reiterating the earlier notions regarding her and by taking note of her blemishes, she was being stereotyped in clear terms and was, thus, subjected to double jeopardy. The postcolonial critics have added yet another dimension to Naidu criticism by raising the important questions of appropriation and representation in order to read her along a new line, extended by postcolonial theory.

I would tend to propose further that there would appear a clear line of distinction if one cared to read these critical responses alongside the Western responses to Naidu. While the broader Indian response is conditioned by nationalist aspirations and discovers her literary merits more in terms of its own literary parameters, the Western response is defined along political terms and Western aesthetic principles. All the readings, though deeply steeped in the critical and sociopolitical climate of the times, reflect their own qualities and limitations. While many of the earlier critics in both the Eastern and Western locations have been given more to exoticizing and stereotyping her than reading her along tough critical/theoretical lines, the newer critics have tried to raise questions and create contexts for reading Naidu. The new critical climate gives us hope and helps us to read Naidu afresh.

The new hath come and now the old retires
'Past and Future,' The Sceptred Flute

Contexts of Reading

Sarojini Naidu's presence in the hall of fame has an air of dubious distinction about it. She has been there for historical rather than literary reasons. As a patriot, a political activist, an enterprising woman, and a poet who wrote in the language of the empire, she could not have been kept waiting in the foyer for long without taking cognizance. Also, she belonged to the first generation of our literary tradition builders like Henry Derozio, the Dutt family, Sri Aurobindo, and Tagore, and had a stake as such. In spite of all these, she remained a peripheral figure, as the ideological, modernist, and urban perspectives brought to bear upon her work did not assign her the status of a major poet. She remained shining and dimming in a conflictual light, between day and night, for long. In a manner, she has been an exiled author, living in the double city, partially accepted and unaccepted by both. Naidu criticism today is obliged to address the questions of her identity and belonging. These questions relate to her language and location, which I should like to suggest, were the two prime concerns of Naidu.

Naidu's linguistic felicity in English and her ability to use it both in prose and poetry with great resourcefulness point towards one important factor: she wished to discover a common language for her expression in writing and speech, a language that had no fixed address and could make sense to a greater number of modern readers and audiences. Language for her was not a mere medium of expressing an idea; it was also sound, rhythm, mood, and condition. In saying that Naidu was too mellifluous, the Eurocentric critics have missed to mark that she was only expressing the genius of the land that could have been expressed in this very kind of language. She was also, in turn, subscribing to the contemporary poetics a point that has been much too insisted upon, both as a sign of her literary resourcefulness and her inability to look ahead of the emerging modernist poetics proposed by Yeats and Eliot. She made her choice of language on proper consideration. This was quite clearly not an easy choice, given the historical context. The decision to be an

Indian writer in the English language was thus a major decision she made for herself and for her readers with whom this language had to stay in future.

Through this chosen language, Naidu also wished to seek her location. This location had a wider meaning for her. It related to her presence in a particular time and space, an emotional and ideational make-up, and a historical and cultural context. It related to her basic identity as a citizen and as a writer. She wished to define her status in time and place and make it relevant. She wished to underline the basic tension that characterized her time and her location in that. This location had several faces: political, cultural, economic, linguistic, and philosophical. It also had its own pulls. These pulls helped her define an identity for herself that was developing along the indigenous and the British poetics.

As Naidu worked towards the birth of the Indian republic from its renaissance, she also worked towards defining her literary identity which was neither unitary nor perfunctory. She evolved a set of sociocultural markers in her poetry, worked towards identifying her historical signs, and sought her readership on this strength. She was a cultural historian who wished to obliterate the distinction between the literary and the non-literary. For the purpose of knowing Naidu better and giving her a place in the literary canon, we need to set a new discourse with a clear shift of focus. We need to contextualize her and to read her in her given location. She needs to be disengaged from all conditioned response that insists on certain ideological and aesthetic principles; she needs to be read more broadly in terms of history, culture, language, and location.

Endnotes

1. See commentary on Mehir Muneer by Makarand Paranjape, *Sarojini Naidu: Selected Poetry and Prose* (New Delhi: Indus, 1993), p. 210.

   I found a printed copy of this poem in the Padmaja Naidu papers, Nehru Memorial Library. The title page reads: '*Mehir Muneer: A Poem in Three Cantos by a Brahmin Girl*. Madras: Printed by Srinivasa, Varadachari and Co., 1893.' There are corrections made throughout the book in a handwriting that resembles Sarojini's, including the title page, where 'A Brahmin Girl' has been scored and 'A Hindu Lady' written in its place. A revised edition, though, was never brought out.

2. See Izzat Yar Khan, *Sarojini Naidu: The Poet* (New Delhi: S. Chand and Co., 1983), p. 6.
3. Meer Ghulam 'Hasan' Dehlavi is popularly known as Meer Hasan. He composed this romance in 1779. The Fort William edition of the poem does not have a title page. In the inner cover at the back of the book, the title and other details are given in English as follows: SIHR – OOL – BUYAN / OR / MUSNUWEE / OF / MEER HUSUN/ BEING A HISTORY OF THE PRINCE / BE NUZEER / IN HINDOOSTANEE VERSE / PUBLISHED UNDER THE PATRONAGE / OF / THE COLLEGE OF FORT WILLIAM / IN BEGAL / CALCUTTA / PRINTED AT THE HINDOOSTANEE PRESS / 1805 (slashes indicate line breaks).
4. Naidu left for England in April 1895. She stayed as a ward of Miss Manning and received education at King's College, University of London, and Girton College, Cambridge University. There she met Arthur Symons, Edmund Gosse, and members of the Rhymer's Club. She also met Yeats and other literary figures in London and was adored by all.
5. See letters of Gandhi to Naidu. Gandhi kept her close to his heart, and she, in turn, assisted him in a number of activities. Her love and reverence for this leader can be seen in the moving homage she paid to him after his assassination in her letter 'My Father, Do Not Rest'.
6. For detailed account of her life, commitments, and services, see especially G.A. Natesan, *Mrs. Sarojini Naidu: A Sketch of Her Life and an Appreciation of Her Works* (Madras: Nateson and Co., 1914); K.A. Abbas, *Sarojini Naidu* (Bombay: Bharatiya Vidya Bhavan, 1980); *Sarojini Naidu: Some Facets of Her Personality* (New Delhi: National Archives, n.d.); Padmini Sengupta, *Sarojini Naidu: A Biography* (Bombay: Asia Publishing House, 1966); Tara Ali Baig, *Sarojini Naidu* (New Delhi: Publications Division, 1975); Vishwanath S. Naravane, *Sarojini Naidu: An Introduction to Her life, Work and Poetry* (New Delhi: Orient Longman Ltd., 1980).
7. A survey of the material available on Naidu, both in terms of books and articles, would illustrate the point well. Reference may be made to books like P.E. Dustoor, *Sarojini Naidu* (Mysore: Rao and Raghavan, 1961); Rameshwar Gupta, *Sarojini, The Poetess* (Delhi: Doaba House, 1975); A.N. Dwivedi, *Sarojini Naidu and Her Poetry* (Allahabad: Kitab Mahal, 1981); Izzat Yar Khan, *Sarojini Naidu: The Poet* (New Delhi: S. Chand and Co. Ltd., 1983); and G. Nageswara Rao, *Hidden Eternity: A Study of the Poetry of Sarojini Naidu* (Tirupati: S.V. University, 1986). Some readings of Naidu in articles and histories of literature that enumerate both her blemishes and merits include K.R. Srinivasa Iyengar, *Indian Writing in English* (New Delhi: Sterling Publishers Pvt. Ltd., first ed. 1962, reprinted 1985), pp. 207–25; C.D. Narasimhaiah, *The Swan and the Eagle* (Simla: Indian Institute of Advanced Study, 1969), pp. 19–23; M.K. Naik, *A History of Indian English Literature* (New Delhi: Sahitya Akademi, 1982), pp. 66–9; and Ranjana

Sidhanta Ash, 'Two Early-Twentieth-Century Women Writers: Cornelia Sorabji and Sarojini Naidu' in *An Illustrated History of Indian Literature in English*, ed. Arvind Krishna Mehrotra (New Delhi: Permanent Black, 2003), pp. 130–34. Narasimhaiah has been particularly ruthless and has not hesitated from making value judgment. After speaking of her 'inferior status as a poet', he continued:

> It is most unlikely she could have written better in Bengali or Telugu or Urdu....For she simply did not have the equipment....It was unfortunate that this young woman got mixed up with political agitators (good for them but it spelt ruin for her) and the patriotic public being lulled by her melody and jewel-tinted words conferred on her the title of 'the nightingale of India' [Narasimhaiah, *The Swan and the Eagle*, p. 20].

'Neither the Victorians nor the Georgians, whose contemporary she was, had in them the power to give her a lead; they had made a mess of their own poetry' [Ibid.].

Better informed readings may be seen in P.V. Rajyalakshmi, *The Lyric Spring: The Poetic Achievement of Sarojini Naidu* (New Delhi: Abhinav Publications, 1977); Makarand Paranjape, 'Introduction', *Sarojini Naidu: Selected Poetry and Prose* (New Delhi: Indus, 1993), pp. 1–20; G.J.V. Prasad, *Continuities in Indian English Poetry* (New Delhi: Pencraft International: 1999), pp. 61–5; and K. Satchidanandan, 'Historicizing Sarojini Naidu', in *Authors, Texts, Issues: Essays on Indian Literature* (Delhi: Pencraft International, 2003), pp. 56–62. For a survey of critical opinion, also see Rajyalakshmi, *The Lyric Spring*, pp. 202–207.

8. See Iyengar, who quotes some of the British responses regarding *The Golden Threshold*: 'This little volume should silence for ever the scoffer who declares that women cannot write poetry' (*Review of Reviews*); 'Her poetry seems to sing itself as if her swift thoughts and strong emotions sprang into lyrics themselves' (*The Times*); 'The pictures are of the East it is true: but there is something fundamentally human that seems to prove that the best song knows nothing of East or West' (*Glasgow Herald*). [Iyengar, *Indian Writing in English*, pp. 214–15.]

Also see Melissa Purdue, 'From Sarojini Naidu's "Curved and Eloquent Little Mouth" to Arundhati Roy's "Mass of Untamed Curls and Smouldering Dark Eyes": Stereotypical Depictions of Female Indian Authors in Reviews of their Work', *Atenea* XXIII (2) (2003): 87–103. She refers to the reviews of *The Golden Threshold, The Bird of Time,* and *The Sceptred Flute* that appeared in *The Academy, The Times,* and *Poetry*, and also to brief studies of Naidu by Edith M. Thomas in *The Critic* and Milton Bronner in *Poet Lore*. All these reviewers and critics extol Naidu for writing a resplendently different kind of poetry. Purdue reads them in a postcolonial theoretical context and highlights how these critics exoticize Naidu as a 'strange gifted daughter of a wonderful race', who comes from 'the mysterious Orient' and 'the land of cobras and those who master them', etc.

9. See Elleke Boehmer, 'East is East and South is South: The Cases of Sarojini Naidu and Arundhati Roy,' *Women: A Cultural Review* 11 (2) (2000): 61–70. Boehmer writes: 'The bizarre and disturbing forces of Naidu's ventriloquism is a fascinating instance of the double-voiced and indeed doubled colonial mimicry of an European aesthetic: it is amply demonstrated, for example, in the decorative and fatalistic effects threaded through the Bird of Time collection.' (63) Further,

> In the criticism we see locked together traditional characterization of the eternal feminine and the eternal orient—an equally traditional interconnection which produces a gendered notion of orientalist typicality that has shifted, as it were, from racial character to text. To overstate the matter in order to make my point: the writing that is deemed most interesting and typical seems to be a writing that is perfumed, decorated, sinuous, sensuous, plural, unruly—most intensely and appropriately so when produced by a woman. Over determined in all its strangeness, abstracted from its local context, stereotyped and restereotyped, the exotic attraction of the once-colonized appears therefore to have been imported into postcolonial criticism, and in the process, to have been commodified and made safe for a western readership. (67)

10. See Purdue, 'From Sarojini Naidu's "Curved and Eloquent Little Mouth" to Arundhati Roy's "Mass of Untamed Curls and Smouldering Dark Eyes": Stereotypical Depictions of Female Indian Authors in Reviews of their Work.' She writes: 'The majority of contemporaneous book reviews on Naidu's writing, whether by male or female, British or American reviewers, positions Naidu as an exotic other.' (89–90)

    'In addition to positioning the colonized writer as exotic, the discourse of infantilization is also prevalent amongst colonizers.' (91)

    'These reviewers do not acknowledge the possibility that Naidu, and other Indian authors writing in English, make the language their own.' (93)

References

Naidu, Sarojini. 1893. *Mehir Muneer: A Poem in Three Cantos by a Brahmin Girl.* Madras: Srinivasa, Varadachari and Co.

Naidu, Sarojini. 1905. *The Golden Threshold*. London: Heinemann.

Naidu, Sarojini. 1912. *The Bird of Time: Songs of Life, Death and The Spring.* London: Heinemann.

Naidu, Sarojini. 1946. *The Sceptred Flute: Songs of India*. Allahabad: Kitabistan.

Naidu, Sarojini. 1961. *The Feather of the Dawn*. Bombay: Asia Publishing House.

Towards the Terms of Reference: Contextualizing Kamala Das

An Excuse for a Preamble

Kamala Das is one of the few Indian English poets to have engaged the attention of a greater number of critics than probably any other poet.[1] Her poetry has, however, been subjected to certain stock responses ever since the late 1960s, that is, when her work started gaining critical attention. All these responses have been based on repetitive readings of Das in her various avatars as a love poet, a confessional poet, an autobiographical poet, and a feminist poet. Although it is difficult to keep these identities separated from one another, some critics have tried to do so and read her poetry along a given line, while others have made efforts to develop a holistic view by referring to her various identities cumulatively. In whatever they have done, their studies have broadly contributed towards essentializing the poet. It is important to assert here that not only has the poet been essentialized in this process, Kamala Das criticism itself stands essentialized for all it has posited so far.

For a critic trying to assess her work today, it is difficult to alter or even resist what has been reiterated over all these years. The poet is in a critical quagmire, and any effort at relocating her as a poet of some other consequence would call for a fresh appraisal of her poetry. We may do this by approaching her poetry with the same old references to *love, confession, autobiography,* and *feminism,* but only after laying down their parameters in a context suitable for the reading of this poet. This revaluation would also be an attempt at disengaging her from stereotypical, exaggerated, or biased readings, and at determining a context for the poet, which is to be found in her own tradition rather than in the one that is borrowed and lies at a farther remove.

Laying the Parameters

Writing love is writing confession; writing confession is writing autobiography; and writing autobiography is writing feminism. These four identifiers are most often, interrelated, as they draw closely upon one another. In this process, they are liable to be meddled and be mistaken for one another, as, I would suggest, has happened in the readings of Kamala Das as a poet.

The poetry of *love* has had a variety of representations in both the Eastern and Western traditions through the ages.[2] Even while the distinction between romantic and erotic poetry has sometimes been too fine, it has been possible to distinguish the two for their obvious or hidden intentionality. Although both underscore male–female relationship, one of them underlines the physicality of this relationship, while the other evokes finer sentiments and emotions. One verges on the earthly, the overtly sexual, and even the pornographic, while the other draws closer to nobler human sentiments. In spite of this basic difference, both remain closely associated with the romance of the human body, underscore sensuality and play of passion, and evolve their own aesthetic principles to sustain as works of art.[3] Another significant facet of this poetry is that it leads, at a higher level, to a realization of the Divine with the help of worldly and secular images.[4] In poems of this category, there is an imagined sexual intervention by gods that ultimately helps the devotee to acquire a kind of superconsciousness. In seeking physical union with the Divine, the poet confesses the suffering experienced in separation and imagines the bliss that might come with union. As such, this poetry becomes a mode of a very personal kind of confession to one that is unseen, but can well be imagined or configured in imagination. To illustrate this point, one may refer to the Tamil love poetry of the Sangam period of the first century AD where gods appear as lovers. These are the poems that belong to *akam* tradition and represent the inner weather of emotions.

Notwithstanding the fact that every expression, including literary expression, is basically an act of *confession*, we have a definite variety of writing available in all literary traditions that verge on the confessional. It is subjective and personal in nature, sometimes overtly or covertly autobiographical, and speaks directly without a persona in between. By this parameter, poetry is more likely to be confessional than fiction or other writings. Even though the word 'confessional' evokes ideas of religious confession, it is far removed from that, especially when used in a literary context. This term, however, acquired a definite connotation with reference to a group of poets who subverted T.S. Eliot's notion of impersonality and made poetry an expression of their personality rather than an escape from it during the late 1950s and 1960s in America.[5] Any poetry, more especially with streaks of the personal, is most likely to be called confessional, but the term is to be used with caution, as it might lead to unfounded conclusions.

The inclusion of confession also leads to the inclusion of autobiography in the matrix of a text. While some texts draw upon memory to create a one-to-one correspondence text, others are imaginative reconstructions and acquire their literary merit for being so.[6] These texts, thus, become the iconographies of the self and have the potential to develop as complex texts. They could be a fine blend of fact, fiction, and fantasy—all leading, in turn, to the creation of a literary text that could be read in a variety of ways. They offer slippages for the readers and are liable to test them on their methodology of reading. In this process, both individual and personal histories find their space on the author's mental map and are delicately balanced in the act of producing a text. Texts of this nature differ considerably from one another, just as lives and autobiographies differ from person to person, or just as histories and historiographies differ from age to age.

Feminism is yet another corollary to romantic love, confession, and autobiography. As a counter discourse to male-centric and phallocentric parameters, feminism interrogates dominant patriarchal ideologies and seeks space for women as potent forces in a social configuration. It is political in its make-up and has acquired a distinct character in each of the locations where it has pursued its agenda, either with essentialist parameters or with relativist ones. In spite of being an ideological construct, it is also a major constituent of the postcolonial discourse. While feminism acquired its ground in the West in the 1960s, it has been a rather new phenomenon in the Indian context.[7] It has manifested strongly in a variety of literary and sociocultural contexts in India, and is now being feverishly debated in public and private domains.

With this brief and general perspective on the four essential constituents of Kamala Das's poetry, one may now try and attempt a reading of the poet for her literary merit. In doing so, I would like to posit how it may be of little use to assess Das as purely a poet of love, how limiting it would be to read her as a confessional poet, how futile to draw upon her autobiography in order to read her poetry, and how very generalizing to call her a feminist poet. I would like to argue that Kamala Das is none of these wholly and completely in the given sense of the terms, although she combines the remoter elements of all of them into a whole and emerges ultimately as a poet of distinct identity.

Finding a Context

In contesting what is generally posited, I would like to assert that love in Kamala Das is not necessarily about romantic love concerned with male–female relationship and various manifestations of this relationship.[8] Love acquires a broader meaning in her poetry; it is a principle of living and of Divine sustenance.[9] It goes beyond the stereotypical male–female syndrome, embraces a larger humanity, and incorporates greater human sympathies.[10] In these poems, one finds an extension of a liberal self that is naturally drawn to the world outside, where she engages with the figure of the male lover, the politically oppressed, socially ostracized, and ethnically marginalized. In relating with this world of myriad manifestations, she also transcends it and looks towards an adorable deity who remains unseen, although he is eminently reachable as a lover. In fact, approaching a deity to seek one's resolution is the ultimate way through which Das defines love.

Love, lust, passion, and erotica have often been used in synonymous ways to discuss Das's poetry. She seeks her solace through love, and this love is not a matter of consummation but of a desire to realize oneself both in physical and spiritual terms. The expression of sensuality/sexuality is only too natural for the human species, and one may only be unjustifiably blamed for sincerely expressing it. This is what has been precisely done in the case of this poet. It is important to say that her love poetry is not so much about the celebration of sexual love for which she has often been blamed, as much as it is about the lack of genuine love. In fact, it is about desire and yearning.

In spite of being deeply rooted in a sacrosanct sociocultural background and heritage, she chose to express herself boldly and uninhibitedly at a time when no one else had thought of doing so. This bold act of frank and free expression was quite clearly liable to be mistaken for her lust. Far from being the poetry of lust or erotica, Das's poetry glosses upon the pangs of love rather than the raptures of flesh. After reading the tamed verse of Toru Dutt and Sarojini Naidu, approaching a poet like Das could not have been such an easily acceptable experience for most of the readers. Das was the first Indian English woman poet to have found her material and medium to express herself in these terms. Hers was an iconoclast's approach, and this could not have been appreciated easily even by serious academic critics. This could be true in particular of those brought upon Victorian and colonial parameters of assessing female roles, or texts, produced by women writers. Misrepresentations of Das as a poet started because of the fact that her readers had yet to be initiated into a new world view and were not still ready to appreciate the new poetics of resistance and representation. Das had offered a unique resistance by altering the stereotypical and initiating a new discourse on freedom, sexuality, and female identity. She did not allow herself to be appropriated as merely a preserve in the male domain, but wished to be taken as a participant in the act of sharing the pleasures of a life that was so easily made liable to misappropriation.

It is appropriate to add here that her poems may also be read as fine specimens of texts that obliterate the distinction between realism and fantasy. It would be rewarding to read many of these love poems of pain and pining as exercises in fantasy. Fantasy, her poetry testifies, springs from the bark and bole of reality and forms an integral part of the real. Real and imagined, thus, join together to create two desperate facets of love, representing desire and disappointment. Yet another form of this fantasy can be seen in her poems where she assumes the persona of Radha and constructs the image of her beloved Krishna to seek solace in Him. The Radha–Krishna relationship is the most celebrated and the most sophisticated one that both mythology and literature have developed and preserved over centuries.

In order to appreciate this aspect of Das's love for the deity of Krishna, a reference to the classical tradition of Indian poetry would be in order. It must be asserted that even though Das appeared to be initiating a new culture of bold and uninhibited expression for the first time in Indian English poetry, she was not actually heralding a new tradition; she was only extending the one that had already been laid and established centuries ago. Right from the Vedic times, through Buddhist nuns, there have been women poets who have written about their lots as derelict and disappointed women, courtesans and nuns, mostly telling the tales of their woe, repression, resistance, and rebellion.[11] This tradition was carried further by the Bhakti poets, who addressed the various moods and manners of *shringara*, or the erotic, in a frank and uninhibited manner. They took both union and separation into account and represented various manifestations of love in and outside marriage that included the lot of the lady already in a nuptial knot (*kanta*), or the one carrying an illicit love affair (*parakiya*), or indulging in a surreptitious rendezvous (*abhisarika*).[12] These women poets have handed down a great tradition of characteristically Indian poetry to their later generation counterparts in how they have chosen their roles, either in bowing down before a god, or negating a nuptial tie, or going against social norms, or marrying a god and living as a saint wife. The example of Virsaiva woman saint called Mahadeviyakka, who wrote in the twelfth century in Kannada, is the most prominent of them all. Other examples of great relevance may be found in the poetry of Antal (eighth century) who wrote in Tamil, Janabai (1298–1350) and Bahnibai (1628–1700) who wrote in Marathi, Lal Ded (fourteenth century) who wrote in Kashmiri, and Mirabai (1498–1565) who wrote in Rajasthani. All of them played their roles as women and as poets, and all of them imparted a philosophical-cum-spiritual halo to their poetic outpourings.[13] It is interesting to note that this tradition was spread far and wide in the Indian subcontinent and covered the length and breadth of the Indian soil. This could be understood in the background of the fact that Hinduism recognizes female principle in the universe as Shakti, and the Hindu mythology has space for sexual relations of the gods who represent the interaction of 'spirit' as male with 'matter' as female. It is on the strength of this argument that I should like to assert that Das's contribution as a poet must be assessed with reference to the indigenous tradition rather than the Western tradition, where love and expressions of love acquire an altogether different proportion and idiom. There is a greater reason for doing so, as Mahadeviyakka, Lal Ded, and Mirabai are venerated as saints in spite of their offbeat stances and relinquishing their robes, while Das is criticized for expressing herself in a frank and uninhibited manner. It is not to assert that Das is a saint in their tradition, but only to say that she draws upon them rather closely. Those poets merged with the Divine and obliterated the distinction between the acceptable and the unacceptable modes of living. This is also what Das tries to do in her own inimitable way. In sum, Das's spirit is akin to those representing the Bhakti tradition of poetry, and she deserves to get a liberal space as is given to those in that tradition of poetry.

This discussion on the forthright and assertive voice of the women poets from the remote past and its manifestation in the poetry of Kamala Das takes us naturally to think of how the expression of intimate and personal material is liable to turn into a confessional act. Broadly speaking, all literary expression is a kind of confession, but what makes poetry characteristically confessional is related to the poet's approach to the material and the method the poet adopts to construct or configure that material. Our response to confessional literature, more especially poetry, has been conditioned in the recent past by the reception of American confessional poets whose poetry turned into a literary fad during the 1960s. They believed in opening doors on their private lives and speaking unabashedly of the psychological states of their being. In doing this, they wrote dramatic monologues of a very intimate kind and unfolded the levels of their psychological stress that would otherwise be kept away from public gaze. Choosing the ordinary idiom of expression, negating a mask or a persona, glossing over their experience of alienation, and throwing the poem open for incorporating any kind of experience whatsoever, these poets privileged the personal over the universal and developed their own mythopoeia. One might argue that many of these qualities are also found in the poetry of Kamala Das, but it should also be kept in mind that the American confessional poetry is rooted in its own sociocultural ethos characterized by the pressures of contemporary American life.[14] The major difference, therefore, lies in the fact that Das represents an entirely different milieu which is simply not comparable with any other milieu, more so the American milieu of the 1960s. Predicaments might, at times, strike a chord of similarity, but they may not necessarily be compatible and comparable, as is the case here. This is one major reason why Das should not be read along with the American confessional poets. There is yet another ground for this as well. If Das's poetry of personal denomination is to be compared with any poet(s), it is to be compared with the Indian women poets, including the Bhakti poets who lived and wrote centuries ago. It is in their company that the individual merit of her poetry would show much more brilliantly than in comparison with the American or any other poet(s) representing a different tradition and milieu.

Much misreading of Das has evolved from uncritical reliance on autobiographical material, personal statements, and sundry prose writings. The main focus has, however, been on *My Story*,[15] which is supposed to be her autobiography, although it is not so in the proper sense of the term. *My Story*, as a title, engaged the attention of her readers at the very outset, precisely because it came from a woman who had already earned a certain reputation as a poet of love, and that same poet, the readers expected, was now going to tell the story of her eventful life much more frankly. The desire to read something revelatory in nature is a typical male desire, which also explains, to a great extent, the notions perpetrated in the male-centric criticism on Das. Most of the readers of this infamous exercise in controversial writing were tempted by it for wrong reasons. They took everything in the book to be true and found easy sources there to annotate her poetry. In fact, *My Story* was neither a sequel nor a key to her poetry; it was a fine blend of fact, fiction, and fantasy. A closer reading of this text would establish that Das was interested more in creating fantasies than in writing a truthful and chronological account of her life. She was allured by the drama that life could offer, and thought that the whole business of living was of passing through odds and evens in the great theatre of life. It was a creative writer's effort who played with her imagination and made experiments with the form of autobiography. Once again an iconoclast's effort, *My Story* is not a sensational work; it is a storyteller's handiwork of imagination. We often tend to forget that she wrote fiction both in Malayalam and English,[16] and it was the storyteller's urge and ingenuity that interfered with the genre of autobiography, turning it into a text defying a category. I would further suggest that the very make-up of this book goes against the essential grain of her poetry, which is all about a genuine exposure to life lived in all innocence, only to be misread rather grossly.

There are several questions I would like to raise in this context. Why should an author be read with the help of bio/autobiographical material or other personal statements? Why should a reader believe all that the author says? Is the text any less important than the annotative material, which sometimes seems to control the response of the reader? Does not the author play tricks with the reader, or is the author also not playful at many a time? Does not the author enjoy the freedom of mixing genres and evolving one's own form, one's own meta-truth? Many more questions can be raised to interrogate the role of the author vis-à-vis the role of the reader. The text is autotelic, New Criticism had already told us, and that we were not required to put a premium on the person of the author. Roland Barthes, in his essay 'The Death of the Author' (1967), carried the argument further to say that the author was not an omniscient being and that the reader had no less a role to play in order to appreciate the plurality of a text. Michel Foucault, in his lecture titled 'What Is an Author?' (1969), interrogated the question of authorship itself and came up with the notion of the anonymous text. With such tools of reading in hand, we cannot go back to misplace our premium on the author's person in place of the text. We must also acknowledge that the author's freedom to use imagination is both infinite and inimitable and cannot be controlled by laying conditions of writing and by questioning or critiquing that author for any deviation from the so-called mode of perception and writing. Das is the kind of writer in whom fact, fiction, and fantasy merge in complex ways, and, thus, they are likely to mislead the reader potentially.

The ways of reading Kamala Das are faulted essentially because the tools of reading her are contextually misplaced. The claim that she is a feminist poet also falls in this category of misreading. Feminism has acquired multiple connotations primarily because of the fact that male–female equations differ from location to location, as do the sociocultural contexts in which these equations grow. India, being a site of great diversity, has a brand of feminism entirely different from those of Western feminism(s). Indian feminism, if we may call it so, has grown out of its own broader indigenous and local conditions. In spite of this, feminism as a broad denominator reminds us of Western feminism(s), just as confessional poetry reminds us of American confessional poetry. It may, thus, be possible to assert in this context that feminism is basically a Western construct and it found its expression in non-Western sites, including India, only recently and quite differently.

In spite of the long history of women's writing in India ever since the ancient and medieval periods, feminist consciousness took the shape of some kind of a movement only with the new postcolonial paradigms emerging in India. Although there have been issues to engage the attention of readers and writers alike, these issues got a shape and a direction only with more informed intervention in the metropolis. With sustained efforts to create sites of resistance, there is an institutional space available now, both in public and private domains. Indian feminist consciousness, however, cannot be subjected to a uniform definition and treatment because of the plural nature of the Indian nation. It is not that all women call themselves feminists, nor that all of them are feminists in the derived sense of the word, but only that the concern for the broader issues of gender are common to all of them.

In most of the appraisals, critics have loosely labelled Das as a feminist. She has been identified as one on account of her being bold and uninhibited in her expressions, which are the broad identifiers of feminists anywhere. What we need to keep in mind is that feminism is not all about being fiercely strong in word and action; it is about configuring the problem as a political one and seeking a resolution in a context along a line compatible with the sociopolitical context of the site in question. By this very definition, Das is not a feminist, just as, in spite of all her female anguish, Sylvia Plath is not a feminist; while Adrienne Rich, on the contrary, is one because of her taking up the women's cause as a political agenda.

Das's feminism, may thus be sought better in a postcolonial context, as she seeks space for the marginalized female and interrogates Indian patriarchal structures of power. She is not a male baiter, as she represents a tradition in which male and female together compose a familial/social structure and the woman is a major participant in that. Her female consciousness should thus be assessed in relation to her racial identity, cultural heritage, historical positioning, and her approach towards acquiring an identity with reference to language, colour, gender, and the contemporary sociocultural make-up. This has to be done with reference to the Indian postcolonial condition, which is clearly different from those of the other postcolonial sites. Writing for Das is in itself a liberating act which has little to do with feminist ideology; it is an individualistic approach towards identifying the odds of life and an effort to seek the evens.

By Way of a Conclusion

Kamala Das is essentially an iconoclast, both in life and literature. She refused stereotypes and evolved a voice and a technique of her own to express the dilemmas and anguish that characterize her poetry. Although a strong tradition of women's writing was available to her in Indian classical and post-classical periods to draw upon, there was none in modern Indian English writing that she could look towards to develop the contours of her own writing. In contrast to Indian English women poets writing a few decades before her, she engaged with issues that concerned identity in a broader sense of the word. As such, she acquired an identity for herself and made way for her contemporaries to do so for themselves. It also amounts to saying that the kind of thematic preferences and stylistic choices that the women poets made after Das owe greatly to Das's own initiation. In this way, she evolved a new norm for women's writing in contemporary Indian English literature.

Neither a feminist nor a confessional in the usual sense of the terms, she acquired her identity primarily as a woman who chose to express her whims and fancies, desires and despairs with remarkable confidence. Neither is she an autobiographical poet, nor one of romantic love in the traditional sense; she culls her material as a woman and as a poet who is capable of apprehending life imaginatively. She does not discount the figure of the male, although she questions the male principle. Male, to her, is not an antithesis in her scheme of things, but only a part of the whole. Love is a desire in her, and submission only a helpless and ironical denial of submission itself. She responded to her predicament as an individual, but she moved beyond herself to embrace a larger world spread brilliantly outside her threshold.

Das writes in two languages—English and Malayalam—and experiments with many forms and genres of poetry and fiction and non-fiction prose. Here again, she crosses the threshold of one language to enter another and of one form or genre to get into the other. In this manner, one writing becomes an extension of the other, and in all her writings taken together, she apprehends and addresses life's larger realities. Her writing has to be approached comparatively and holistically, taking both the languages and all the forms and genres together to develop a comprehensive perspective. A bilingual writer makes greater demands upon the critic, as is evident from this case. Das's critic has to be one who may negotiate with both the languages and the literary heritage available in them.

Das's graph of development is clearly laid out in terms of her thematic and stylistic transformations through different phases of her career. Her reputation rests largely on the poems she wrote in her first three collections, but she grew differently in the later phase of her creative life. Annamalai and Colombo poems, along with those that address her relationship with Allah—the Maker, the Preserver, the Destroyer—redefine herself and her relationship with the world.

Kamala Das did not conceive her role as a creative writer in political terms. Untutored in theory and philosophy, complex principles of poetry and poetics, she thought of creative act as a mode of natural expression. She is a romanticist or a naturalist in her approach, who lays premium on imagination and intuition. In spite of this, she has an unacknowledged theory of her own about language, love, and gender.

Endnotes

1. Kamala Das caught critical attention with the publication of her very first anthology *Summer in Calcutta* in 1965. Her reputation as a poet and prose writer

kept growing with the years as she published more of her works. Apart from a considerable number of research engagements on her, both in India and abroad, innumerable articles (in books and journals) and at least a dozen books, wholly devoted to her work, have appeared so far. These books include: Devinder Kohli, *Virgin Whiteness: The Poetry of Kamala Das* (Calcutta: Writers Workshop, 1968); Devinder Kohli, *Kamala Das* (New Delhi: Arnold-Heinemann, 1975); Anisur Rahman, *Expressive Form in the Poetry of Kamala Das* (New Delhi: Abhinav Publications, 1981); S.C. Harrex and Vincent O'Sullivan, eds, *Kamala Das: A Selection With Essays on Her Work*, CRNLE Series No. 1 (Adelaide: Centre for Research in New Literatures in English, 1986); A.N. Dwivedi, *Kamala Das and Her Poetry* (New Delhi: Doaba House, 1983); A.N. Dwivedi, *Kamala Das and Her Poetry*, second revised and enlarged edition (New Delhi: Atlantic Publishers, 2000); Iqbal Kaur, *Untying and Retying the Text: An Analysis of Kamala Das's My Story* (New Delhi: Bahri Publications, 1990); Vrinda Nabar, *The Endless Female Hungers: A Study of Kamala Das* (New Delhi: Sterling Publishers, 1994); Iqbal Kaur, ed., *Perspectives on Kamala Das's Poetry* (New Delhi: Intellectual Publishing House, 1995); Iqbal Kaur, ed., *Perspectives on Kamala Das's Prose* (New Delhi: Intellectual Publishing House, 1995); Rajeshwar Mittapalli and Pier Paolo Piciucco, eds, *Kamala Das: A Critical Spectrum* (New Delhi: Atlantic Publishers, 2001); N.V. Raveendran, *The Aesthetics of Sensuality: A Stylistic Study of the Poetry of Kamala Das* (New Delhi: Atlantic Publishers, 2000); and Irshad Gulam Ahmed, *Kamala Das: The Poetic Pilgrimage* (New Delhi: Creative Books, 2005).

2. Innumerable examples may be drawn from ancient Arabic and Sanskrit poetry, as also from the Greek, Roman, English, and other Western languages down the ages. From Sanskrit, one may refer to Meghaduta (fifth century) and Sringastaka (seventh/eighth century). From the Arabic, reference may be made to Hamasah and the Mu'allaqāt (tenth century). Other examples may be drawn from Persian and Turkish poetry of the Middle Ages. From the Western tradition, we may cite examples from Sappho and Anacreon of the Greek, and Catullus, Propertius, and Ovid of the Roman. There are other examples in Medieval Latin poetry. This tradition was carried forward in the subsequent ages from Renaissance to the present times in both the Eastern and Western poetic traditions.
3. See an example from Sanskrit in a poem entitled 'A Love Poem' by Vidya (seventh century) from the post-classical period: 'The luck is yours that you can talk about/your lover's playful glance, his words and touch./For me, I swear that once he puts his hand/upon my girdle, I remember nothing' (trans. Edwin Gerow and Peter Dent). [Katharine Washburn and John S. Major, eds, *World Poetry: An Anthology of Verse from Antiquity to Our Time* (New York: Quality Paperback Book Club, 1998), p. 222.]
4. Interesting examples of erotic love in relation to gods may be seen in ancient Tamil padams that draws upon bhakti. Annamayya (1408–1503) says: 'Make love, get close, ask for more—/but it's hard to separate and burn' ('A Woman

Talking to Herself', p. 51), 'Some woman has made love to you,/ Lord of Venkata hill,/ plundered your body's perfumes./Soon after, you came into my arms./ How can I blame you? My weariness is gone' ('A Woman to her Lover', pp. 52–3). Ksetrayya configures this experience differently: 'She says, "I can't sleep./ Let's do what men do."/ Thinking "she" was a woman,/ I get on top of him./ Then he doesn't let go: he holds me so tight/ he loses himself in me. Wicked as ever, he declares:/"I am your Muvvagopala!"//and makes love to me./Those women, they told me he was a woman!' ('A Young Woman to a Friend', p. 72); 'Listening to my moans as you touch certain spots,/ the parrot mimics me, and O how we laugh in bed!' ('A Woman to her Lover', p. 127). All these quotations are taken from A.K. Ramanujan, Velcheru Narayana Rao, and David Shulman, trans. and ed., *When God is a Customer: Telegu Courtesan Songs by Ksetrayya and Others* (Berkeley: University of California Press, 1994).

5. A very pertinent example is that of the twelfth-century saint Mahadeviyakka, a major precursor of discourse on women's emancipation. She was a devotee of Shiva who renounced society, moved out of her marriage, made friends with birds and animals, and wandered in search of her guru. She found one in Allama Prabhu. Mahadeviyakka relinquished clothes and walked naked—a practice unheard of among women, although male ascetics are known to have chosen this path of walking naked in their spiritual quest for the Lord. It is believed that hair grew all over her body that protected her from all odds.

   Another example of equal interest is to be found in the fourteenth-century saint Lal Ded. Popularly and endearingly remembered as 'Lalla', 'Mother Lalla', 'Granny Lalla', and 'Lalla Yogeshwari', she also suffered in her family and society which she relinquished in search of the Lord. A devotee of Shiva, she too went around naked and found her guru in Sidh Srikanth.

   Mirabai, who was born towards the end of the fifteenth century, offers yet another example in this category. She, too, had a strong individualistic perception of the ultimate, as she refused to perform sati and chose, instead, to seek her salvation by dancing and singing in the temple. A devotee of the archetypal lover-god Krishna, she was detested by her family for her idiosyncratic ways of spiritual communion. She entered the sanctum of the temple in a state of ecstasy, and the door was closed only to be opened later, revealing that her sari had wrapped the Lord in whom she had blissfully culminated.

   There are many other saints who happen to be male like Tukaram, Kabir, Guru Nanak, Chaitanya, etc. Their lives tell of the ways they chose to communicate with their lords, and how they wrote verse which explored the mysterious ways of men to God and of God to men.

6. Confessional poetry came to be associated with the American poets W.D. Snodgrass and Robert Lowell, who published their volumes of poetry *Heart's*

Needle and *Life Studies* respectively in 1959. Others who joined this mode of writing were John Berryman and Theodore Roethke, and two women poets—Anne Sexton and Sylvia Plath—who added yet another variety to this mode of poetic expression, and who ultimately completed their act of confession by committing suicide one after another.

7. These are the two broad categories of autobiographical writing. While St. Augustine's *Confessions* fall in the category of the intensely personal account of the self, Rousseau's *Confessions* is an imaginative reconstruction. Many examples may be quoted from different literary traditions.
8. For a broader perspective, see Susie Tharu and K. Lalitha, eds, *Women Writing in India*, two volumes (1991, 1993); Urvashi Butalia, *The Other Side of Silence: Voices from the Partition of India* (1998); Malashri Lal, *The Law of the Threshold: Women Writers in Indian English* (1995); and Jasbir Jain and Avadesh Kumar Singh, eds, *Indian Feminisms* (2001).
9. See, for examples, some earlier poems like 'The Freaks', 'In Love', 'The Music Party', 'A Relationship', 'An Apology to Gautama', in *Summer in Calcutta* (New Delhi: Everest Press, 1965); 'The Prisoner', 'I Shall Someday', 'The Old Playhouse', 'Gino', 'The Stone Age', in *The Old Playhouse and Other Poems* (Madras: Orient Longman, 1973); and 'Substitute', 'The Descendants', 'Captive', in *The Descendants* (Calcutta: Writers Workshop, 1967). Some other poems of this category may be seen in her later collections *Tonight, This Savage Rite: The Love Poems of Kamala Das and Pritish Nandy* (New Delhi: Arnold-Heinemann, 1979); *Collected Poems*, Vol. 1 (Trivandrum: Navakerala Printers, 1984); *The Best of Kamala Das* (Kozhikode, Bodhi Publishing House, 1991); and *Only the Soul Knows How to Sing* (Kottayam: DC Books, 1996).
10. See, more specifically, poems like 'Radha' and 'Radha Krishna', in *Summer in Calcutta*; 'The Maggots', in *The Descendants*; 'Ghanshyam', in *An Anthology of Indo-English Love Poetry*, ed. S.C. Saha (Calcutta: Prayer Books, 1976); and 'Lines Addressed to a Devadasi', in *An Anthology of Indo-English Poetry*, ed. Gauri Deshpande (New Delhi: Hind Pocket Books, 1974).
11. See Kamala Das's six poems called 'Colombo Poems' that include 'Fear', 'The Sea of Galle Face Green', 'Smoke in Colombo', 'After July', 'A Certain Defect in Blood', and 'Shopper at Cornell's Colombo'. These poems record her response to the long-drawn Sinhalese–Tamil conflict in Sri Lanka. These are included in *Collected Poems*, Vol. 1. Also see a sequence of pensive or self-reflective poems called 'Annamalai Poems' (1985) that underline the poet's inner weather as a woman and a writer. Some of them are 'The Annamalai Hills', 'Home is a Concept', 'Smudged Mirror', 'A Widow's Lament', 'A Feminist's Lament', 'Larger Than Life Was He', and 'Stock Taking'. Eleven of these poems were published in *The Best of Kamala Das*, pp. 149–58; and six in *Literature and Criticism* 2 (1) (2000): 156–57.
12. For poems by several women writing on their experiences in various female roles, see Margaret Macnicol, ed., *Poems by Indian Women* (Calcutta: Association Press, 1923).

13. A detailed discussion on women saints, bhakti, and Shaiva poetry, etc. may be seen in the six essays of A.K. Ramanujan in a section entitled 'Essays on Bhakti and Modern Poetry', in *The Collected Essays of A.K. Ramanujan*, ed. Vinay Dharwadker (New Delhi: OUP, 1999).
14. It would be instructive to look at some examples from this kind of poetry in order to see how Das echoes them. In one of her poems entitled 'Someone Else's Song', Das says that she is 'a million million people /talking all at once'. Mahadeviyakka says in one of her compositions: 'Not one, not two, not three or four/ but through eighty-four hundred thousand vaginas/ have I come...' (trans. A.K. Ramanujan) [Tharu and Lalitha, *Women Writing in India, Vol I: 600 B.C. to the Early 20th Century*, p. 80]. Janabai and Lal Ded reach their Lords through surrender of their selves and dance in a state of trance, which reminds, interestingly enough, of the Sufi dance in a similar state of ecstasy and surrender. Janabai says: 'Cast off all shame,/ and sell yourself/ in the marketplace; then alone can you hope/ to reach the Lord' (trans Vilas Sarang) [Ibid., p. 83]. Lal Ded echoes in a strikingly similar fashion: 'My teacher told me one thing,/ Live in the soul.// When that was so,/I began to go naked,/ and dance'. (trans. Coleman Barks) [Washburn and Major, New York: p. 583]. Craving for physical union is yet another important facet of this poetry. Mirabai says: 'There is a longing, it is for his body, for every hair of that dark body./ All I was doing was breathing, and the Dancing Energy came by my house'. (trans. Robert Bly) [Ibid., p. 582]. Quite in keeping with this tradition, Das also surrenders to her Lord Krishna, whom she lovingly addresses as Vitthal, Hari, Vishnu, Narayan, Rama, Puroshottam, and Mohan. Also in keeping with this tradition, she considers herself to be a devadasi, in the service of the Lord.
15. Discussion on American confessional poetry may be seen in M.L. Rosenthal, *The Modern Poets: A Critical Introduction* (New York: Oxford University Press, 1960); R. Phillips, *The Confessional Poets* (Carbondale: Southern Illinois University, 1973); Frances Bixler, ed., *Original Essays on the Poetry of Anne Sexton* (Conway: University of Central Arkansas Press, 1988); Jacqueline Rose, *The Haunting of Sylvia Plath* (London: Virago Press, 1991); and Adam Kirsch, *The Wounded Surgeon: Confession and Transformation in Six American Poets* (W. W. Norton and Company, 2005).
16. *My Story* (1977) received instant attention on its publication, primarily because it was projected as a sensational piece of writing. Reviewers and critics did not look at its literary merit as much as they took the extra-literary features of the book into consideration. The popularity of this text, based on its reputation as a sensational text, may be gauged by the fact that it has since been translated into fifteen languages of the world.
17. Her fictional works in English include *Alphabet of Lust* (1976) and *A Doll for the Child Prostitute* (1977). However, she has been much more prolific in Malayalam since the mid-fifties. *Mathilukal* (Walls) appeared in 1955, *Pathu Kathakal* (Secret Stories) in 1958, *Naricheerukal Parakkumbol* (When Little Bats Fly) in 1960, *Ente Snehitha Aruna* (My Friend Aruna) in 1963, *Pakshiyude Manam* (A Bird's

Honour) in 1964, and *Thanuppu* (Cold) in 1967. Her collected short stories *Ente Cheru Kathakal* (My Short Stories) appeared in two volumes in 1985.

References

Das, Kamala. 1965. *Summer in Calcutta*. New Delhi: Everest Press.

———. 1967. *The Descendants*. Calcutta: Writers Workshop.

———. 1973. *The Old Playhouse and Other Poems*. Madras: Orient Longman.

———. *My Story*. 1977. New Delhi: Sterling Publishers.

———. 1979. *Tonight, This Savage Rite: The Love Poems of Kamala Das and Pritish Nandy*. New Delhi: Arnold-Heinemann.

———. 1984. *Collected Poems*, Vol 1. Trivandrum: Navakerala Printers.

———. 1991. *The Best of Kamala Das*. Kozhikode, Bodhi Publishing House.

———. 1996. *Only the Soul Knows How to Sing*. Kottayam: DC Books.

Phillips, R. 1973. *The Confessional Poets*. Carbondale: Southern Illinois University.

Ramanujan, A.K., Velcheru Narayana Rao, and David Shulman, trans. and ed. 1994. *When God is a Customer: Telugu Courtesan Songs by Ksetrayya and Others*. Berkeley: University of California.

Ramanujan, A.K. 1999. 'Essays on Bhakti and Modern Poetry'. In *The Collected Essays of A.K. Ramanujan*. Ed. Vinay Dharwadker. New Delhi: OUP.

Rosenthal, M.L. 1960. *The Modern Poets: A Critical Introduction*. New York: Oxford University Press.

Tharu, Susie and K. Lalitha. 1993. *Women Writing in India, Volume 1: 600 B.C. to the Early 20th Century*. New Delhi: OUP.

———. 1993. *Women Writing in India, Volume 2: The 20th Century*. New Delhi: OUP.

Washburn, Katharine and John S. Major, eds. 1998. *World Poetry: An Anthology of Verse from Antiquity to Our Time*. New York: Quality Paperback Book Club.

The Calligraphy of Coils:
The Poetry of Agha Shahid Ali

A Contrapuntal Rhetoric

With the typical imagery of the 'calligraphy' and the 'coil', Agha Shahid Ali[1] (1949–2001) revealed his Oriental connections rather unwittingly when he wrote: 'The earth is a calligraphy of coils' ('From Another Desert': *ANMOA*). This implies further that he perceived the earth as a complex script that recorded myriad conditions of being, as it moved in a circle. Ali's poetry seeks sustenance from earth's vitality, and it connects those conditions of being together in a synchronous whole. As such, persons, places, and predicaments; love, death, and loneliness; and language, form, and poetry are richly coiled together in a remarkable calligraphy. This calligraphy has no breaks or discontinuities; in fact, one extends into the other and creates what Edward Said called a 'contrapuntal rhetoric', marked by similarity of occurrences.

A strong rhetoric persuades strongly, as does Ali's poetry, which seeks to connect the constituents of this calligraphy in an organic whole. His poetry is essentially a manner of seeking an address, a name, a way of belonging. He finds an address for himself in each of these conditions individually, as in all of them wholly. He creates an extremely rich community of beings composed of human and non-human, reverberating with life and invoking a rare empathy. Poets always yearn to achieve this state, but Ali does it differently with different attributes and baggage. He has his own space, his own people, his own influences, and his own longings. It is a longing for an individual identity, a form, or a language to speak in.

Kashmir Shrinks into My Mailbox

Places are vital presences in Ali's poetry. He has a large space to operate upon in physical and poetic terms. A poet who lived and wrote in America was in America, and yet not in America. Ethno-racial labels of Indian-American, Asian-American, or Kashmiri-American did not work for him like neat labels or addresses of belonging. In calling himself a Kashmiri-American, he made vital pronouncements of being a Kashmiri at both the ends, as the label suggests, and remaining an American at the centre from where he could look back and forth. In hyphenating his locus, he achieved a metaphoric connectivity while retaining his space for himself with great conviction. Even though Kashmir is not at the centre of his identity tag, it remains so in spirit and has its constant pull on him. The very titles of these collections of poems—*Rooms are Never Finished* [*RANF*] (2001), *The Country Without a Post Office* [*TCWPO*] (1997), *A Nostalgist's Map of America* [*ANMOA*] (1991), and *The Half-Inch Himalayas* [*THIH*] (1987)—are indicative of his being space-centric. 'The Blessed Word: A Prologue' spells it out rather dramatically:

> Let me cry out in that void, say it as I can. I can write on that void:
> Kashmir, Kaschmir, Cashmere, Qashmir, Cashmir, Cashmire,
> Kashmere, Cachemire,
> Cushmeer, Cachmiere, Casmir. Or Cauchemar in a sea of stories? Or:
> Kacmir, Kaschemir, Kasmere, Kachmire, Kasmir, Kerseymere?
>
> (*TCWPO*: 3)

This is like calling a beloved by many names. The poem invokes various images of Kashmir: its glorious past, its murky present, the festival of Id-ul-Zuha, chinar leaves, songs of the legendary Habba Khatoon, Jhelum, and Zero Bridge. More importantly, he is moved by Osip Mandelstam, a Russian poet, whom he quotes in the epigraph to this poem—'We shall meet again, in Petersburg'—and appropriates this reference for his own sake in saying: 'He reinvents Petersburg (I, Srinagar), an imaginary homeland, filling it, closing it, shutting himself (myself) in it'. (3)

Several other poems[2] invent and reinvent the images of Kashmir and confirm Ali's concern vigorously. In all these poems, Kashmir emerges as a point in space that suffers and resuscitates, but remains a living entity both in memory and reality. It shines in its glory and remains a constant historical, political, and cultural reference:

> I will die, in autumn, in Kashmir,
> and the shadowed routine of each vein
> will almost be news...
>
> ('The Last Saffron', *TCWPO*: 13)

> IT'S WAR:
> It's 1994: ARMY LAYS SIEGE TO SHRINE...
>
> ('I Dream I am the Only Passenger on Flight 493 to Srinagar', *TCWPO*: 18)

> Again I've returned to this country
> where a minaret has been entombed.
>
> ('The Country without a Post Office', *TCWPO*: 25)

> The Mansion is white, lit up with roses. He is driven
> through streets in which blood flows like Hussain's.
> Our hands won't return to us, not even mutilated, when
> Death comes—thin bureaucrat—from the plains.
>
> ('Muharram in Srinagar', *TCWPO*: 57)

> No one now comes from Kandahar,
> dear Ali, to pitch tents by the Jhelum,
> under autumn maples,
> and claim descent from the holy prophet.
>
> ('Cracked Portraits', *THIH*: 10)

Kashmir is a constant refrain in Ali's poetry. It is a refrain of love, anger, and despair. The examples quoted earlier underline his concern with his home and his identity. He assembles them, image by image, spread all around in the land of his birth. The place is rehabilitated in reality, memory, and fantasy.

His cartographic imagination works to create a map of belonging for him. While he can identify his locus, he can also extend its frontiers liberally, allowing one to enter into the other. As such, one place becomes all places and all places become one. Kashmir melts into Amherst ('Lenox Hill', *RANF*), Pennsylvania, Ohio, and Arizona into Calcutta ('In Search of Evanescence', *ANMOA*), Delhi into Arizona ('Snow on the Desert', *ANMOA*), the valleys of Kashmir into the peaks of Zabarvan ('A History of Paisley', *TCWPO*), and so on. The memories of the place are not evoked in Ali in the way they are evoked in those living in a state of forced exile. In his case, they are evoked out of his intense concern for the land. This concern is both political and cultural in nature, and has significant implications in the growth of Ali as a poet, a citizen, a political being, a cultural historian, and a myth-maker.

Living away from Kashmir is a matter of Ali's own choice, but it relates him to the place more intensely and fervently. It is yet another act of imaginative and emotional belonging to the place while being away from there. He reconstructs this sense of belonging through history, memory, and myth-making. This is the result of his liberal imagination and free associations that erase all boundaries. In this process, many other spots intermingle, constructing a new mental geography of belonging. The poet, like a navigator, then takes on a route of discovery through various places: Chile, Brisbane, Armenia, Chechnya, Bosnia, Naples, Athens, Isfahan, Kashgar, and Syria. They emerge in various contexts, reincarnate each other, and reflect his catholicity and imaginative vitality. The endless, open space is the home he needs to explore for himself and to know his moorings through them. He defies demarcation and creates his own terms of spatial reference, not as one in exile but as one who belongs.

My Mother Is My Poem

Persons, like places, enliven Ali's poetry. The poem and the mother are not two different entities for him, as both of them give him a context and make the context real. They inspire and help him grow. In turning the mother into a poem, he also turns the poem, as he identifies with both of them with equal intensity.

Some of the finest poetry that one may read in remembrance and veneration of a mother is put together in section I—'From Amherst to Kashmir'—in *Rooms are Never Finished.* This sequence of twelve poems is commemorative rather than elegiac in nature in the way it brings the mother back to life. In travelling with her dead body from Amherst to Kashmir, the poet passes through phases of suffering, memory, and realization, and experiences strange echoes in natural and human manifestations:

> Mother,
> they asked me, *So how's the writing?* I answered *My mother*
> *is my poem.*
>
> ('Lenox Hill', *RANF*: 18)

> Only Karbala could frame our grief:
> The wail rose: How could such a night fall on Hussain?
> Mother, you remembered perfectly that God is a thief
> when memory is a black and white film again
> (*Dark Krishna,*
> *don't let your Radha die in the rain*)
>
> ('Summers of Transition', *RANF*: 31)

> ...*How dare the moon*—I want to cry out,
> Mother—*shine so hauntingly out*
> *here when I've sentenced it to black waves*
> *inside me? Why has it not perished?*
> *How dare it shine on an earth*
> *From which you have vanished?*
>
> ('By the Waters of the Sind', *RANF*: 52)

In his sequence, representing a variety of situations, the central voice relates together the sorrows of Karbala, the lament of Zainab, the devotion of Radha and Krishna, and the voices of Faiz and Ghalib to configure his suffering over the disappearance of his mother. The poet constructs a unique sequence of correspondences between characters and situations and seeks his sustenance through them. Many conditions are evoked by history and memory. They offer strength to him while he is with her ephemeral human memory. They offer strength to him while he is with her ephemeral human body on the earth and also in the air while flying back home. The mother, along with the father and the ancestors, also appears in earlier poems like 'A Lost Memory of Delhi', 'Dream of Glass Bangles', 'Snowmen', 'Cracked Portraits', and 'The Season of the *Plains*' (*THIH*). The poem and the mother are always lively and sympathetic; they keep him going through the act of living and exploring life.

There are other figures also who inhabit Ali's poems and impart a conviction to the poet as he evolves a lasting relationship with them. Among such figures are the great ghazal singer Begum Akhtar and the major Urdu poet Faiz Ahmad Faiz. They appear and reappear as vital sources of identification from place to place. Some of the most poignant lines written for Begum Akhtar may be read in the poems where she emerges now as a phantom, now as a reality:

> Exiling you to cold mud,
> your coffin, stupid and white,
> astounds by its ignorance.
>
> It wears its blank pride,
> defleshing the nomad's echo.
> I follow you to the earth's claw,
>
> shouldering time's shadow.
> This is history's bitter arrogance,
> this moment of the bone's freedom
>
> ('In Memory of Begum Akhtar', *THIH*: 28)
>
> (*My silk is stained,*
> *How will I face my Lord?*
> she'd set in Pain—
> her chosen raga that July in Srinagar.)

A week later: GHAZAL QUEEN BEGUM AKHTAR
IS DEAD. She had claimed her right-to-die:
She had sung 'Everyone Will be Here But I.'

('I Dream I Am the Only Passenger
on Flight 493 to Srinagar', *TCWPO*: 17)

Wherever you were, Faiz, that
language spoke to you; and when you heard it,
you were alone—in Tunis, Beirut,
London, or Moscow. Those poets' laments
concealed, as yours revealed, the sorrows
of a broken time.

('Homage to Faiz Ahmed Faiz', *THIH*: 30)

Ali has a whole lot of persons who influence him rather deeply in his poetic make-up and in acquiring a voice. Neruda, Cavafy, Pessoa, Paz, Darwish, Dickinson, Eliot, and Merrill, representing different cultural and literary traditions, help him work his way through. While these poets give him a rare conviction, Begum Akhtar, the inimitable singer, helps him recognize the beauty of the human voice and its deep impact in discovering a tone of voice for himself. He creates a small island for himself, an island of undefined geography and no boundaries. It is spread far and wide, and gathers grace from all corners. It has its own community of beings drawn from the past and the present, who stand by him in apprehending life and making it a worthy experience. It has space for Zainab and Hussain, Radha and Krishna, Sufism and Bhakti, Buddhism and Hinduism. It is a rich kaleidoscope of human images and conditions of being, all richly calligraphed in the coil of life and its varied manifestations.

A Language Will Die With Me

Like places and persons, language is the other essential concern of Ali. How does he acquire, refurbish, and appropriate it in a context? For one interested in his poetic evolution, this would be an important question to answer.

A poem for Ali is a linguistic construct of an unusual kind. It states and echoes; it is full of associations with other languages and cultural conditions. He tests and tries his English to find if it acquires a different tenor. While he grew up with the canonical English texts and automatically chose to write in the English language, as he said in a paper presented in a workshop,[3] he also had an auditory intermixing of Persian, Urdu, and Kashmiri into his sensibility. He carried it on as he developed, and found them entering his ways of perception and expression. As he realized the value of sense and sound independently, he could also discover the vital relationship between the two. He, therefore, enriched his literary baggage by testing and trying the potential of one language interfaced with the other. One may overhear the Urdu–Persian rhythm in his lines:

> Separation
> Can't be borne when the rains
> come: this every lyric says.
>
> ('The Season of the Plains', *THIH*: 17)

> Again I've returned to this country
> where a minaret has been entombed.
> Someone soaks the wicks of clay lamps
> in mustard oil, each night climbs its steps
> to read messages scratched on planets.
>
> ('The Country Without a Post Office', *TCWPO*: 25)

> All night I'm awake I'll keep you awake
> take this vow that I am yours I am yours
> dark god you are all I have all I have.
>
> ('Film *Bhajan* Found on a 78 RPM', *RANF*: 41)

> 'In the Name of the Merciful' let night begin.
> I must light lamps without her—at every shrine?
> God then is only the final assassin.
>
> ('God', *RANF*: 44)

The atmosphere and the turns of phrases are indicative of the poet's association with a different cultural set-up. He revives the spirit of that set-up in a language and in a manner that distinguishes him from the poets of the typically Western tradition. Ali came to the magic of Urdu not through the script, but through the sensuous voice of Begum Akhtar singing Faiz, and the two went deep into the making of his poetic sensibility and imparting his language a certain complexion:

> Was Begum Akhter singing Faiz when the lights went out? He is always with me, often in her voice. I have brought them with me to America, with absolute ease, taken them back to the subcontinent, then again brought tem back to America. I have not surrendered any part of me; rather my claims to both Urdu and English have become greater. The way the raga and the poem become each other's for Begum Akhter, so have Urdu and English become for me. My two loyalties, on loan to each other, are now so one that the loan has been forgiven. Not, forgotten.[4]

Ali, however, repaid the loan by translating Faiz, a poet profusely praised by Edward Said, whom he quoted in the paper 'The Rebel's Silhouette: Translating Faiz Ahmad Faiz' as 'one of the greatest poets of this century' (3) for the quality of his wider sensuousness. There again, he wanted to see, as he did elsewhere in the paper, if he would be able to 'make English behave outside its aesthetic habits?' (3) The other reason he gave for rendering Faiz into English was that no one seemed to know this poet of great sociopolitical conviction in America when he reached there. He took it to be a 'terrible insult' (3) to his culture. The loan was rather well paid when having realized this, he translated Faiz into the English language. The fact that another American poet Naomi Lazard had already translated Faiz into English with certain distinction was quite naturally a delightful discovery for him. Ali's bilingualism and biculturalism, subjects now being hotly debated in literary, cultural, and critical circles, had 'political, and cultural and aesthetic implications' (2) for him, as he acquired an identity and a language for himself through this process of double loyalty.

Ali's translations of Faiz in *The Rebel's Silhouette* (*TRS*), however, bring forth several other issues concerning his method, his aesthetic perception, and his treatment of language. It is an act of lending out a part of one's heritage to oneself as passing it over to the other literary counterparts. Ali's translations are curious efforts at representing the spirit of Faiz. These are a poet's translation, reconceived and reworked in the English language. They acquire their own assertive power when they negotiate with the demands of the Urdu–Persian tradition. As the poems are given a new linguistic framework, they develop their own form and acquire their own value. The ghazals and the other regular poems bear marks of his playfulness and his frank treatment into a tightly knit whole. A ghazal's couplet is rendered thus:

> He bet both this life and the next
> and gambled all night for your love
> he first lost earth then eternity
> Now he departs from his night of grief
> defeat visible in his eyes. (*TRS*: 7)
>
> When I remember you
> the morning is essence it is perfume it is musk
> And the night
> when I kindle our sorrow
> is longing caught in itself. (*TRS*: 31)

For a reader brought up on the English literary tradition, this is an entirely new concept of love, typically Eastern in approach, imagery, and phraseology. Each line refers to a stock image, is treated afresh, and enlivens the given context. Several other poems of this anthology like 'Don't Ask Me for That Love Again', 'Solitude', 'A Prison Evening', 'We Who Were Executed', 'Before You Came', and 'Be Near Me' may also be read along this line, where an English reader may easily discover a different world and a different aesthetic principle brought to negotiate with the demands of the English language, sensibility, and poetic form. Ali is fully aware of the demands and negotiates with them as he negotiates with the Urdu couplet. His concern with the ghazal/couplet ultimately turned out to be a major concern for him. This is well borne out by the collections of his poems—*The Country Without a Post Office and Rooms Are Never Finished*—where ghazals regularly punctuate the titles of the poems on the contents page, as if to create an air of individual poetic identity and impart new structures of poetic rendition. For him, writing a ghazal was an act of evolving a new linguistic reference, a new code of composition. He seemed to reconfirm what Adrienne Rich had said in one of her ghazals—every existence speaks a language of its own. With every composition, the language fades out in Ali, and with every situation, it fades in with a new vitality. When he said that 'a language will die with me' in the poem 'In search of Evanescence' from *A Nostalgist's Map of America*, he was only underlining the principle of living, perishing, and reliving from context to context. This concern matured ultimately in the collection of ghazals called *Ravishing DisUnities: Real Ghazals in English*, where he put together one hundred and nine poets, mostly American, trying their hand on this curious literary form which he saw acquiring a certain face.

Ali's collection of ghazals, *Ravishing DisUnities*, is his way of testing as to how far this form had acquired its root in a different literary tradition. In helping create a new language and evolve a new poetic form, he also introduced a new imaginative space the poets had not known so far while writing their regular poems in English with a beginning and an end, if not a middle. Ali made a major case in this collection concerning form, language, and sensibility, to name the important ones only. In his 'Introduction', he wrote:

> Through ghazals, English can again employ full rhymes, even the most cliché-ridden, without apology or embarrassment....further, the ghazal also offers English a chance to find a formal way, a 'legal' way out, to cultivate a profound respect for desperation—something that American poetry has not altogether lost. As for the English, let me leave it there. (11)

The ghazal offered these poets a way of exiting from the contemporary aesthetics of formlessness and an entry into a new world of great creative promise and delight. In popularizing the ghazal, Ali was offering a new aesthetic formulation which could enrich the contemporary poetic scenario of America.

I Always Loved Neatness

In saying that Ali is a poet of great technical virtuosity, one would only be making a safe and sound assertion. One may further qualify this statement by adding that among his contemporaries, there may be only a few to have such a feeling for the language, such a sweep of imagination, such magical configuration of reality, and all these with such a tight control over the form. Every poem is a different experience, creates a different condition, and writes a different language, and none of these can ever be repeated. The language and the form are born and reborn in each context, making a way through the real and the eerie, the magical and the mundane.

Even a general reading of his poems in a chronological sequence would establish the markers of his development only too clearly. A technical virtuoso, he exhibits a certain confidence at every stage. He chooses to follow a strict discipline in whatever he cultivates: a canzone, a sestina, or a terza rima; a sonnet, a ghazal, or a prose poem. He insists upon the regular syllables, absence of enjambment, rhyme, refrain, and the unitary existence of the couplet in the ghazal without which it would not be a ghazal at all. He considers the form not as a constraint, but as a mode that liberates and surprises. He has been constantly preoccupied with the idea of an order which emerges out of the seemingly disparate elements. Ali is a literary enricher for two reasons: first, he creates a new formal and linguistic order and, second, he imparts an entirely new set of textual and cultural references to the Western literary tradition. He is not one of those poets who would like to take an easy way and avoid the technical demands of the chosen form. His verse acquires a rich texture as he attends to the technical requirements of his composition. This poetic method turns him into an intense artist whose commitment to the architectonics of the poem is total and complete.

Where does one place a poet like him? A keen observer of the European-American literary and cultural tradition, he always had a strong pull towards the Orient. Located geographically in America, he would swing back and forth. Living in a particular point in time, he looked beyond the present and the immediate. Totally committed to the formal finesse, he could be intense as well. He saw conditions, characters, and languages mixing liberally into each other. He does not offer neat classification or neat answers, as history defies such a pattern. His is an example of liberal imagination taken to its height. His text is not unitary; it lends itself to multiple readings and works through the principle of interface. Reading his poetry is like deciphering complex visual and verbal patterns. He is a multiple exile, but at home everywhere. His poetry poses questions concerning myth and memory, history and culture, location and language, and form and technique. He raises political and cultural questions. He is a compulsive poet; he knocks at the readers' consciousness and wishes him to join his world of strange affinities and correspondences. In joining him, the reader acquires a supplementary personality and is left amply surprised at receiving the gift his poetry offers.

Endnotes

1. He published eight collections of poems between 1972 and 2001: *Bone-Sculpture* (1972), *In Memory of Begum Akhtar and Other Poems* (1979), *The Half-Inch Himalayas* (1987), *A Walk Through the Yellow Pages* (1987), *A Nostalgist's Map of America* (1991), *The Beloved Witness: Selected Poems* (1992), *The Country Without a Post Office* (1997), and *Rooms Are Never Finished* (2001). He also published his translations from the poetry of Faiz Ahmad Faiz in *The Rebel's Silhouette* (1991), edited *Ravishing DisUnities: Real Ghazals in English* (2000), and made a critical study entitled 'T.S. Eliot as Editor' for his PhD. His poems were subsequently collected in *The Veiled Suite* and published by W.W. Norton and Company in 2009 and later by Penguin, India, in the following year.
2. See especially, among others, 'Postcard from Kashmir', 'Snowmen', 'Cracked Portraits', and 'The Season of the Plains' (*THIH*); 'I See Kashmir from New Delhi at Midnight', 'A History of Paisley', and 'Son et Lumière at Shalimar Garden' (*TCWPO*); and 'From Amherst to Kashmir' (*RANF*).
3. In his paper entitled 'The Rebel's Silhouette: Translating Faiz Ahmad Faiz' presented at a workshop on 'Language, Culture, and Translation', organized by Katha, New Delhi (31 October–1 November 1992), Ali wrote:

> Poetry was part of the air we breathed. In Srinagar during the summer of 1989 (when my mother helped me translate Faiz), my grandmother, then eighty eight, quite by chance quoted Milton during a conversation. In English. Ever since I can remember, she quoted Shakespeare, Keats, and Hardy, in English; Hafiz and Rumi in Persian; Ghalib and Faiz in Urdu; Habba Khatun, Mahjoor, and Zinda Kaul in Kashmiri. But I'd never heard her quote Milton. I was ecstatic: once again I didn't need proof of my rights to the English canon...Significantly, not only was my training in school in English (I mean that I grew up with English as my first language), but, paradoxically, my first language was/is not my mother tongue, which is Urdu. When I wrote my first poems, at the age of ten, they were in English. I did not 'choose' to write in English., it just happened that way. Naturally. (p. 2)

4. Ibid., p. 11.

References

Ali, Agha Shahid. 1987. *The Half-Inch Himalayas*. Middleton, CT: Wesleyan University Press (referred to as *THH*).

———. 1991. *A Nostalgist's Map of America*. New York: W.W. Norton and Co. (referred to as *ANMOA*).

———, trans. 1991. *The Rebel's Silhouette.* New Delhi: OUP (referred to as *TRS*).

———. 1997. *The Country Without a Post Office.* Delhi: Ravi Dayal (referred to as *TCWPO*).

———. 2000. *Ravishing DisUnities: Real Ghazals in English.* Middleton, CT: Wesleyan University Press (referred to as *RD*).

———. 2001. *Rooms Are Never Finished.* New York: W.W. Norton and Co. (referred to here as *RANF*).

REALISTIC CONFIGURATIONS

Indian English Fiction: Multiple Receptions and a Rejoinder

Posts and Signposts

Let me begin by creating a timeline of Indian English fiction and make an attempt to prepare a paradigm of fictional narratives by selecting two out of many texts from each of the eight consequential decades from 1930s onwards. I want to do so to be able to posit a case in favour of new Indian English fiction that has acquired greater space and critical attention compared with other literary forms and genres in any of the Indian languages. Beginning with *Rajmohan's Wife* (1864/1935)[1], Indian English fiction resumed its course, almost seven decades later, with *Swami and Friends* and *Kanthapura* in the 30s, *Twilight in Delhi* and *All About H. Hatterr* in the 40s, *Zohra* and *Train to Pakistan* in the 50s, *Sunlight on a Broken Column* and *A Bend in the Ganges* in the 60s, *The Day in Shadow* and *Fire on the Mountain* in the 70s, in order to reach a major landmark in *Midnight's Children* in the early 80s. With the movement well-defined and the map well-laid-out, while the 80s brought forth *The Circle of Reason* and *The Trotter-Nama* to the attention of the ever-growing number of discriminating readers, the 90s witnessed more celebrated ones in *A Suitable Boy* and *The God of Small Things*. The turn of the century enriched and problematized the scenario still further with *Family Matters* in 2002 and *The Namesake* in 2003, and *Gods Without Men, River of Smoke*, and *The Artist of Disappearance* in 2011. One waits for *A Suitable Girl* now, by Vikram Seth, which is likely to receive the same amount of hype, if not more, than A *Suitable Boy*.

I have selected twenty texts, to be precise, for their representational and narrative varieties, and to draw an atlas of the Indian narrative in the English language. Before we proceed, I should like to offer a clarification—the texts that do not figure in the aforementioned inventory of sorts are by no means negligible; in fact, they form the larger cartography of authors' imagination and help us chart out the route that this so-called 'postcolonial' Indian English fiction is taking now. All these texts, both listed or implied otherwise for their merit, offer a comprehensive view of the growth and maturity of Indian English fiction. As indicators of a major narrative tradition in the making, these texts underline the worth of a mode of expression that acquired its value through decades of engagement with the novelistic form and the experiential variety. I have drawn this framework with an intention to posit that the development of the Indian English fiction has been a steady one over the last eight decades. It has been a process of growth with patience, which may be marked in the manner the contours of the narrative grew with greater clarity, decade after decade. The plot thickened with the appearance of Salman Rushdie on the scene, who made bold experiments in the much-contested domain of language and decolonized it finally that only three authors—R.K. Narayan, Raja Rao, and G.V. Desani—had done before him. To my mind, Rushdie is the first sign post of the postmodern narrative after whom the generation that followed him in historical terms may rightly be called the post-Rushdie generation.

In the post-Rushdie generation, Indian English fiction has emerged as a site of major contestation in a wider variety of domains, compared with the more popular areas of study in other postcolonial sites. Apart from its intense engagement with form and language, it has indulged in a discourse concerning the evolution and efflorescence of the Indian nation state in relation to its local correlates, cosmopolitan connect, political dilemmas, social stratifications, cultural spaces, regional variations, historical configurations, and linguistic negotiations. The fictional works produced over all these decades have been preoccupied with ideological and stylistic issues, as much as they have been concerned with the problematic of textual formation or the evolution of narrative. With the growing number of fictional works published in each succeeding decade, this fictional harvest has become a subject of serious concern both for the author and the reader. This phenomenon accounts for the increasing number of serious critical studies over the past decade, compared with the studies carried out during the pre-Rushdie decades.[2] The critical reception of Indian English fiction is in itself a subject of closer scrutiny, as is the phenomenal growth and merit of the narrative itself which it attempts to situate. I would like to make a reading of some of them produced during the past one decade or so to chart out the way in which Indian English fiction may possibly be read in the future decades.

Reception

In *Myths of the Nation: National Identity and Literary Representation* (1999), Rumina Sethi engages with some of the most central issues relating to nation, identity, and literary representation, which have, in any case, acquired the status of serious discourse with the intervention of postcolonial theory. With a sound baggage of theoretical postulates available to her, she determines her points of reference in Indian freedom struggle, evolution of nationalism, nationalist ideology, and cultural iconography. She relates the evolution of Indian English narrative in a historical framework and accounts for the concrescence of myths and ideologies. In situating an earlier narrative like *Kanthapura* within such a framework, she also creates, by implication, a parameter for reading history, fiction, myth, identity, and ideology in postcolonial terms. It may be seen that texts drawing closely upon history lend themselves easily for underlining nationalistic discourse, which, in the case of India, is marked by multiple trajectories. In an earlier essay entitled 'The Writer's Truth: Representation of Identities in Indian Fiction' (1997), she had laid down her perspective in clear terms:

> I have argued against the polemics of nationalist sentiments generalized through religious and other stereotypes, and pointed to the paradoxical nature of nationalist writing that begins to assume identification with European accounts of India. The 'recovery' of an 'authentic' Indian

> tradition, it follows, has to be examined against Orientalism which has provided impetus to Indian writing to a large extent. (951–52)

A set of several Indian English narratives rooted in historical time like *Waiting for the Mahatma* (1955), *Midnight's Children* (1981), *The Shadow Lines* (1988), *Raj* (1989), *Delhi* (1990), *A Suitable Boy* (1993), *Looking Through Glass* (1995), and *A Fine Balance* (1995) raise a variety of such questions and make way for a complex interaction of ideological constructs and our reading of them in this perspective.

An entirely different point of view emerges in Makarand R. Paranjape's *Towards a Poetics of the Indian English Novel* (2000), where greater emphasis is laid on civilizational dimension of the narrative in terms of its genealogy. He goes back in time to revive the framework of *purushartha*s enunciated in *Manusmriti, Mahabharata*, and *Natya Shastra.* He makes a case for the espousal of *dharma, artha, kama, and moksha* as the proper ways of life and living. He further develops a thesis to categorize the narratives into imperial and sub-imperial with respect to their thematic concerns and methods of rendition. He casts a wider net to study the novelistic oeuvre spread over a larger historical period of a century and a half, and refers to a variety of concerns like form, Anglo-Indian and Indo-Anglian heritages, language, class, cultural bases, gender, and sociopolitical linkages. He carries forward his argument in yet another essay on 'Situating the Contemporary Indian (English) Novel' by making a case for the Indian narratology, cultural baggage, ideological structures, and the collectivity of Indian consciousness. While he denies that the categories of 'class, caste, religion, ideology, or even aesthetics' (9) in any of these categories would lead to 'flawed understanding' (9) of the Indian novel, he lays greater emphasis on 'national consciousness'. He puts forward his conclusive remarks in a comprehensive manner:

> To sum up the Indian novel, unlike the Western novel, is expressive not of individualism but of collectivity. As such, the Indian novel is best understood in its wider context of literary creativity in all Indian languages. Though written by various elite groups, the Indian novel is

> actually concerned with the experience and expression of this Indian collectivity. This collectivity may be defined as the modern Indian nation, which itself is a combination of usable elements from its past and critical elements of Western modernity. Since this collectivity is both the manifestation and the instrument of an ongoing civilizational enterprise, the novel also bears the self-representations and self-apprehensions of this civilizational enterprise. Taken together, the works that constitute this collectivity, regardless of their class, caste, gender, and other markers, are really parts of a wider and deeper narrative of the Indian consciousness. (12)

The stance so developed opens a huge vista for experiential, ideational, and creative negotiations by a huge variety of narrators, representing multiple associations with history and culture.

At yet another remove, we have Tabish Khair's *Babu Fictions: Alienation in Contemporary Indian English Novels* (2001) that develops the metaphor of 'babu' and 'coolie' as stereotypes to examine and develop upon the Marxian notion of 'alienation'. This metaphor serves as a major leitmotif of his work. He raises a basic question, dealt with many a time earlier, whether the stories of those who have limited access to English will have the narration in that language. In outlining the purpose of his work, he says:

> how [...] is it possible to write Indian fiction in English and fiction about Indians in English (henceforth 'Indian English fiction') without appropriating from a position of power or occluding Coolie/non-Babu realities and discourses? And to what extent does this socio-economic and discursive alienation shape Indian English fiction, including such common critical 'myths' as those of the 'interminable narration' of India, of 'hybridity', of chaos on the margins, of the centrality of the colonial, even of what passes for Indian English? How does it, for example, induce a certain style, a certain worldview, a certain approach, to say, the theme of the saint? These are some of the questions sought to be addressed in this book. (x)

He engages with issues of narratology and language, contexts of babu and babu fictions, the rhetoric of exile and belonging, and the ever-present dilemma of hybridity and cosmopolitanism. While doing this, he also engages with the questions of language and expression, spatial landscapes, and social positioning in relation to caste, class, and gender. Khair qualifies the authenticity of the narrative that has emerged in some of the major authors like Narayan, Rao, Naipaul, Rushdie, and Ghosh in a creative-cum-critical framework he has developed for his purpose.

We come across a well-defined and focussed study in Neelam Srivastava's *Secularism in the Postcolonial Indian Novel: National and Cosmopolitan Narratives in English* (2008). Instead of indulging in the general dynamics of Indian English fiction, she engages with the given issue of 'secularism', which calls for a scholarly engagement in the context of fictional narratives. She examines the various constructs of secularism as a backdrop of her study to discuss minority identity, syncretism, realism, historical configurations, language formation, the construct of nation, cosmopolitanism, and globalization. The notion of the secular Indian nation engages her attention insofar as she tries to locate it in selected fictional narratives of the consequential 80s and 90s. Her choice of authors—Seth, Rushdie, Ghosh, Tharoor, and Mistry—bear good testimony to her case, as they represent both the mainstream and minority notions of secularism. She lays down her aim as such:

> In this book I have attempted to show how the postcolonial Indian novel employs the dialogism of the novel form as a privileged space for the representation of different worldviews. Novelistic language is in clear contrast to the more monologic language of the social sciences (as they are constituted at present, though I have also mentioned the recent historiographical trends that seek to 'dialogize' history, such as *Subaltern Studies* collective). The novels discussed in this book directly address the problems arising from the conflict between previous religious and communitarian identities and the national secular identity that constitutionally defined Indian citizenship after 1947. This book has identified two representative positions in

> narratives of India in English. On the one hand, there is a secular rationalist position, which relegates religion to the 'private' narrative of the novel, and translates bhasha terms in a national metalanguage, namely English. On the other hand, there is an ongoing critique of Nehruvian secularism and an engagement with the complexities of religious belief in the sphere of novel. (182)

Her engagement with modern Indian history, the fall of the Nehruvian ideal, the promulgation of Emergency, the threat to secular democracy and India's pluralism, and the onset of postcolonial India and the postcolonial Indian impart a broader base to her study. She reads the selected fictional narratives as history written from both the colonialist and nationalist perspectives. The narrative of India written in the colonial language, becoming a part of Indian consciousness, mark this study in relation to identity formation, secularism, and the larger framework of cosmopolitanism. While developing a close focus on the problematic of secularism and minority-majority discourse, Srivastava develops a larger view of modern Indian history and its remarkably multifaceted narrative.

In his broad-based study of modernity, transmodernity, nationalism, time, language, reality, and a plethora of their constituents in *Genres of Modernity: Contemporary Indian Novels in English* (2008), Dirk Wiemann works out the complex projections of postmodernism and postcolonialism to study the already established Indian English fiction writers. In discussing Salman Rushdie, Shashi Tharoor, Vikram Chandra, Kiran Nagarkar, Vikram Seth, Amit Chaudhuri, Amitav Ghosh, and Arundhati Roy, he engages with many modes of narrating the Indian nation and Indian modernity. He develops his stance on theoretical parameters, and redefines modernity while interrogating the homogenizing Western constructs to bear upon the Indian post-coloniality and subalternity—'time' and 'space'—as represented in Indian English fiction. He states his critical intention unreservedly:

> What I offer is a reading of some exemplary novels from the corpus of Indian writing in English *not simply* from a white male European perspective, even though this is actually and undeniably the location I

> happen to inhabit. I am not trying to disavow that privileged position but I wish to question it as the ultimate and insurmountable horizon of my reading... (11)

Wiemann's is a study of the contemporary Indian modernist context by drawing upon historiography, postcolonial feminism, and a wide variety of social and political theory, as reflected in heterogeneous texts of sociological, historical, and philosophical nature from a perspective justifiably European but relevantly Indian.

Postcolonial Literary History and Indian English Fiction (2008) is Paul Sharrad's postcolonial reading of history, theory, and select fictional narratives. He resorts to epistemic constructions of diaspora, place, nation, and myth in relation to texts from a mix of authors like G.V. Desani, Namita Gokhale, Anita Desai, Ranga Rao, Bharati Mukherjee, Mukul Kesavan, Salman Rushdie, Amitav Ghosh, and Vikram Chandra. He explains his basic premise to develop his readings with the following logic:

> Rushdie's phrase 'Handcuffed to history' suggests the argument that Indian modernity is the product of a series of historical moments (1757, 1835, 1857, 1919, 1948, and so on) and the nation is an invention derived, in part, from overseas ideas of proper governance. From a literary perspective, it also hints at the submission of one kind of textuality and constructed reality (Literature) to another kind (History) accorded a far greater priority (in both senses of the word). Without history—the succession of past events—there would be no Indian novel, and certainly no Indian novel in English. (6)

Sharrad engages with the idea of history at multiple levels, as it seems to regulate Indian English writing which must attest to the historicity of the modern age. History, as such, is an aggregate of multiple manifestations of/in time reflected in a nation's ideological currents, political conflicts, and social and economic predicaments. Sharrad explores the interconnectedness of fiction with literary history, and literary history with historiography. He argues that since there is a tendency to situate or contextualize a literary text, there emerges a 'relativised conception of literary history and critical value' (18), even though it does not necessarily provide a strong theoretical framework.

Priyamvada Gopal's *The Indian English Novel: Nation, History, and Narration* (2009) lays down a broad map of Indian English fiction with reference to thematic concerns and narrative strategies employed. She classifies fictional types by choosing some of the important concerns of modern literary reading that include gender, ethnography, history, and nation. She qualifies her reading of nation by examining the idea of India in greater detail. By drawing upon a complex of narratives representing the heterogeneity of the Indian nation, she also examines some other seminal figures and moments in the history of the nation like Gandhi, the partition of India, and its legacies in terms of the historic migration of the people and its aftermath. The significance of the book lies in the way it examines various constructions of the nation as an idea, or as a complex site of realities, which characterize its varieties and contradictions. The book is an attempt at contextualizing the Indian English narrative in terms of the debates built in the texts.

The Postcolonial Indian Novel in English (2011) by Geetha Ganapathy-Doré is the latest of the studies carried out in the field. It once again takes the canonical figures into consideration from Desani to Jhumpa Lahiri. She charts out the development of the genre in terms of the major historical marks in literary history. While doing this, she also appropriates the postcolonial methods of approaching texts rooted in a given historical and cultural site. In order to develop this perspective, she marks the signposts that define the nature of narrative discourse. These include the identifying marks of colonization, the emergence of the Indian nation, gender and social stratifications, and finally the signifiers of globalization. Doré also underlines the intertextualities writ large in texts of multiple affiliations and of hybrid nature. This affords her with the possibility of examining the linguistic oeuvre of the texts that develop in shifting and polyvalent currents of signification in the process of textual formation. Beginning her study with a mapping of theoretical bases of postcolonialism, she goes on to examine the issues, mentioned earlier, to be able to bring her argument to a close with defining the essential markers of the postcolonial Indian fiction. This is an exhaustive reading of all major issues involved in reading Indian texts within the defined parameters of postcolonialism with additional space devoted to examining self-writing, the typicality of our palimpsest, the polyvalent nature of the narrative, and the given space. The book engages with the poetics of narration and the English language used in the narration with all its individualities, oddities, and specialities.

Rejoinder

There are quite a few issues that emerge from this overview of the select studies of Indian English fiction carried out from 1999 to 2011. While we come across a repetitive pattern in all these studies taken together, there are certain issues that are specific and have been dealt with theoretical rigour. In all these studies, however, there is a constant engagement with recurrent concerns in a huge variety of fictions, which include nation, nationalism, and nationalist discourse on the one hand, and colonialism, postcolonialism, history, and historiography on the other. These are studied with the tools of literary and postcolonial theory that frequently tend to situate ideology, subaltern, caste, class, gender, and identity in the texts of the typically Indian postcolonial site. The studies engage with the issues of hybridity, polyvalency, polyphony, and heterogeneity with equal attention, as they examine related issues like cosmopolitanism and globalism, and modernity and postmodernity. These issues emerge in all these studies like inevitable refrains, leading to conclusions closely bearing upon one another. Although each study presents an individual stance, the issues and texts chosen are almost always of the same stock and orientation. While Rumina Sethi, Tabish Khair, Neelam Srivastava, Dirk Wiemann, Paul Sharrad, Priyamvada Gopal, and Geeta Ganapathy-Doré approach texts and contexts as postcolonialists and theorists, Makarand R. Paranjape evolves his stance as an essentialist and taxonomist. While Sethi examines what she calls the myths of the nation, Khair makes a definite attempt to test his thesis on the problem of 'alienation' with a variety of arguments related to the metaphoric subaltern and the privileged. As Srivastava draws upon the theme of secularism to scan the Indian scenario socially, historically, and theoretically, Dirk moves towards a definite privileging of Western theory to mark modernism in a more liberal perspective. In Sharrad, there is an open space for historicizing the text and the context, but in both Gopal and Doré, there is a definite attempt to develop a broader view of this narrative by exploring history, culture, and the major marks of the Indian nation as a postcolonial site of theoretical inquiry. All these critics, drawing invariably upon Western theoretical constructs, develop their readings of the Indian texts and root them in the Indian context, but with essentially non-Indian tools. Perhaps, Makarand R. Paranjape is the only critic who, as an essentialist and taxonomist, chooses to develop a more fundamental view of this narrative by taking it back to civilizational bases. There is no denying the fact that while postcolonialist methodology is a more popular and a critically viable method to approach these texts, the validity of nativist position may not also be denied altogether. It, however, calls for a much more inclusive and broader base of cultural references than those often reiterated by the typical nativists.

Let me take this argument further by proposing some possible lines of inquiry for reading of the modern Indian English fiction. Let me propose that the post-Rushdie fiction has broken entirely fresh grounds not only for creative writing, as is generally supposed, but also for critical reading. This is clearly distinguishable from the fictional heritage handed down to us by the triumvirate of Anand, Narayan, and Rao, which most of the critics, one after another, have noted down from corresponding angles. Let me propose further that this fictional capital, which is of comparatively recent origin in the Indian English literary history, may not be quite properly and justifiably read by proposing and pursuing neat categories of authors, thematic registers, or stylistic methods. As categories can be limiting, and sometimes even formulaic and misleading, on account of their being too general and prescriptive in their very approach, they are liable to make way for partial or incomplete readings. For example, how can we negotiate with different types of authors, even though they may be categorized for certain broad similarities or correspondences? How can we, shall I ask, necessarily study Anand, Narayan, and Rao together, as is most often done, even though they are so different from each other in their essential concerns, both with experience and execution? Is their falling together in a certain historical period of time and their being canonical good enough reason for doing so? Can we justifiably club Amitav Ghosh and Vikram Seth together only because they are on the way to canonization? Similarly, can we really undertake the study of those like Rohinton Mistry, Shashi Tharoor, and Alllan Sealy together simply because they bear huge promises? Can we consider widely different authors like Mukul Kesavan, Amit Chaudhuri, and Upamanyu Chatterjee together, simply because they deserve serious critical attention? Similarly, can we possibly take the slew of diasporic authors like Bharati Mukherjee, Kiran Desai, Shauna Singh Baldwin, and Tabish Khair together, in spite of the fact that they construct their diasporas so differently from each other? In the same vein, can we sort the still uncategorized ones like Pankaj Mishra, Aravind Adiga, Anurag Mathur, Ruchir Joshi, Amit Chaudhuri, Sunetra Gupta, and so many others into one group for the simple reason that they are in good focus now and are making their ways together? Can we, by the same logic, read a different class of authors like Chetan Bhagat and Shobhaa De together because they have created a new readership of the young and racy professionals for themselves? Like the problems in the category of authors, there are problems with the category of themes as well. Can we, for example, study Shashi Deshpande only for representing women's voice and Githa Hariharan for unveiling the starkly political? In the same manner, is it possible to read Manohar Malgonkar or Khushwant Singh together only because they chose to write their own kinds of partition narratives, or Raja Rao, Amitav Ghosh, and Mukul Kesavan for constructing their own versions of history and nation? Similarly, can we study Kamala Markandaya for cross-cultural interaction alone, and Anand merely for his social realism? Further still, can we read Mistry and Attia Hosain only for constructing minority discourse, and Narayan and Rushdie for creating mythopoeic narratives of their own make and mix? In fact, the very categories of the historical, regional, political, philosophical, and such other fictions can be too constraining and severely limiting.[3] This would also apply in the case of another category representing experimentation in form and language that we have in Rushdie, Seth, and Ghosh. Studied in a given perspective, the worth of these authors could be appreciated, but only partially, as their other aspects would fall out of the critics' purview. Categories are easy to formulate; they pave ways for schematic studies, but they may also be constraining and partial. One might argue, however, that categorizations do make way for comparative studies, but it must also be stressed that comparative studies are not only a matter of creating categories and noting down similarities. In fact, they go much deeper to study impact and response, mark the evolution of form and meaning, and project interrelationships between constructs of various denominations in literary histories.

Instead of studying the modern Indian English fiction in terms of categories, it may be considerably rewarding to examine it in terms of how it carries forward a narrative tradition and how it makes innovations in the process of evolving and narrating the story. The new fiction may be read better by projecting the merits of non-linearity and hybridity that it often draws upon in order to evolve a form entirely different from the ones evolved and practiced earlier. It may be read for its treatment of the material as multiple texts of history, culture, location, ideology, and gender; for linguistic intermixing; for Englishing the native and nativizing the English. The narrative strategies may be identified to mark the characteristically Indian narrative in terms of its nature and character. It may also be read in relation to genealogy of Indian as well as Anglophone fiction, and how it projects the Indian postmodern and the Indian postcolonial condition. It must be noted that our marks of postmodernism and postcolonialism are remarkably different from the constructions of postmodernism and postcolonialism developed by the Western academia. The reading of Indian English fiction has to be rooted in and related with Indian literary history, Indian space and landscape, the idea of India, and its secular nature. It has to be examined for its linguistic intermixing, polyphonic ensemble, polyvalent nature of text, as also its syncretism, intertextuality, and hybridity, and most importantly, its narrative structure and character. This fiction has to be read for its unique process of textual formation and evolution of the narrative as social and cultural discourse. An Indian text is, by nature, multiple in its essential character, which comes into being through the principle of interface at the communal and cultural levels, rather than strictly regional, rural, metropolitan, provincial, national, or even cosmopolitan levels.

While there are certain very special ways in which Indian English fiction may be studied, one may do well to consider its narratology as a separate area of inquiry. K. Ayyappa Paniker has identified ten models of Indian narratology[4] as Vedic, Purana, Itihasa, Srnkhala, Anyapadesa, Mahakavya, Buddhist, Dravidian, Multiple, and Mixed, representing folk/tribal and miscellaneous narratives. Based on these, he concludes the essential traits of Indian narratology in ten different ways, which he chooses to designate as Interiorization, Serialization, Fanatasization, Cyclicalization, Allegorization, Anonymization, Elasticization of Time, Spatialization, Stylization, and Improvization. I would posit that Indian narrative is a different proposition compared with the monolingual and monocultural narratives of the West. It acquires its mark through its multiple histories, its cultural multiplicity, linguistic variety, regional exclusivity, and authorial individuality. It is rooted in the great traditions of the ancient, the medieval, and modern India. It is traceable in the shifting methods of narration ever since the *shruti* and *smriti* traditions of constructing and disseminating religio-philosophical narratives like the Vedas, the Upanishads, the *Ramayana*, and the *Mahabharata*. It is richly embodied in *dharma shastra*, *itihasa*, *purana*, *sutra*, *agama*, and *darshan*. Apart from Sanskrit, Prakrit, and Pali, there are extremely rich traditions available in Buddhist tales, Perso-Arabic narratives, and in the huge ensemble of narratives from Dravidian languages. These narratives matured into yet another kind of secular narratives, as in *Kathasaritsagara* and *Panchatantra*. The themes and methodologies of narration underwent further changes in medieval India, which saw life in a state of constant flux and experienced the emergence of new sociopolitical dynamics. With medieval India becoming a repository of multiple discourses marked by rich interaction between

Hinduism and Islam, a plethora of Bhakti–Sufi narratives came into being. This is well exemplified by narratives from Guru Nanak in Punjabi, Mirabai in Rajasthani, Kabir in Khariboli, Tukaram in Marathi, Tulsidas in Awadhi, Narsinh Mehta in Gujarati, and many more from many more linguistics clusters of India. The coming together of Awadhi, Braj, and Khariboli led further to the evolution of new narratives, new literary equations, and new literary histories. Representing a vibrant kaleidoscope of languages and literatures, medieval India saw the emergence of secular literatures and narrative modes in all Indian languages, irrespective of regions and faiths. Folk narratives and *dastan* are the other rich fares to negotiate with, along with the plethora of narratives that came into being ever since the consequential era of print capitalism. Coming to modern British and post-British India, we come across extremely complex predicaments in the history of the nation. It faces multiple issues characteristic of a multicultural site, of a much contested civil society, and of complex governance since independence. It has seen the rise and consequential revision of Nehruvian agenda, based on economic development and social equality. It has passed through the oppressive days of Emergency, the instability of the Indian state since the 1970s, the rise of extremist parties since the 1980s, and the never-ending communal strife since India's independence. The discontents of the modern nation state are contained in the politics of ethnicity, caste, class, community, and regional separatism on the one hand, and economic liberalization and globalization on the other.

India is a site of multiple and unending stories—of long *katha*s and *dastan*s, of smart snippets told in a jiffy by a playful companion, a dreamy tale recounted by a grandmother to a mesmerized child, or a most interesting story narrated by a master narrator at the village *chaupal*. These stories, written in black and white, or kept to heart, are narrated to entertain, instruct, or win a contest. They are available in various linguistic, cultural, and regional spaces. Very few of them, however, are available in the English language. There are stories at each step, in each region, in each language, and in each historical period. Indian English writers are yet to open their doors to these fictions of the past and the present. Indian English fiction writers are in a position of great advantage like no other writer of any postcolonial site. They carry with them the heritage of at least one or two more languages and literary cultures, apart from the English. They are the ones who may narrate the stories of this great variety, and they are the ones who have more than one narrative tradition to fall back upon in order to enrich their own narratives. Indian English writers may distinguish themselves and their chosen genres by repositioning and recontextualizing themselves. Their significance would lie in evolving multiple ways of narrating the nation from many more perspectives still not appropriated. The new history of Indian English writing lies in the belly of a future that is replete with great possibilities. Perhaps, the fictions of future would call for new parameters of reading, adding perhaps a fresh perspective to postcolonialism.

Endnotes

1. Supposed to be the first Indian English novel, Bankimchandra Chatterjee's *Rajmohan's Wife* was serialized in a Calcutta weekly *Indian Field* in 1864. This novel also happened to be the first and the only novel by him, although he wrote fourteen novels in Bangla, which was his mother tongue. In 1935, almost seven decades later, Brajendra Nath Chatterjee published *Rajmohan's Wife* as a complete text. In 1996, Meenakshi Mukherjee brought it back to modern readership with a critical foreword, afterword, notes, and bibliography, which situates the novel in a framework and a perspective and underlines its historic significance.
2. There have not been many sound critical studies of Indian English fiction in the past. Probably, the best of the earlier studies is Meenakshi Mukherjee's *The Twice Born Fiction: Themes and Techniques of the Indian Novel in English* (1971), which was followed by Uma Parmeswaran's *A Study of Representative Indo-English Novelists* (1976). William Walsh's edited *Readings in Commonwealth Literature* (1973) and C.D. Narasimhaiah's *Swan and the Eagle: Essays on Indian English Literature* (1969) deal partly with Indian English fiction, but they present incisive early studies in the area.
3. M.K. Naik mentions categories of Indian English fiction as regional, historical, political, philosophical, etc. and laments the lack of a comprehensive development of English novel in India. In making his case, he frequently draws upon Western examples and refers to known and little-known paucity of Indian English fiction. See M.K. Naik and Shyamala A. Narayan, 'Epilogue: Thoughts on the Present Discontents Concerning Recent Indian English Fiction,' in *Indian English Fiction: A Critical Study* (New Delhi: Pencraft International, 2009).

4. A very succinct account of Indian narrative may be found in K. Ayyappa Paniker, *Indian Narratology* (Delhi: Sterling Publishers, 2003).

References

Dirk, Wiemann. 2008. *Genres of Modernity: Contemporary Indian Novels in English.* Amsterdam, New York: Rodopi.

Ganapathy-Doré, Geetha. 2011. *The Postcolonial Indian Novel in English.* Newcastle upon Tyne: Cambridge Scholars Publishing.

Gopal, Priyamvada. 2009. *The Indian English Novel: Nation, History, and Narration.* Oxford: OUP.

Khair, Tabish. 2001. *Babu Fictions: Alienation in Contemporary Indian English Novels.* Delhi: OUP.

Paniker, Ayyappa. 2003. *Indian Narratology.* Delhi: Sterling Publishers.

Paranjape, Makarand R. 2000. *Towards a Poetics of the Indian English Novel.* Shimla: Indian Institute of Advanced Study.

———. 2009. 'Situating the Contemporary Indian (English) Novel.' In *Another Canon: Indian Texts and Traditions in English.* New Delhi: Anthem Press.

Riemenschneider, Dieter. 2005. *The Indian Novel in English: Its Critical Discourse 1934–2004.* Jaipur: Rawat Publications.

Sethi, Rumina. 1999. *Myths of the Nation: National Identity and Literary Representation.* Oxford: Clarendon Press.

———. 'The Writer's Truth: Representation of Identities in Indian Fiction.' *Modern Asian Studies* 31 (4) (1997): 951–65.

Sharrad, Paul. 2008. *Postcolonial Literary History and Indian English Fiction.* Amherst, New York: Cambria Press.

Srivastava, Neelam. 2008. *Secularism in the Postcolonial Indian Novel: National and Cosmopolitan Narratives in English.* London and New York: Routledge.

Premchand: Premises and Problems

Premises: Time and Place

If dates are important, they must not be so only to help us contextualize historically but to seek greater meaning behind and beyond them. In the particular case of Premchand[1] (1880–1936), dates acquire enormous significance for one prime reason—he wrote at a time when India was rewriting its history, both in terms of how it was dealing with the British empire, and how one of its socially conscious authors, who wrote in two major languages of north India, Urdu and Hindi, was making an individual effort to discover a different language and narrative in order to relate with a readership that was still fed upon the typically romantic notion of literature and literary readership. This must make Premchand a very innovative author. The account of his achievements is thus one of considerable significance in how he determined his basic aim and how he strove all along to meet the expectations he set for himself in various roles as a writer and a commentator on life and letters. Apart from creating short and long fictional narratives, he also committed himself to developing serious discourses in his non-fiction prose that included his sociopolitical essays, editorials, notes, book reviews, and letters on personal and topical issues. This made all the difference towards making him a canonical figure that he became in his lifetime, and which also made way for the huge critical attention that he received from Hindi, Urdu, and English readers and critics ever since his death.[2]

It should be significant to note here that Premchand pursued two very distinct careers in his life rather simultaneously: one concerned his perseverance to seek a livelihood as an individual, and the other related his intellectual growth as a writer. The first one was quite certainly much too variegated and painfully demanding in physical terms, but the second one showed steady growth and remarkable worth. It is in this particular respect that his significance as a socially conscious individual and a literary artist can be appreciated. An individual of virile sociopolitical and literary imagination, he matured over the years both as a social philosopher and a creative writer. The evolution of his scientific temper, his acute realism, and his creative skills may best be comprehended in the background of the broader predicament that he suffered since his formative years. Beginning as an avid reader in the early twenties, he emerged as a keen observer of the conditions both in and outside India. This was completely revolutionary in itself, as he was redefining the role of author, literature, and reader as well as of society, politics, and the economics of survival.

In order to put Premchand in a context, let me consider some of the major premises he envisaged in the process of finding his own moorings. An iconoclast at core, it is only natural that he should have moulded his thought and action in response to the dynamics of his times. It should, thus, be pertinent to mention, for example, that even while he critically assessed the role of the Arya Samaj towards the eradication of the prevailing social evils, he grew in the mould of a typical nationalist and opposed the British rule over India. In continuation of this, and in behaving like a committed nationalist, he worried little about reprimands and bans imposed by the British and continued his political and literary preoccupations with conviction. Similarly, while he sympathized with the Russian Revolution (1917) and refused to be a part of the celebrations at the end of the World War I (1918), the massacre at Jallianwala Bagh (13 April 1919) inflamed his imagination and the Gandhian philosophy kept him positively oriented. It was quite in keeping with his ways of pursuing his preoccupations and expressing his conviction that he decided to resign from the government job to sell spinning wheels and to support the Non-Cooperation Movement. It was in this very spirit that he also decided to decline the title of Rai

Bahadur and write extensively on nationalist movement, Hindu–Muslim unity, and the possibility of Hindi and Urdu blending together to become India's national language. Although far removed from home, but with bearings on affairs back home, things as varied but as significant as Simon Commission, the rise of Hitler, the Round Table Conferences (1930–32), and the working of the British Labour party caught his attention. Similarly, issues as divergent as capitalism, internationalism, and Soviet Russia on the one hand, and zamindari system, Hindu society, and swaraj on the other engaged him seriously. He pondered and struck a balance, in his own imagination, with as diverse personalities as Mazzini and Garibaldi, Tilak and Gokhale, Vivekananda and Tolstoy, and Bhagat Singh and Gandhi. As Premchand passed through a meandering passage, he touched many a pole before he arrived at the final destination. This was not the arrival of an Arya Samaji or a socialist, a Marxist or a Gandhian, a nationalist or an advocate of communal harmony, or linguistic unity, but of an iconoclast. He clearly showed the signs of a composite personality, and his evolution can be appreciated as organic in the best sense of the word. His interests were all-inclusive rather than unitary, his growth was round rather than flat, and his words and deeds were those of a visionary rather than of an unimaginative and derivative individual.[3]

In the backdrop of this sociopolitical context, it would only be appropriate to consider how he tried and found his literary mooring in the way he explored himself. For a curious individual graduating into an author, it was only proper that he determined his path with an amount of clarity and certainty. It would thus be important to note that he charted his literary path with remarkable discrimination. He realized quite early in his formative years that his literary and non-literary predecessors, whom he had to fall back upon, could bring him only a truncated view of the society that was at best unitary rather than composite. There were literary writers given to creating fanciful worlds in fanciful language, or there were others who pursued their sociopolitical preoccupations which varied considerably from his own. Premchand was different from both these types of writers in the sense that he chose to obliterate the distinction between the literary and the non-literary. As times had changed and demanded an altered perspective, it was only natural for him not to separate the sociopolitical domain from the literary one, as the two, he justifiably thought, were inextricably linked and could be separated only at a big risk. His approval of the founding of the Indian Progressive Writers' Association (although he did not like the word 'progressive', as writers could not be writers if they were not progressive) and his association with it only explains his basic premise: the two domains representing the social and the literary must stay together to create a sound basis for a harmonious social order and respectable human existence. This is extended further in how he looked at the question of the national language, which, he thought, may flourish best not in the division of Urdu and Hindi, but in a happy amalgamation of the two and the formation of a new language called Hindustani. Premchand was a healthy negotiator between heterogeneities and believed in reconciliation with profit and without cost.

To put the aforesaid argument in perspective, it would be appropriate to refer to his presidential address at the Progressive Writers' Conference held in Lucknow on 9 April 1936, exactly six months before his death. Coming at the fag end of his career, after Premchand had already passed through the travails of his life as an individual and an author, this address is of immense significance as it sums up his major concerns as a committed author and literary activist. He defined the basic aim of literature with reference to its major constituents that included his reflections on the role and nature of language, concept of beauty, definition of author, meaning of realism, and significance of change and progress. It would be relevant to quote from the end of his address, which refers to his major concerns and also defines the role of literature, author, and the recipient of the author's work. He said with hitting precision:

> The only literature that will pass our test is that which contains *high thinking, a sense of freedom*, the *essence of beauty*, the *soul of creativity* and the light that emanates from *the truths of life*, a literature which instills in us *dynamism; not sleep*; because *to go on sleeping now would be a sign of death.*[4] [Emphasis added]

Although the address was prescriptive in many respects, it was also definitive in the manner he defined language as a means (and not as an end), literature as criticism of life, writer as one who gives shape to an image, beauty as a creation of harmony, and individual as an integral part of society. These were significant views that he evolved with patience, and over a long period of time, on contemplating over the issues of life and art. Considering his contemporary context, it may not be possible to disagree with his predilections, as he was essentially given to developing his own ideological bases for the expression of his literary and non-literary preoccupations. Subsequently, Premchand emerged as a figure to reckon with, and he still remains one who made immense sense then as he makes now. It would be proper to quote the following passage that sums up his image and his reception quite appropriately:

> In many respects, Munshi Premchand has become a hoary icon, a sometime sentimentalist from a bygone age, firmly established in the dubious immortality of a curricular classic. He has become part of our cultural shorthand, the familiar and rubbed-down currency of our social imagination. Embalmed in textbooks, routinely rehearsed in classroom and examination hall, Premchand is obviously dead—rendered innocuous by being made part of the deadening and hypocritical tedium of the education system. To the young, his idealistic vision may well appear merely sentimental—and the icon 'Premchand', almost complicit with the establishment that honours him, like a distant ancestor who is both remembered and, in the very act of remembering, forgotten.[5]

In view of the given passage, it may be justifiably asserted that Premchand stands at a vital juncture of a certain kind of prevalent sociopolitical condition on the one side, and a soon-to-be-outdated literary tradition on the other. Both of these had to undergo stages of transformation without much delay, as would appear if examined critically, and Premchand had to emerge as a harbinger of new consciousness. It would be appropriate here to consider some of his relevant works to demonstrate how he developed as a socially committed being and a creative writer ever since he started writing in the first decade of the twentieth century. His writings that reflected his views on society, culture, literature, politics, and imperial design appeared in a number of journals, the more important of them being *Zamana* (Urdu), *Hans* (Hindi), *Jagran* (Hindi), *Awaz-e-Khalq* (Urdu), *Pratap* (Hindi), *Madhuri* (Hindi), *Kaleem* (Urdu), *Samalochak* (Hindi), and *Asmat* (Urdu).[6] For some of these he wrote quite regularly, and they ultimately came to be associated with his name in a big way. He worked in multiple domains that may be broadly classified as political, sociocultural, and literary. In the political domain, he wrote extensively on India's struggle for independence, capitalism, Swadeshi Movement, swaraj, and satyagraha, and by implication, nationalism. His ideas and ideals got reflected in a huge variety of literary and extra-literary writings, where he obliterated the distinction between a socially and politically engaged being and a creative writer. Quite unlike a political activist, a social reformer, or a philosopher, he worked like an ordinary human being with his pen in hand towards moulding public opinion and creating a healthy human condition that had been severely damaged by imperialist powers.

Premchand firmly believed that the struggle for independence would bear fruits only if the society could understand its own drawbacks and make efforts to meet its responsibility. He critically viewed the extent of success that the call for non-cooperation could achieve, and he knew the problems in the way of practical politics. He could realize that personal considerations of people concerning their security in the event of violence would keep them away from meeting their commitments. In saying so, he also exhorted them to action, as it would lead to a secure social order and economic prosperity. He considered that people still were the victims of a seeming clash between rationality and call of the soul. He also viewed the clash between the landed gentry and the peasantry, and firmly believed that the bugle of democracy had been blown and it would surely be heard all over. He imagined a collective community that did not discriminate on the lines of religion and language. Premchand held a holistic view of life and society and thought that independence could only be achieved with honest participation and proper understanding of the conditions around. He spoke much more clearly, as if presenting a manifesto for freedom, when he advocated for communal peace and the need for propaganda in the villages to prepare people for realizing the significance of freedom and for making their collective efforts to achieve it.

Premchand stood for complete independence as against dominion status that would only be a political tool to divert and delay the materialization of independence. Swaraj, he believed, was a movement in the interest of the common people to secure common good and to reap the benefits of political freedom. The best beneficiaries of swaraj, he thought, would be the poor, the honest, and the most sincere, while those who thrived on exploitation, injustice, and pretence would be the worst hit by this revolution.[7] Premchand worked through persuasion in the typical humanist tradition rather than raise slogans and coax people into action. The concept of swaraj went well with the concept of the swadeshi, which created a fair space for indigenous products. The swadeshi movement could succeed only when the producer and the buyer joined their hands in selling and buying the product with the same spirit, that is, the producer offered the material in good spirit and at an affordable rate, and the buyer bought it with the same spirit of respect and acceptance. It had to be a matter of mutual acceptance and self-esteem, and it was symbolic of one's regard for the nation. The swadeshi material could be bought and promoted even if it cost higher than the foreign products, as it showed trust in one's own potential.[8]

Just as swaraj was a political value system for Premchand, satyagraha too had its much deeper implications than the usual. It symbolized a philosophical system that had a liberal space for broader understanding and larger human catholicity. It represented a principle of life and living, respect for human dignity and sympathy, clemency and dissent, and regard for truth and justice.[9] He naturally went against political, imperialist, and economic exploitations as the means of exercising power by dividing communities to retain control over the colonized. It is in this context that his concern for the role of the Congress party towards ensuring social justice and political freedom, and the role that Gandhi and Nehru played in this direction become important.[10] It is in this overall perspective that Premchand's concept of nationalism may also be assessed, which is not based on narrow or romantic notions but on a broader philosophy of homogeneity, balance, and accommodation.[11] Although the concept of the nation state had not yet emerged when he wrote, he looked towards a condition that approximated closely the very concept of the modern nation state and the role of the individual in that complex sociopolitical construction.

Given this background, it was only natural for Premchand to make a choice for socialism rather than capitalism. He wrote openly against the European capitalist practice of production and supply which resorted to cutting down on production when demand fell, and for increasing the same when the demand rose. The idea was to ensure the accumulation of capital and retain control over the market. He took it to be a general phenomenon and severely criticized similar practices being followed in India. He did not hesitate in disapproving of even Lakshmi, the Goddess of Wealth, and equated Her with a witch, as She had brought greater harm to society than the devil himself. His advocacy for a collective society, he believed, would keep those away who had monopolized the power to exploit that came naturally with the acquisition of money and material. He had a natural abhorrence for the amassers of wealth and their pretension for art and culture. He looked at society as divided between two classes of the producer and the exploiter, who is incarnated as a capitalist and who could only promote evils like repression, ill will, dishonesty, falsity, and other such evils that corroded the society.[12] Many other related issues engaged his attention all through his literary career, which include his concern for exploitation, picketing ordinance, need for unity, round-table conferences, economic independence, imperial policies of retaining dominance, British legal system and their degradation, etc.[13]

Premchand's interest in the sociocultural domain was as intense as it was in the political domain. In fact, they may not be separated as they complement each other and largely reflect upon his literary writing. He believed in a collective community constituted of Hindus and Muslims, a common language composed of Hindi and Urdu, and a common predicament born out of the prevailing social, political, and economic ethos. He believed that social justice could be ensured only when people of different classes and different faiths, raising inflammable slogans of 'Har Har Mahadev' and 'Allah-hu-Akbar' in charged times, could learn to live together in harmony. He wished to break stereotypes that put a particular faith and its followers in a predetermined frame. His criticism of Chatursen Shastri's book *Islam ka Vish Vriksha* (The Poison Tree of Islam) (1933), irrespective of the onslaught he had to put up with, bears this out too well. When he said that communalism swears by culture and it took both the communities to task for their failings, he was making a bold proclamation that was as relevant when he said so as it is today. Hindu–Muslim relationship remained a major concern through his career. While the temple and the mosque became his metaphor for this problem, he wrote extensively on the dearth of human values and the bane of communalism, the orthodox pundit and the mullah, the Quranic message of unity and the Prophet of Islam, Hindu Sabha and Muslim League, and persons like Gandhi and Nehru, Mohammad Ali and Shaukat Ali, and the bitter critics like Chatursen Shastri and Bhai Parmanand.[14]

Premchand thought that the curse of untouchability was corroding the Indian society, and he revered Gandhi for the efforts he made to save the society from this curse. He stood for the rights of the Harijans to enter the temple which had become controversial and went against the very spirit of general humanity.[15] Along with the Harijans, he was also concerned with the problem of the peasantry with equal intensity. He believed in Bolshevik Revolution and thought that the future belonged to the peasants and workers who could not be neglected any longer. He lamented over the lack of organization in them and wrote about their misfortunes, solutions for their misery, and the need for consolidation of land.[16] Similarly, much before issues relating to gender discrimination caught academic attention, he thought of it and advocated for women's emancipation. He wrote about their rights as equal to those of their counterparts, the rising number of divorces, the new consciousness among the prostitutes to redeem themselves, the miseries of widowhood, the curse of dowry, and widow marriage.[17] All these issues project the image of a person who was deeply touched by the major concerns confronting the society. He attended to these issues in his essays and editorials, as we have seen before, but he chose to do so in his fictional writings as well.

Problems: Fiction and Non-Fiction

Let us now consider Premchand's literary heritage and his improvisations to create his own kind of a literary world. We have instances from his career that he read voraciously from the available literary sources in Urdu, which consisted largely of quixotic, magical, and adventurous tales reflecting abundant exuberance, surfeit of passion, and magic of romantic imagination. Known in Urdu as *dastan*, *qissa/fasana*, and *tilism*, they were orally narrated and then recorded as literary texts to engross the readers and keep them mesmerized with lavish linguistic fare and emotional turns of events. So curious and enthused he was by these literary feats that at an early age of thirteen, he started reading a version of the classic text of this kind called *Tilism-e Hoshruba* (2009), spread over thousands of pages. He came later to the fictional narratives of Pandit Ratan Nath Dhar Sarshar and Deputy Nazir Ahmad Dehlvi, who wrote during the late nineteenth century, and Mirza Muhammad Hadi Ruswa, who wrote just before Premchand started writing his own stories. His readings also included the Urdu translations of widely divergent texts like George W.M. Reynolds's extremely popular saga called *The Mysteries of the Court of London* (1848–1856), written during the mid-nineteenth century, and the Puranas, published by the legendary Newal Kishore Press of Lucknow. As he was swayed by his fancy to read fictional narratives, he managed to get them with great difficulty in order to discover his own possible way of constructing and narrating a story. All these texts that Premchand could lay his hands upon were essentially rhetorical in nature, undefined in form, and filled with fanciful similes and metaphors, and sentimental exuberance of the heroes and the heroines.

Such was the literary tradition that Premchand inherited. He scrutinized it with the curiosity of a literary quester, but found little in them to draw upon. So, he developed a narrative of his own kind which would be carved along a different line. This was significant insofar as it showed that he had an acute critical sense and was going to chart his path in his own manner. There is no doubt about the fact that his first few stories, written originally in Urdu during the first decade of the twentieth century, like 'Duniya ka Sabse Anmol Ratan' (published in his first collection of stories *Soz-e Watan* in 1908), 'Ishq-e Duniya aur Hubb-e Watan' (published in Urdu monthly journal *Zamana* in April 1908 and collected *in Soz-e Watan* in 1908), and 'Yehi Mera Watan Hai' (published in his first collection of stories *Soz-e Watan* in 1908) seem to be stemming from these sources in many respects. Premchand started writing his stories just six years after the first Urdu story 'Nashe ki Pehli Tarang' was written by Sajjad Haider Yaldram in 1900. As Premchand was laying the foundations of storytelling in Urdu, his stories could not have been much different from a novice's work. It is not surprising that he fumbled for an idiom and groped for a form in the beginning of his literary career. The important point is that he took little time to realize that he needed to discover a different language and a distinct form of his own. In this respect, his growth was rather swift as can be gathered from the stories he wrote only a few years later. Instead of going for the long-winded and exaggerated narrative, he had realized the significance of telling a precise tale with more realistic characters, plausible turns of events, and in a less embellished kind of language. This was his journey towards acquiring a style and a voice of his own, and this is surely one of the features that distinguished him as a story writer of the modernist temper.

Just as reading was a passion, writing too became a passion with Premchand. Both became a part of his make-up, and both went hand in hand as he developed his own world view. It is in this process that Premchand came to realize that literature represented life and was, at best, a criticism of life. This is precisely why he had little consideration for the purely romantic and the exuberant in literature, and this is also why he insisted upon altering the concept of beauty which, he thought, lay in the starker realities of life than in the visually beautiful and the emotionally fascinating. He held a robust and masculine attitude towards life, which is explained largely in how he chose to engage with the more engrossing realities of life as he advanced in his career. Apart from the ideas expressed in his presidential address about literature in general, he expressed himself in equally strong terms in his long and short essays on his own poetics and practice, as also of other writers and works of Urdu, Hindi, and Sanskrit. He was centrally preoccupied with the pace of literature in his times and the possible path it might take in future. As such, he thought it proper to develop a holistic view as he wrote on both the contemporary and the classical writers of the present and the past, and wanted the Urdu–Hindi readers to acquire a broader and comparative perspective. This was like educating the reader and creating new canons for an objective literary reading and appreciation. As such, he emerged as a conscious author, the architect of a virile text, and the creator of a conscious reader. This put him in a separate class, where he stood by himself without a companion who could even remotely approximate his thematic preoccupations and literary techniques.

Premchand's literary oeuvre is both varied and rich. It is worth asserting that he may not be justifiably read in isolation as a story writer or a novelist, but only in totality as an editor, a playwright, a writer for children, an essayist, a reviewer, a translator, a letter writer, a biographer, and a fiction writer to top them all. All these identities merged well in him, as each one served as an extension of the other, and all of them, taken together, complimented one another towards constructing his identity as a writer and a social philosopher of his time. It is equally important to note that just as his various writings have to be read together, his Urdu and Hindi writings must also be read along with each other. He was a littérateur in a broader sense of the word, a littérateur who was given to projecting a larger view of life and letters during the first three decades of the twentieth century. We have examined his oeuvre in relation to his major commitments, as reflected in his non-fictional writing, but it is also important to develop a perspective on how he approached these issues in his letters to some of the important figures of his time.

In most of his letters, Premchand seems to be preoccupied with the writing and reception of his fictional works, as also his financial gains and losses, but he also chose to express his aesthetic principles in clear terms in many of them. In a letter, written early in his career (1911–12), to Daya Narayan Nigam, the editor of *Zamana*, where he published frequently and respected the editor greatly, he wrote, 'For its theme, literature is concerned with morals and manners, scrutiny of emotions, revelation of realities, and expression of the conditions of heart and soul.'[18] In this letter, he is extremely critical of artificial exuberance, emotional exaggeration, sheer romantic outbursts, and the traditional themes and techniques, as employed in poetry. This speaks of his intent to create space for masculinity in literary writing. In another letter to the manager of *Zamana*, written about eight to nine years later in 1920, he said as much, 'I want literature to be masculine. Whatever be its form, I have no liking for the feminine.'[19] He explained that it was only a part of his nature, and that is why he did not like most of Tagore's poems. He maintained this stance in the next decade as well. While responding to a fellow Hindi writer Harihar Nath's story, which he found to be too poetic, passionate, and sentimental, he wrote in 1930:

> If your taste ties that way, do it by all means but avoid sentimentalism. A creative mind should create—what? Situations to illustrate characters. A young man should write in an optimistic mood, his optimism should be infectious, it should infuse the same spirit in others. I think the highest aim of literature is to uplift, elevate. Even our realism should not lose sight of this fact.[20]

As would appear from the graph of his development as a writer, Premchand paid premium to creativity as a mark of modernity and believed in exploring new areas of experience with certain depth and precision. He made this quite known in the early 30s, when he commented on the lack of these in his fellow Hindi writers whom he addressed as Jainendra, Sudarshan, Kaushik, Ugra, Jaishankar Prasad, and Rajeshwari. More than an objective criticism on the contemporaries, it was a way of defining one's own terms of development. This is borne out by his acknowledgment of Tolstoy, Victor Hugo, and Romain Rolland as major influences on him. As he looked for an ideal condition, he looked for ideal characters also who could constitute a remarkably fresh world view. 'I have in each of my novels,' he wrote to Indranath, 'an ideal character, with human failings as well as virtues, but essentially ideal. In *Premashram* there is Premshankar, in *Rangabhoomi* there is Surdas, similarly in *Kayakalp* there is Chakradhar, in *Karmabhoomi* there is Amarkant.'[21] This was recapitulating his idealism in 1934. While assessing his role as a writer, he wrote the same year to the publisher of the Urdu magazine *Nairang-e Khayal* with a sense of finality, 'My stories are often based on observations. I try to infuse some dramatic element in them. I do not write stories only for describing an event. I want to express some philosophical and emotional reality in them. Unless I find a ground, or a basis for all these, I do not lift my pen.'[22] These are the views of a writer who was approaching the end of his literary career, and who had obliterated the distinction between genres and forms insofar as the expression of his basic intents was concerned. Shortly before his death, he wrote to Banarasi Das in a philosophical vein in 1935:

> I am growing younger everyday....Of course there is a healthy youth and a mad youth. Healthy youth consists of a progressive and optimistic view of life, at the same time avoiding pitfalls. Mad youth consists of rashness and exaggeration of one's own capacities and dreams. I have not ceased dreaming and am a bit rash as well. The exaggeration has happily gone. So even of madness I have the better part.[23]

Premchand's fiction and non-fiction bear closely upon one another. While fiction appealed to one section of the readers, his other writings found space in yet another set of recipients. While his fiction was an imaginative reconstruction of the actualities of life, his non-fiction engaged with those actualities of life in more concrete terms. Real characters engaged with the questions of swaraj and swadeshi, *shuddhi* and communal harmony, satyagraha and peasant activism, morals and manners, creeds and credo, and margins and peripheries acquired remarkable proportions in his stories and novels. These characters annotated the life they lived and the conditions they engaged with. In trying to create a new condition for life and living, Premchand was also formulating a new condition for the acceptance of his writings. In this respect, he was a revolutionary both in life and art.

If one were to appreciate Premchand's perspectives on life and times, one could do so even at the risk of sounding traditional and prescriptive by broadly dividing his stories into thematic clusters or categories. This would help us understand his basic commitments and to develop a broader understanding of his oeuvre. It may thus be asserted that his stories broadly fall into three categories: (a) morals and manners, (b) creeds and credo, and (c) margins and peripheries. While stories about morals and manners focus on ethics, conscience, and integrity, those about creeds and credo concern spiritual, material, traditional, and national issues, and the ones about margins and peripheries relate with the worlds of the subaltern, women, children, and animals.

Premchand was a realist at core. He perceived his plot with some of the real and imagined characters and situations that underlined his basic affiliation to realism and reality. While he was creatively real in some of his stories like 'Meri Pehli Rachna' (1930) and 'Adeeb Ki Izzat' (1931), he was imaginatively so in many others like 'Poos Ki Raat' (1930) and 'Muft Ka Yash' (1934). His stories concerning morals and manners underline issues relating to integrity and scruples ('Paap Ka Agnikund', 1910), ethics of life and living ('Panch Parmeshwar', 1916), crime and punishment ('Pandit Mote Ram Ki Diary', 1934), deceit and duping ('Swang', 1935), as also the awakened human conscience ('Namak Ka Daroga', 1915). Premchand's constructions of the subaltern have been much debated upon, and the stories falling in this category have also been frequently referred to in general and critical discussions ('Thakur Ka Kuan', 1924). In several other stories, he relates with the very innocence of beings and constructs images of childhood ('Idgah', 1933) and the animal world ('Sailani Bandar', 1924). Human beings in their various interfaces have been the major concern of Premchand. There are remarkable stories of encounter ('Bade Bhai Sahab', 1934), endurance ('Vaishya', 1933), and enterprise ('Beti Ka Dhan', 1915) that constitute his character-situation study and mark his art of storytelling. Similarly, facets of womanhood interested Premchand, which he chose to represent in a number of his stories. Broadly, his women are either submissive ('Beton Wali Vidhwa', date unconfirmed) or assertive ('Cricket Match', 1937), although pitiably and ironically, even both at times ('Mritak Bhoj', 1922), as they try to negotiate with the odd conditions of their life and living. Given the historical point of time when Premchand lived and wrote, the Indian nation had to be one of his prime concerns right from the very beginning of his literary career. His constructions of the nation are many, and all of them taken together reflect his broad concern with the integrity of the land and the people ('Rajhath', 1912), as they happened to negotiate with their condition in pre-independent India. Another aspect of life that caught his imagination intensely concerned the experience of love and longing. There are flawed characters and situations that interest him ('Rasik Sampadak', 1933), as are the persons and situations that are contingent and compliant ('Triya Charitra', 1913), obsessive and compassionate ('Manawan', 1912), worldly and sublime ('Wafa Ki Devi', 1935), and forbidding and secretive ('Virodhi', 1921). Creeds and credo interested Premchand as a storyteller as well as a concerned individual. Stories that fall in this category relate to aspects spiritual and ethereal ('Karmon Ka Phal', 1915), material and mundane ('Pashu Se Manushya', date unconfirmed), and fantastic and superstitious ('Naag Pooja', 1922).

Although this categorization is in no way conclusive, and cannot be so for obvious reasons of thematic overlapping and subjective readings,[24] it must be said that he is surely the first modern writer to create a form for short fiction in Urdu and Hindi. Premchand was neither overtly conscious of being a literary artist, nor he had any claims to the fine tunings of literary art and craft. He neither was a literary chronicler, nor a social philosopher in definitional terms, but he was surely all these—a literary artist, a chronicler, and a philosopher of his times, without any conscious reaching after art, history, and social philosophy.

Reading an Indian text by an author like Premchand implies a reading of the Indian context and its various representations. It involves a reading of, say for example, how he resisted sociopolitical stereotypes, how he configured history and its attendant denominators, how he strove to evolve an identity for himself and his world, and how he constructed his typically Indian narrative. Precisely because of these reasons, this author is important to a literary historiographer as well as to the modern reader. Equally important is the fact that he is the one who brought a form to the short and the long fiction in Urdu and Hindi, who invented a language for his fictional narrative, and who created new aesthetics for his generation, even while he lived life as a nationalist and held iconoclastic views on life and times and morals and manners.

The stories of Premchand represent the dynamics of the location he was deeply steeped into. They also represent a possible vision of the Indian nation that had to configure in the decades to come. It would be interesting to examine whether his stories represent facets of Indian histories and historiographies, and whether they represent a certain vision of the people and their predicament. It would be important to know whether Premchand strove to discover a new form for his narrative, and whether he was preoccupied with inventing a contemporary idiom to compose his text. One may propose straight and positive responses to these questions, as he was making an effort to address these issues for himself as well as his contemporaries. He was trying to evolve responses to diverse racial, historical, cultural, and individual conditions, and in a literary form that had to be evolved through the existing Urdu–Hindi literary traditions and canonical formulations. Premchand's quest was clearly one for individual expression and for constructing a modernist text that his imagination afforded him. A typical Premchand text is replete with numerous subtexts drawn from society and culture; they grow upon him as his own vision of society grows and matures with time. He is an improviser upon form and value and draws his sustenance from his individual strength as a storyteller. His text acquires its vitality in the way it identifies and creates a readership, as also formulates appropriate conditions for his acceptance in terms of thematic significance and stylistic innovations. In this respect, he is the author of the archetypal text that represents the historical predicament of a people, and in a literary form that is essentially revisionist in spirit.

Premchand's contemporary relevance can be appreciated along these parameters which are typically postcolonial in nature and significance. History, being the essential denominator of this postcolonial parameter, is writ well in all his writings, and it acquires its relevance through the myths that he broke to create new ones and the stereotypes that he resisted to develop a different vision of time and space. He fictionalized history with a view to construct an identity for a people. In this respect, he is a part and parcel of the new Indian literary culture. His stories revolving round the themes of morals and manners, creeds and credo, and margins and peripheries, as enumerated earlier, are central to the Indian ethos and make room for him among the modern Indian authors of significance. His views on a variety of social, political, and economic issues, as embodied in his fiction and non-fiction, are incarnations of historical moments in the life of a nation that compose and constitute the basic oeuvre of Premchand as a writer.

Endnotes

1. He was named Dhanpat Rai by his father, Munshi Ajaib Lal Srivastava. His uncle, Mahabir Lal, chose the pen name of Nawab Rai for him when he started writing. When he published his slim collection of patriotic stories called *Soz-e Watan* under this pen name in 1907, the district magistrate took severe exception to it and charged him for writing these stories that smelt of sedition. As such, Nawab Rai was made to surrender the seven hundred unsold copies of the book. This was the time for him to change his name in order to continue writing. Munshi Daya Narain Nigam, the editor of *Zamana*, chose the name Premchand for him. The first story that he published with this new name was titled 'Badey Ghar ki Beti' (1910).
2. Premchand has received considerable critical attention in India from critics and commentators in Hindi, Urdu, and English—the three languages in which he has been read, sometimes with great attention, while at others rather informally, but most often without much critical application and sensitivity which he richly deserved. The number of individual studies devoted to him and his broad spectrum of writings in terms of books and articles, as well as dissertations and projects, carried out in the academia both in and outside India bear ample testimony to this fact. While many studies essentialize him, there are others that historicize him or simply read him as a typical representative of the north Indian milieu. On the one hand, several editorial ventures have been made to determine an acceptable chronology of his works both in Hindi and Urdu; on the other hand, efforts have been made to read, teach, and translate him for a wider readership

in English. A reference to available scholarship in Hindi, Urdu, and English, howsoever adequate or inadequate, may be made in this connection.

3. Interested readers may like to see two most authentic and informed works that reflect upon the life and times of Premchand: *Premchand Ghar Mein* (1956) by Shivrani Devi and *Premchand: Qalam Ka Sipahi* (1976) by Amrit Rai [English translation *Premchand: His Life and Times* by Harish Trivedi in 1991]. There are many other biographical and semi-critical works available in Urdu and Hindi that include *Premchand* (1950) by Hans Raj Rehbar, *Premchand: A Literary Biography* (1964) and *Qalam ka Mazdoor* (1965) by Madan Gopal, *Premchand: His Life and Work* (1980) by V.S. Naravane, and *Ek Chitratmak Jeevani* (1986) by Kamal Kishore Goenka. References may also be made to the commemorative issues of *Hans* (May 1937) and *Zamana* (Jan–Feb 1938) that amply record the warm response of his contemporaries on Premchand as a writer and as a person. Critical responses to his works both in Hindi and Urdu are traceable right from these two publications.
4. Premchand, 'The Aim of Literature', in *The Oxford India Premchand*, trans. Francesca Orsini (New Delhi: OUP, 2004), not paginated.
5. Alok Rai, 'Introduction,' in Amrit Rai, *Premchand: His Life and Times*, trans. Harish Trivedi (New Delhi: OUP, 1990), p. ix.
6. He also edited some of these journals—*Maryada* (Feb–July 1922), *Madhuri* (1927–31), *Hans* (1930–36), and *Jagran* (1932–34).
7. See further 'Swaraj ke Faidey' (The Benefits of Swaraj), 'Swaraj se Kiska Ahit Hoga' (Who would be Harmed by Swaraj), 'Swaraj Sangram Mein Kis Ki Vijay Ho Rahi Hai' (Who Is Winning in the Revolution for Swaraj), and 'Swarajya Mil Kar Rahega' (We Shall Surely Have Swarajya). See Ramvilas Sharma, ed., *Premchand Rachnavali* (New Delhi: Janvani Prakashan, 1996), vols. 7 and 8.
8. See further 'Swadeshi Andolan' (Swadeshi Movement), and 'Swadeshi' (Swadeshi), ibid.
9. See further 'Satyagraha' (Satyagraha), ibid.
10. He wrote on the roles of the Congress party, Gandhi, and Nehru apart from others leaders of the independence movement. References may be made to his editorial notes on the Congress party: 'Congress' (Congress), 'Congress aur Socialism' (Congress and Socialism), 'Congress Committee Kya Karegi' (What will the Congress Committee Do Now), 'Congress ka Naya Programme' (The New Programme of Congress), 'Congress Zindabad' (Long Live Congress), 'Congress ka Sarkar se Sahyog' (The Cooperation of the Congress With Government), 'Congress Ki Arthik Yojana' (The Economic Programme of Congress), 'Shiksha Vibhag Aur Congress' (Education Department and the Congress); notes on Gandhi: 'Mahatma ji ka Upwas' (The Fast of the Mahatma), 'Mahatma ji ka Yatra' (The Tours of the Mahatma), 'Mahatma ji ka Safal Taap'

(The Successful Penance of the Mahatma), 'Mahatma ji ke Appeal Per Sarkar ka Jawab' (Government's Reply on the Mahatma's Appeal), 'Mahatma ji ki Vijay Yatra' (The Victory Tour of the Mahatma), 'Mahatma ji ki Swadheenata' (The Independence of the Mahatma); notes on Pandit Nehru: 'Pandit Jawaharlal Nehru ki Giraftari' (The Arrest of Pandit Jawaharlal Nehru), 'Pandit Jawaharlal Nehru ji ki Nirasha' (The Disappointment of Pandit Jawaharlal Nehru), Pandit Jawaharlal Nehru ki Arthik Vyawastha' (The Economic Programme of Pandit Jawaharlal Nehru), etc., ibid.

11. See further 'Rashtriyata Aur Antar Rashtriyata' (Nationalism and Internationalism), and 'Azadi ki Ladai' (Freedom Struggle), and 'Rashtriyata Ki Vijay' (The Triumph of Nationalism), ibid.
12. See further 'Mahajani Sabhyata' (The Capitalist Culture), 'Mahajan Aur Kisan' (The Capitalist and the Peasant), 'Andha Poonjiwaad' (Blind Capitalism), ibid.
13. To develop a broader perspective on this issue, references may be made to his essays and editorial notes: 'Mansik Paradhinta' (Mental Slavery), 'Vibhajak Rekha' (The Line of Division), 'Danda' (The Rule of Baton), 'Daman' (Exploitation), 'Daman ki Seema' (The Limits of Exploitation), 'Picketing Ordinance' (Picketing Ordinance), 'Nav Yug' (The New Era), 'Vartaman Andolan ke Raaste Mein Rukawatein' (Obstacles on the Path of the Present Revolution), 'Azadi ki Ladai' (The Struggle for Independence), 'Arthik Swaraj' (Economic Independence), 'Ekta' (Unity), 'Ekta ke Viruddh Sampradayikta ka Shor-o-ghul' (The Clamour of Communalism Against Unity), ibid.
14. From among many writings on the issue, references may be made to some like 'Islam ka Vish Vriksha' (The Poison Tree of Islam), 'Quran Mein Dharmic Ekta ka Tatwa' (The Elements of Religious Solidarity in Islam), 'Manushyata ka Akaal' (The Dearth of Humanity), 'Hindu–Muslim Ekta' (Hindu–Muslim Unity), 'Maulana Shaukat Ali ki Gehri Soojh' (The Inner Wisdom of Maulana Shaukat Ali), 'Ekta Sammelan' (Unity Conference), 'Hindu Samaj ke Vivatsa Drishya'—vols 1, 2, 3 (The Unpleasant Scenes of the Hindu Society), 'Maulana Hasrat Mohani' (Maulana Hasrat), 'Bhai Parmanand ki Sandeha Drishti' (The Suspicions of Bhai Parmanand), 'Bhai Parmanad ji ka Bhashan' (The Address of Bhai Parmanand), and 'Samradayikta aur Swarth' (Communalism and Selfishness), ibid.
15. See further 'Hamara Kartavya' (Our Duty), 'Acchooton ko Mandir mein Janey dena Paap hai' (It is a Sin to Allow the Harijans to Enter Temples), 'Paawan Tithi' (An Auspicious Date), and 'Mandir Pravesh aur Harijan' (Entry to Temple and Harijan), ibid.
16. See further 'Aaraazi ki Chakbandi' (The Consolidation of Plots), 'Hatbhagey Kisan' (The Unfortunate Farmers), and 'Zabardasti' (By Force), ibid.

17. See further 'Nari Jaati ke Adhikar' (The Rights of Women), 'Ek Dukhi Baap' (A Miserable Father), 'Auraton ka Krya Vikrya' (The Sale and Purchase of Women), and 'Vaivahik Lain Dain aur Qanoon' (Dowry and Law), ibid.
18. Exact date and place is not mentioned. It was written in Urdu under the signature of Premchand, probably in 1911–12, from Mahoba. See *Premchand Rachnavali*, trans. Anisur Rahman, p. 20.
19. Written in Urdu under the signature of Dhanpat Rai from Normal School, Gorakhpur on 14 September 1920. See ibid., p. 110.
20. Written in English under the signature of Dhanpat Rai from the office of *Madhuri* (Lucknow) on 22 January 1930. See ibid., p. 270.
21. Written in English under the signature of P. Chand from 168 Sarswati Sadan, Dadar, Bombay 14, on 26 December 1934. See ibid., pp. 431–32.
22. Written in Urdu under the signature of Premchand from Saraswati Press in February 1934. See ibid., p. 434.
23. Written in English under the signature of Dhanpat Rai from the office of *Hans* on 1 December 1935. See ibid., p. 497.
24. A reference may be made here to David Rubin, who, in *The World of Premchand* (1969), tried to classify stories in terms of location, 'the village', 'the town', and 'the World', and in terms of women characters as 'widows, wives and other heroines' in his collection entitled *Widows, Wives and Other Heroines: Twelve Stories by Premchand* (1998).

References

Premchand. 1996. *Premchand Rachnavali*. Ed. Ramvilas Sharma. New Delhi: Janvani Prakashan.

Premchand. 2004. *The Oxford India Premchand*. New Delhi: OUP.

Rai, Amrit. 1990. 'Introduction' by Alok Rai. In *Premchand: His Life and Times*. Trans. Harish Trivedi. New Delhi: OUP.

Versions of Subversion: Michael Ondaatje's *Running in the Family*

Michael Ondaatje's *Running in the Family* (1982), considered by many a postmodernist text, lends itself to a variety of readings.[1] One may also read it along a different line as a text of subversion—both thematic and formal—and underline its essentially subversive nature by which it acquires its intriguing individuality. This partly biographical, and partly autobiographical, retrieval of subliminal images draws upon the surrealist mixing of facts and fiction, truth and hearsay, narrative prose and evocative poetry, and words and snapshots. These seemingly desperate modes of discourse, balanced together in this text, may be explored and connected consequently to approach its possible meaning and form.

All the constituents of verisimilitude and imagination, word and image, and place and displacement, to name a few, seem to form a complex structure in this text. In writing the lives and times of his people, as also of his own, Ondaatje depends, to a large extent, on the method of destroying and overthrowing, reconstructing and delimiting the traditional tenets of linearity. He administers a test to himself to find out if his word may endure his world and this world may stand up to negotiate with the word. Ondaatje tries to test the limits of art and its vulnerability in a mode where distortions of images, as in an incurvate mirror, ultimately create a sense of the real.

Versions of subversion in *Running in the Family* may be studied both in terms of the subjects of narration and narratology. The two, subverted in the typical Ondaatje manner, merge together to create an elusive text, bringing shocks of recognition to a curious reader. Ondaatje lays down a part of his strategy in the very first sentence of his 'Acknowledgements', which he chooses to subvert at the end of the book: 'A literary work is a communal act,' he says and 'this book could not have been imagined, let alone conceived, without the help of many people' (205). A traditional reader approaching this act of 'communal' and 'imagined' writing, this text of 'confused genealogies and rumour' (205), is put into doubt regarding the vital questions of authorship and credence, just as one finishes reading the book, although he/she has to his/her credit Paul Fussell's definition of travel books as 'a sub-species of memoirs' claiming 'literal validity by constant reference to actuality' (203).[2] His reading strategy is questioned further on the following page of Ondaatje's 'Acknowledgements':

> While all these names may give an air of authenticity, I must confess that the book is not a history but a portrait or 'gesture'. And if those listed above disapprove of the fictional air I apologize and can only say that in Sri Lanka a well-told lie is worth a thousand facts. (206)

Ondaatje's concern for 'portrait' or 'gesture' rather than for 'actuality' spells out his writerly concern and makes demands upon the traditional reader to alter his/her conditioned response. The author confronts the problem of making a credible choice in writing, while the reader prepares to negotiate with his/her various modes of discourse: photographs, journal entries, newspaper reports, quotations, commentaries on Ceylon by visitors, brass plaques on church walls, etc. By constructing a myth of his people and their land, he is, in reality, aware of constructing a credible lie, for lies underline the facts in a subversive order. The search for the plausible would, otherwise, limit the infinite space that this text aspires to create. *Running in the Family* makes a promise to thematize a condition of 'being' out of the abstract and the illusive. It is achieved in the book by defamiliarization and exaggeration, and by charting the map of virile human imagination. Both the acts of writing this book (on the part of the author) and reading it (on the part of the reader) are, therefore, complicated. 'No story is ever told just once' (26), we are told at the beginning of the book which is subverted at the end: 'You can write it once' (201). The long journey from the initial to the final stage, which comes after about one hundred seventy-five pages, underlines the impossibility of the ultimate in writing what Linda Hutcheon calls Ondaatje's 'historiographic metafiction' (139). This movement from the position of hope and faith to that of despair and fatigue does not point towards the failure of the word, but, in an inverse order, signifies its strength with which it holds the world. This and many other instances of reversal of order, leading ultimately to an order of the new, punctuate the movement of the book from the beginning to the end.

Running in the Family is a complex detour into time, space, and text. One wonders if it is an attempt at writing 'an absolutist history' with 'minimalist insights' (44), as John A. Thieme would have it. It does not really matter if 'there is little sense of linear movement in *Running in the Family*—a clear historical pattern fails to emerge' (44). Historical relations are straightened in this book in much the same manner as the textual correlatives are sought to create a rarefied atmosphere in the text. Putting together a composition of over two hundred pages with forty seemingly unrelated sections, and disengaging from the fetters of sustained linear narrative is, in fact, Ondaatje's major authorial design. Variations in the treatment of language from pure narrative to evocative poetry and vice versa emerge as an important aspect of his writing technique. Mixing in a whole the past and the present tenses, the observer and the participant, and the lonely and the inhabited places contribute simultaneously to the organization of the text. Similarly, cartographic, linguistic, and human relations undergo consequential transformation as the text moves from one stage of blurring and sharpening the focus to another. It draws automatically that the reader does not receive an organized text; one has to reorder the fragments of time, space, and text. Ondaatje has evolved his individual mode of writing after his mother's 'sense of the dramatic' (168) and his father's 'sense of secrecy' (168). These figures acting as 'strong influence', to use a bloom phrase, contribute to his writing of the text. He writes:

> My father loved books and so did my mother, but my father swallowed the heart of books and kept that knowledge and emotion to himself. My mother read her favourite poems out loud, would make us read plays

> together and acted herself, even running a small dance and theatre school that people still remember in Colombo. Her reading out loud demanded the whole room, and while young her grace and dancing caught everyone's attention. Later, it was her voice, her stories with that husky wheezing laugh that almost drowned out the punch lines. She belonged to a type of Ceylonese family whose women would take the minutest reaction from another and blow it up into a tremendously exciting tale, then later use it as an example of someone's strain of character. If anything kept their generation alive it was this recording by exaggeration. (168–69)

It is by following these modes that Ondaatje wishes to retrieve the past images stored in his memory 'like frozen opera' (22) and wants to 'touch them into words' (22). Author Ina Ferris makes a subtle point while discounting the use of mimetic theories of art and suggesting that in *Running in the Family*, 'there is no transcription, only inscription' (76). It is in this context that one might explore continuity and coherence in Ondaatje's writing, especially when he refers to such seemingly varied material as the fifteenth-century graffiti poems on the rock face of Sigiriya,[3] the poignant lines from the poetry of Lakdhas Wikkrama Sinha,[4] and the wall writings by students on the campus during the 1971 insurgency.[5] He turns the banal into mythic, the concrete into the abstract, and tries to contextualize them all on a broader scale. 'I write as a reader' (240), he told Canadian novelist Catherine Bush in an interview. By doing so, he joins the peripheries of reading and writing into one. His efforts at writing without a palpable plot or design, abandoning the text, and letting it remain unfinished contribute to the cumulative effect of his subversive writing.

Subversive modes in *Running in the Family* engage the readers' attention from page to page. Ondaatje's wish to locate his place is writ large at the very beginning of the book, as one opens it to find a map with all the major points of reference which constitute his areas of myth-making. It is a geographical entity with its characteristic contours. There is a simple way of identifying it in these times: 'Ceylon falls on a map and its outline is the shape of a tear. After the spaces of India and Canada it is so small. A miniature (147).' He wishes for yet another way to help it materialize on a different plane with images which may not be quite concrete or real, as all such images are liable to be false. His quest for the imagined takes him to disown all stereotypes as such:

> On my brother's wall in Toronto are the false maps. Old portraits of Ceylon. The result of sightings, glances from trading vessels, the theories of sextant. The shapes differ so much they seem to be translations—by Ptolemy, Mercator, Francois Valentyn, Mortier, and Heydt—growing from mythic shapes into eventual accuracy. Amoeba, then stout rectangle, and then the island as we know it now, pendant off the ear of India. Around it, a blue-combed ocean busy with dolphin and sea-horse, cherub and compass. Ceylon floats on the Indian Ocean and holds its naive mountains, drawings of cassowary and boar who leap without perspective across imagined 'desertum' and plain. (63)

Ondaatje's concern is not for a geographical space of a new name Sri Lanka given to it in 1972, but a mighty space, a condition of mind. It has passed through the vicissitudes of history to acquire its new identity. It has been, in the past, the route for invaders and traders, rumoured in Greece, Rome, Arab, and China, the award of Adam and Eve on their fall from the heavens, the seducer of the Portuguese, the Dutch, and the English. It has had various identifiers: Serendip, Ratnapura, Taprobana, Zeloan, Zeilan, Seylan, Ceylon, and Ceylone. He underlines its innocent lacking rather ironically in the two epigraphs on the page facing the map. One of them is a Franciscan Friar of the fourteenth century: 'I saw in this land fowls as big as our country geese having two heads ... and other miraculous things which I will not here write of' (unnumbered p. 9), and the other is from Douglas Amarasekera who wrote in *Ceylon Sunday Times* of 29 January 1978: 'The Americans were able to put a man on the moon because they knew English. The Sinhalese and the Tamils whose knowledge of English was poor thought that the earth was flat' (unnumbered p. 9). Ondaatje puts his epigraph to new uses. He subverts them to develop yet another view of the land, and the book may be read as an effort at underlining this difference. The two journeys to this place in

1978 and 1980 turn out to be his stark honeymoons. He makes efforts to locate and recognize himself among a host of people and places, memories and records, images and metaphors. There is an underlying irony in his return journey, as he does not come to stay here permanently but goes back to his chosen place of adoption. The very act of planning his 'journey back' (22) and searching out 'possible routes to Ceylon' (22) in the maps on quiet afternoons highlights the vital pull of his soil, which he feels even after a long separation. The journeys undertaken are more emotional than physical, and help in composing both the fragments of life and the text.

In the seven sections of the book—'Asian Rumours', 'A Fine Romance', 'Don't Talk to Me About Matisse', 'Eclipse Plumage', 'The Prodigal', 'What We Think of Married Life', and 'The Ceylon Cactus and the Succulent Society'—subversion takes place at various levels. Before the reader enters this strange world, verging on fantasy and reality, he/she is initiated into it in a manner which characteristically entwine the two strains together. A beginning like this prepares the reader to bank upon the author's memories, which are akin to 'rumours' and swarm, as if, over the reader and make him/her believe in an incredibly fabulous narrative of life and art.[6] As the narrative moves on, strange situations and characters appear. The traditional concept of courtship stands reverted, as an engagement is meant to be broken too soon followed by another engagement.[7] Marriages are not kept up as expectedly traditionally, as fidelity does not stand the lure of romance.[8] Idiosyncrasies rule over normalcy, and loquacity comes after gulping the tongue of horrid reptile called Thalagoya[9]. Travels though the land present a picture of disorder reflected in the imaginative horizon of the author.[10] The loss of sharing the warmth of understanding lingers in the memory. Ultimately, all historical relations turn eerie, events defy dates, and alphabets turn into hieroglyphics. Suitably enough, the book ends not with the last evening but with the 'Last Morning' (202).

Running in the Family is a surrealist picture gallery. It is concerned with image-making and mediation, intertextuality and decoding. It is a map of human concern, a son's book for his father written together with brothers, sisters, aunts, and other relatives. The father remains present all through the narrative, but occupies greater space as the text approaches its end. It is a way of catching up with the unspent force of a character and his interminable story. His family is traced right from the sixteenth century, and in the entire family tree the father appears to be the most lovable wretch. He has passed through stages of life from one of great splendour to complete loss, from ethnic glory and exoticism of the past to the effacement of all magnificence in the present. The book on an irresponsible, subversive, and erratic father ends on a note as if he has not been read fully: 'And yet he is still one of those books we long to read whose pages remain uncut' (200). This observation comes at the end after Ondaatje has finished writing about his life, times, and place. This may create an impression of the failure of the text. It is, in fact, an acknowledgment of the immense potential the world holds, and that every text is only an attempt at coming to terms with the world, and also that it remains, at best, an unfinished act. The story of an extended family broken into many nuclear families and scattered over many lucrative spots across the globe highlights the status of a family in our times and the postcolonial search for, what Rushdie calls, the 'imaginary homelands'. This loss of centrality emerges as an important aspect of *Running in the Family*, and this is adequately expressed in the following passage:

> Before my mother left for England in 1949 she went to a fortune-teller who predicted that while she would continue to see each of her children often for the rest of her life, she would never see them all together again. This turned out to be true. Gillian stayed in Ceylon with me, Christopher and Janet went to England. I went to England, Christopher went to Canada, Gillian came to England, Janet went to America, Gillian returned to Ceylon, Janet returned to England, I went to Canada. Magnetic fields would go crazy in the presence of more than three Ondaatjes. And my father. Always separate until he died, away from us. The north pole. (172)

Running in the Family has been approached variously, applying modern wisdom with reference to 'subjugated knowledges' (Foucault), 'intertextuality' (Foucault), 'biographemes' (Linda Hutcheon), and 'myth of excess of belonging' (Aijaz Ahmad). It is, however, a book of love and romantic hangover, warmth and large human catholicity, which the reader makes out only after he/she has negotiated with Ondaatje's subversive methodology of treating life and art.

Endnotes

1. See, for example, Ajay Heble, 'Rumours of Topography: The Cultural Politics of Michael Ondaatje's *Running in the Family*', in Michael Ondaatje Issue, ed. Karen E. Smyth, *Essays on Canadian Writing* 53 (1994): 186–203; Graham Huggan, 'Exoticism and Ethnicity in Michael Ondaatje's *Running in the Family*,' *Essays on Canadian Writing* 57 (1995): 116–28; Linda Hutcheon, '*Running in the Family*: The Postmodernist Challenge', in *Spider Blues: Essays on Michael Ondaatje*, ed. Sam Solecki (Montreal: Véhicule Press, 1985), pp. 301–14; Ernest Macintyre, 'Outside of Time: *Running in the Family*', in *Spider Blues*, pp. 315–19; Winfried Siemerling, *Discoveries of the Other: Alterity in the Work of Leonard Cohen, Hubert Aquin, Michael Ondaatje, and Nicole Brossard* (Toronto: University of Toronto Press, 1994), pp. 137–53; John A. Thieme, '"Historical Relations": Modes of Discourse in Michael Ondaatje's *Running in the Family*', in *Narrative Strategies in Canadian Literature: Feminism and Postcolonialism*, ed. Coral A. Howells and Lynette Hunter (Milton Keynes: Open University Press, 1991), pp. 40–8.
2. Paul Fussell writes: Travels books are a sub-species of memoir in which the autobiographical narratives arise from the speaker's encounter with distant or unfamiliar data, and in which the narrative—unlike that in a novel or a romance—claims literal validity by constant reference to actuality.' [Fussell, *Abroad: British Literary Traveling Between the Wars* (Oxford: Oxford University Press, 1980), p. 203].
3. 'In the 5th century B.C. graffiti poems were scratched onto the rock face of Sigiriya—the rock fortress of a despot king. Short verses to the painted women in the frescoes which spoke of love in all its confusions and brokenness. Poems to mythological women who consumed and overcame mundane lives. The phrases saw breasts as perfect swans; eyes were long and clean as horizons. The anonymous poets returned again and again to the same metaphors. Beautiful false compare. These were the first folk poems of the country.' (84)
4. 'Don't talk to me about Matisse ... the European style of 1900, the tradition of the studio where the nude woman reclines forever on a sheet of blood. Talk to me instead of the culture generally—how the murderers were sustained by the beauty robbed of savages: to our remote villages the painters came, and our white-washed mud-huts were splattered with gunfire.' (85–6)

5. 'When the government rounded up thousands of suspects during the insurgency of 1971, the Vidyalankara campus of the University of Ceylon was turned into a prison camp. The police weeded out the guilty, trying to break their spirit. When the university opened again the returning students found hundreds of poems written on walls, ceilings, and in hidden corners of the campus. Quatrains and free verse about the struggles, tortures, the unbroken spirit, love of friends who had died for the cause. The students went around for days transcribing them into their notebooks before they were covered with whitewash and lye.' (84)
6. 'Once a friend had told me that it was only when I was drunk that I seemed to know exactly what I wanted. And so, two months later ... a trick which seemed only possible when drunk and relaxed—I knew I was already running ... I was running to Asia and everything would change. It began with that moment when I was dancing and laughing wildly within the comfort and order of my life. Beside the fridge I tried to communicate some of the fragments I knew about my father, my grandmother. 'So how *did* your grandmother die?' 'Natural causes.' 'What?' 'Floods.' (22–3)
7. 'The Courtship.' (31–5)
8. 'Flaming Youth' (44–7), 'The Babylon Stakes' (48–52), 'Tropical Gossip' (53–4), 'Aunts' (110–12), and 'The Passions of Lalla.' (113–29)
9. 'Tongue.' (72–5)
10. 'The country is crossed-hatched with maze-like routes whose only escape is the sea. From a ship or plane you can turn back or look down at the disorder. Villages spill onto streets, the jungle encroaches on the village.' (147)

References

Bush, Catherine. 'Michael Ondaatje: An Interview.' *Essays on Canadian Writing* (53) (1994).

Ferris, Ina. 1985. 'Michael Ondaatje and the Turn to the Narrative.' In *The Canadian Novel: The Present Tense.* Ed. John Moss. Toronto: NC Press.

Fussell, Paul. 1980. *Abroad: British Literary Traveling Between the Wars*. Oxford: OUP.

Hutcheon, Linda. 1985. '*Running in the Family*: The Postmodernist Challenge.' *Spider Blues: Essays on Michael Ondaatje*. Ed. Sam Solecki. Montreal: Véhicule.

Ondaatje, Michael. 1984. *Running in the Family*. London: Picador.

Thieme, John A. 1991. '"Historical Relations": Modes of Discourse in Michael Ondaatje's *Running in the Family*.' In *Narrative Strategies in Canadian Literature: Feminism and Postcolonialism*. Ed. Coral A. Howells and Lynette Hunter. Milton Keynes: Open University.

History, Poetry, Politics: A Reading of Khushal Khan Khattak

Genealogies: Personal and Political

As a Persian lexical item, 'Khushal'[1] means 'prosperous' in English and it also qualifies a person who enjoys the pleasant conditions of life. While naming their son Khushal, who, in future years, was destined to be a warrior, diplomat, poet, and philosopher, the parents must have desired all pleasures in the life of their son. The cunning movement of history, however, belied much of their hopes. Khushal, who came to be known as Khushal Khan Khattak (1613–1689), and emerged as a prominent chieftain of the Khattak tribe of Afghanistan, could not live a life as desired, or play his role as he wished. In the hiatus between illusory hope and historical reality lies the meaning of life and art that Khushal sought to achieve both as a warrior and a poet. A redoubtable progeny of his tribe,[2] Khushal stood at a crucial juncture in the history of Mughal–Afghan relationship, where he found favour with Shah Jahan (1592–1666) but disfavour with Aurangzeb (1618–1707), which ultimately led him to become a rebel of the Mughal empire. He recounted and reconfigured all these as a sensitive poet and projected a larger vision of his life and times, as also of history, poetry, and politics.

Widely revered as the father of Pashto literature and the national poet of Afghanistan, Khushal was a keen witness to the dispensations and machinations of two rulers of Mughal empire, which his forefathers had been serving since Akbar (1542–1605) in southern Afghanistan. The Mughal rule, which had started there with Babur (1483–1530) and continued until the reign of Aurangzeb, came under strain with Aurangzeb's stern policy towards Khushal, although it was the promising demeanour of Khushal that had persuaded Shah Jahan to appoint him as a *mansabdar* at the young age of twenty-eight in 1641. During the reign of Shah Jahan, Khushal proved his worth expected of him, but he came into greater prominence when he carried out his successful expeditions in Balkh and Badakhshan to the great appreciation of the emperor. While he enjoyed his confidence and emerged as a controlling hand, he also had jealous counterparts at home making their way to the governor of Kabul after the succession of Aurangzeb following Shah Jahan. On being maliciously briefed about Khushal by the governor of Kabul, and becoming suspicious of his growing power and popularity, Aurangzeb got him arrested and imprisoned in Ranthambore Fort in 1658 only to be set free a decade later in 1668. Khushal administered with the best of his capacities for seventeen years, that is, from his appointment as *mansabdar* in 1641 to his arrest and condemnation in 1658. Considering his services to the Mughals and the treatment he received from them, Paul Smith has succinctly observed:

> After he was permitted to return to Pashtun dominated areas (Eastern Afghanistan and Western Pakistan), Khushal had been deadly shocked by the unfriendly treatment he received from Mughal authorities and Emperor Aurangzeb whose indifference and coolness towards his plight had wounded Khushal's ego. He used to say, 'I had done nothing wrong against the interest of the king or the empire'. Mughal authorities continued to offer him temptations in order to reclaim him to their service but Khushal resisted all such offers and made it clear to the Mughals that 'I served your cause to the best of my honesty, I subdued and killed my own Pashtuns to promote the Empire's interests but my services and my loyalty did not make me a Mughal'. According to Khushal, he was burning inside for exacting revenge, but preferred to keep silent. Nevertheless the Mughals were not inclined to bear his aloofness and therefore he was challenged either 'to be friend or foe' as the interests of Empire knew no partiality'. (11–12)

On being utterly dejected, he declared himself a rebel of the Mughal empire, chose to align with the Mohmand, Safi, and Afridi tribes, and donned the mantle of the son of his soil. He called for Pashtun revolt against the Mughals in 1672 with a view to unite the Afghans and assert their position in the newly emerging political climate of the land. The shocking defeat of the Mughals in Khyber in 1672 and the closure of Attock–Kabul trade route in 1674 proved to be the two major causes that led to the disintegration of the Mughal rule in Afghanistan. These may also be considered as the important events that helped inculcate the spirit of Afghan nationalism in the people. It did not, however, succeed the way Khushal wished, but it certainly redefined the Mughal–Afghan relationship in a significant way and contributed towards the revisioning of Mughal politics in India. Sir Olaf Caroe, an administrator in British India, who has been quoted by the Afghan diplomat Ravan Farhâdi, has appropriately taken note of this phenomenon by acknowledging further that Khushal acted with his sword as much as he did with his pen: 'The armed resistance which he encouraged by his pen and emphasised by his sword is "to be counted among the causes that brought about the dramatic collapse of the Mogul Empire in India"' (72). As the Mughal machinations to break the Afghan unity continued behind the veils, Khushal did not wholly succeed in his mission, but he surely created a consciousness of self-assertion among his people before he finally sought a private space for himself to ruminate and write of his life and times. The desperate Mughals even set Khushal's son Behram Khan to capture or kill him, but before he could succeed in doing so, Khushal found his deliverance among the Afridis with the help of his two sons Nusrat Khan and Gohar Khan. It should be proper to conclude that the worth of Khushal can be examined only in relationship to imperial politics of his time as well as his personal prowess as a warrior and a poet who remain inseparable in terms of their individual strengths. C.E. Biddulph, in his 'Introduction' to *Afghan Poetry of the Seventeenth Century*, has summed up Khushal's accomplishments and limitations in precise terms as follows:

> He appears to have been indeed a man of the most extraordinary vigour of mind and exceptional versatility of talent; there is no subject which could ordinarily occur to a human being, not a specialist, which he does not discuss. Such a development of intellect and power of observation

> and appreciation of the gravity and profoundness of the problems affecting human life as are exhibited in his works are all the more astonishing to us when we consider his career, the age he lived in, and the almost utter state of barbarism of the social surroundings amidst which he spent the best part of his life. (xv)

A person and a poet of this stature, Khushal has remained a point of reference in Afghan history for the past three centuries and has also evoked contemporary interest for a contextual reading of his multiple merits in the disciplines of history, politics, and literature. He may be considered a warrior who fell prey to politicking, as a harbinger of Afghan nationalism who made way for futuristic engagement over the issues of nation and nationalism, and as an untutored genius who learnt his art on his own and drew upon the linguistic and stylistic resources of Dari and Persian to evolve a tradition of literary writing in Pashto.

Poetry: Self and the Other

The life that Khushal lived as well as the kind of poetry he wrote are mirror images of each other. It would be pertinent to mark how his poetry annotates his life. In a long autobiographical poem, spread over two hundred twenty-two verses in eleven stanzas, he has charted out a particular course of his life. This begins with a description of a long journey in terms of the places he arrived at, the people he met with, and the cruel behaviour he received from Aurangzeb and his officers. This poetical account begins with Naushahra as the first destination, which led further to Peshawar, Surai, Attock, Pindi, Lahore, and Delhi. In this long trail, he met his own people who wailed on seeing him on a journey of suffering and no return. He also describes the perpetrators of injustice against him that included his own treacherous uncle, one of his sons, the Mughal governor, and other representatives of the empire. He further narrates his days in captivity, the suffering of his family, the kindness of Shah Jahan in retrospect, and the cruelty of Aurangzeb who took command in Afghanistan after him. He describes his arrest: 'Down they brought me from my fort, when I fell into their hands;/Quickly the kotwal placed shackles on my feet; ten pounds was their weight' (Biddulph: 46). In an act of political astuteness, he advises his family not to raise arm or shed blood, but to maintain calm lest the foe should be happy that his own people caused a ruckus and brought ruin to him. Refusing to pay a sum for release, he asserts his moral strength and underlines the treachery of those aligned against him. He goes on to describe his captivity, his petition to the emperor, and the commotion amongst his people back home. He also expresses his deep anger against Aurangzeb: 'Such is our Emperor, such his justice, such his conduct;/Yet, please God, no favour may be shown the tyrant on this earth' (Biddulph: 54). He curses him in many more verses like this one here, which draws upon an allusion from Islamic history: 'May evil be his end, and the fate of Yezid upon him!/May the curse remain upon him as of Hussein and Hassan's death!' (Biddulph: 55).

In retrospect, Khushal also narrates the advent of Muslim rule in Delhi, the splendour of the city of Delhi, the grandeur of Diwan-i-Aam, and the magnificence of the Mughal court. He praises Shah Jahan in all humility: 'Had I art of poetry and verses/Many are the praises of my Emperor I should have sung' (Biddulph: 59). Khushal's responses to his adversaries may be traced back to his Afghan heritage that makes him proud of himself and of his people on the whole. He writes about himself thus: 'It is for the Afghan honour that my sword I have bound beside me,/I Khushhal Khatak am the only proud Afghan of the day!' (Biddulph: 65). He was aware of himself as a poet as much as he was conscious of his chieftainship. He thus combines and balances both the roles together to write about his life and times, without which he could not have been acclaimed as a son of the soil and a poet of his people. He wonders at how he could negotiate with himself to be able to write his poetry: 'Surprised indeed am I at how it leads me on,/This strange art of mine they call devilry and magic' (Biddulph: 68). All these references he makes to himself and to the people around him create a historical condition in which he himself was both a sufferer and a witness.

Khushal's domain of poetry is as widespread as that of an emperor's domain. As a prolific literary figure, Khushal has eight collections of poetry and six of prose to his credit, where he found space for subjects as varied as individual, communal, and national histories; metaphysics and morality; social and natural justice; love and romance, apart from nationalist aspirations; philosophical musings; and systems of knowledge like medicine, ethics, and falconry.[3] He is also supposed to be the one who experimented with metrical and poetical forms to help develop a strong tradition of poetry in Pashto. Khushal's individuality lay in his art of blending the common speech and song rhythms of Persian with Dari in order to develop a modernist tradition of poetry in Pashto. His reputation as a poet outside Pashto literary tradition, however, has been appreciated mostly through translations[4] of his works in English, French, Italian, Russian, and Urdu. Let us develop a map of his poetical output with reference to his major concerns.

In writing the history and politics of his times, Khushal developed a view of peoples and places in quite frank and unambiguous terms. These are, however, not always completely free of contradictions or discrepancies, but these may be read with reference to his shifting perspectives on them with the change of time and sociopolitical dispensations. Some of his observations appear rather stark, which also refer to his own people. The following verses would bear these out:

The Iranis are of a friendly disposition—they are true and faithful:
They have urbanity, and breeding—are respectable and deserving.
The Afghans are malevolent, and ruthless, and contentious;
But give them for their modesty and valour due praise.
Whether Baluch or Hazarah, both are dirty, and abominable:
They have neither religion nor faith—may shame attend them!
Whether Hindustani or Sindhi, may their faces be blackened;
For they have neither modesty nor shame; neither bread nor meat!
The Kashmiris, whether male or female—may they all be undone!
They have none of the chattels of humanity amongst them.
Behold! They are not of the human race—what are they?
May perdition swallow them—both Uzbak and Kazalbash!
The Laghmanis, Bangashis, Suwatis, Tirahis—all of them,
Are dancers and fiddlers—and who will be friends with such?

Unto him, all matters are manifest, regarding other folks' ways;
Then render unto Khushhāl's shrewdness, its due need of praise.
(Raverty: 187)

As fine specimens of his vivid cartographic imagination, these verses represent a picture gallery of locations that have had a long history of their own and have mattered significantly in the political map of his time. Such individual perceptions may be subject to varied interpretations, but they are frank expressions of Khushal's personal understanding of peoples and places which also fluctuated with changes in historical conditions. Similarly, his attitude towards Afghans is also critical, even while he takes pride in them rather unreservedly. At certain places, he praises them in comparative terms, while at others, he rejects them on the whole:

The Afghans are far superior to the Mughals at the sword,
Were but the Afghans, in intellect, a little discreet. (Raverty: 152)
If the Afghan people are of the human race,
In disposition and ways they are very Hindus. (Raverty: 223)
They are possessed of neither skill, nor intellect;
But are happy in ignorance, and in strife. (Raverty: 224)
Neither do they obey the words of their fathers;
Nor do they unto the teacher's instruction give ear. (Raverty: 224)
When there may be one worthy man amongst them,
They are the destroyers of his head and life. (Raverty: 224)
They ever lie in wait, one to injure the other;
Hence they are, always, by calamity, remembered. (Raverty: 224)
They neither possess worth, nor do others esteem them,
Though they are more numerous than locusts or than ants.
(Raverty: 224)
But still, O Khushhāl! Thank God for this,
That they are not slaves, but free-born men. (Raverty: 224)

Khushal's uncharitable attitude towards the Yusufzais, as well as his own Khattak tribe, is expressed with equal frankness. This sharp cleavage between the two tribes had stayed for long, but Khushal chose to mend fences with the Yusufzais in order to resist and defeat the Mughal onslaught and end their rule in Afghanistan. Expressing his earlier anger against the Yusufzais, he had written: 'The dogs of the Khattaks are far better than the Yūsufzīs,/Though, in disposition, the Khattaks are more worthless than dogs' (Raverty: 150). He also challenged their sense of honour, thus: 'See how many battles have been fought on all sides;/Yet still, amongst the Yūsufzīs, there is no sense of shame' (Raverty: 150). This anger reached a point of total rejection, as in this verse: 'Now that I have beheld the Suwāt valley, I have this much discovered,/That there is no tribe more abject and contemptible than the Yūsufzīs' (Raverty: 182). What is remarkable here is that Khushal emerged as an iconoclast and struggled for a cause that led him to work for ending tribal enmity and promoting the cause of larger unity in the interests of the Afghan land.

In a similar fashion, he came down upon the Mughals but became much more devastating when he thought of Aurangzeb who appears as a refrain of hatred in his poetry. Some verses would bear this out:

The dark night of Aurangzeb's prison, I hold in remembrance,
When all the night long, 'O God! O God!' continually, I cried.
(Raverty: 206)

His evil name only will remain behind in the world;
Knowing, as he doth, whether he as Kasrā, or as Hujāj acteth.
(Raverty: 155)

I am well acquainted with Aurangzeb's justice, and equity—
His orthodoxy in matters of faith—his self-denial and fasts; (Raverty: 188)
His own brothers, time after time, cruelly put to the sword—
His father overcome in battle, and into prison thrown! (Raverty: 188)
Tho' a person dash his head against the ground a thousand times,
Or by his fastings, should bring his navel and spine together; (Raverty: 188)
Until coupled with the desire of acting with virtue and goodness,
His adorations, and devotions, are all impositions and lies. (Raverty: 188)
Since the arm of Khushhāl cannot reach the tyrant here,
In the day of doom, may the Almighty have no mercy on him!
(Raverty: 188)

Khushal's poetry can be easily divided into two parts. In one, he writes about the history and politics of his times, but in another, he acquires an entirely new identity as a love poet as well as a metaphysical poet. One may posit that both these aspects of his poetry represent his basic predilections that identify him as an intensely private person, in spite of his tribal or militarist affiliations. His love poetry is rich with resplendent images and metaphors. This may be seen in how he configures the lady love in different verses as silver-bodied and as tall as a cypress. He compares her teeth to pearls and diamonds, lips to sugar and rubies, eyebrows to arches, dark eyes to javelin, nose to rosebud, and chin to jasmine. He praises her for her moles, raven locks, hair's perfume, and rose-coloured and gold-embroidered dress (Biddulph: 79). He adores her for bearing the qualities of a partridge, peacock, falcon, leopard, hawk, antelope, and lamb for her ways on the lover. She is the one who assumes many postures and allures in many ways that characterize the humans, the animals, and the birds (Biddulph: 80–1). Khushal's lady-love is a human being made of flesh and blood, but vibrates with energy and acts variously, embodying the best of the qualities that the birds and animals represent. She is not shy or withdrawn, but vivacious and participating. Although romanticized in extreme, she is the one with whom he relates in dream and in reality and celebrates the bliss of romantic love. Khushal's ability to create the figure of the lady-love may be noticed in these verses:

These dark waving curls, they are thine, thou dear one,
so beautiful, so gay!
Black narcissuses are those eyes of thine, thou dear one, so beautiful, so
gay! (Raverty: 164)
Now that I have with mine eyes gazed on this, thy lovely cheek,
I know that it is the tulip, thou dear one, so beautiful, so gay!
(Raverty: 164)

Her two eyes are a falcon, and her waving locks are the king-feathers:
The falcon pounced on, and carried from me the pigeon of
my heart. (Raverty: 171)

He, who may have turned Malang, requireth but
a carpet for prayer;
And in the end, too, a Malang will she make of me—that dear one.
(Raverty: 175)

No gem-studded ornament hath she inserted in her nostril;
But with a single black clove she resteth satisfied—that dear one.
(Raverty: 175)

People say unto me, 'Verily thy colour is become sallow—thou
art in love!'
I do not deny it: truly, my friends, I am in love! indeed, I am!
(Raverty: 196)

Say not unto me—'Why swearest thou by me?'
If I swear not by thee, by whom shall I swear? (Raverty: 204)

Truly, I am thy lover, and thine, thine only:
And this, I, Khushhāl, by thy sweet face, swear! (Raverty: 204)

The rose, the hyacinth, the wild rose, the tulip, and the buds—
Thou didst bring with thee, on thy coming, the whole spring.
(Raverty: 218)

When I press her unto my bosom, she looketh towards me,
Like a young gazelle inebriated with the milk of its dam. (Raverty: 218)

Looking at the beauty of fair women I have found my God,
Short is the distance between metaphor and fact' (Biddulph: 76)

I said, 'If I come to thee, wilt thou greet me with a kiss?'
Said she, 'Hast thou a thousand heads that thou askest this of me?'
(Biddulph: 79)

I said, 'Thy raven tresses are like so many black cobras.'
Said she, 'Why trust thyself within the cobra's reach?' (Biddulph: 79)

Both her lips has she now parted,
Pearls she pours upon her lover. (Biddulph: 81)

Her black locks are as a chain, her face the Kaaba,
With both hands seize those locks if thou wouldst made the Hajj.
(Biddulph: 83)

My sweetheart, soaked in wine stupor
Drowned in musk and rosewater
With unveiled scattered tresses
Gave me a kiss, sweeter than sugar. (Rahman: 4)

Khushal's love poetry is rooted in the romantic tradition of the Eastern poetry, which is characterized by exuberance of emotions and opulence of imagery. This poetry, thus, develops a definite correspondence with romantic poetry in Arabic, Persian, and Sanskrit languages. In this respect, Khushal's poetry belongs to a larger tradition of poetry in the Oriental languages.

This aspect of Khushal's poetry may be explored further in what we may designate as his poetry of metaphysical affiliations. Here again, he corresponds with the greater Oriental tradition of metaphysical poetry that combines ethics, morality, and philosophy together. He emerges in these verses as a poet of ideas who has developed a liberal understanding of the role of man in this universe, which is characterized by antinomies of the physical world and the ambivalences of human nature. In one of his verses, he rethinks and reconsiders himself variously as a 'fiction', a 'treasury of mysteries', 'a moth', 'a stranger unto the world', and 'a pearl in the ocean' (Raverty: 184). We may consider the following verses to appreciate his philosophical understanding of phenomenon:

You are a talisman of unreliable birth
Made of wind, water, fire and earth

A non-entity before, a non-entity after
For God's sake, know your worth. (Rahman: 3)

In my poor judgment, death is more preferable than life,
When existence can no longer, with honour, be enjoyed. (Raverty: 153)

Cast thine eyes upon the bubble in the stream!
What is it? and what its origin and its base? (Raverty: 168)

Concerning thyself, thou knowest nothing:
Alas! alas! verily, thou knowest naught. (Raverty: 168)

What are all thy grief and misery about?
And why becomest thou again overjoyed? (Raverty: 168)

The nightingales and the parrots fly about the wilds, astounded;
And crows and ravens caw and croak above the beds of flowers.
(Raverty: 179)

Without the parrot, the cage is useless—be convinced of this!
And the soul is like unto the parrot—the body like unto its cage.
(Raverty: 186)

In another verse, Khushal defines the qualities of an ideal man. The qualities enumerated here are the ones that have been reiterated endlessly in all cultures, but these verses may be read in the context of the life he lived, which brought him this vision to sustain himself as a human being with a sense of pride rather than of defeat:

A man is he, who is courageous, and whom success attendeth—
Who is gentle and affable, unto all people, as long as life lasteth.
(Raverty: 189)
His face, his real face—his word, his word—his promise,
his promise:

With no falsehood in him, no deception, not witless and lewd.
(Raverty: 190)
His words few, but his deeds many, and in silence performed—
With mouth closed, but bosom laid open like the bud of the rose.
(Raverty: 190)
When humility may be necessary, or when stateliness be required,
To be in loftiness, like the heavens—in humbleness, like the dust.
(Raverty: 190)
In dignity, like the cypress—in generosity and bounty, like the vine—
Its branches, on all sides, under the weight of its clusters bending.
(Raverty: 190)
Like unto a fresh and fragrant full-blown rose in the parterre,
Around which the sweet nightingales raise their plaintive songs.
(Raverty: 190)

Khushal's poetry in Pashto is considered to be highly rhythmical. In one of his compositions, he expressed his poetics with remarkable clarity. He disapproved of those who wrote 'without rhythm, without measure' (Biddulph: 76). He further said that he learnt Persian poetry, but he preferred Pashto poetry as it was his own language which he loved more. He also proclaimed: 'In measure, in meaning, in nicety, in metaphor,/Have I the Pushtoo language made to rival with the Persian' (Biddulph: 76). Even though he wrote in Pashto, he knew well that it was not an easy language to master with 'its measures hard to find'. He considered himself a self-taught poet and mentioned only one poet, Mirza Khan Ansari, from whom he could learn his art: 'There is no one that has taught me the art of Pushto poetry,/ The Mirza who wrote verses, it is long since he was dead' (Biddulph: 76). His reading of Persian poetry must have contributed to his own understanding of poetical norms, and helped him acquire a supplementary personality to develop as a rounded poet by absorbing influences and evolving his own methods of expression. Poetry was a mode for him to redeem himself; it was a personal panacea at both the political and personal levels, as it afforded him salvation from the onslaughts of life he suffered and negotiated with.

In his 'Introduction' to Sami ur Rahman's *The Rubaiyat of Khushal Khan Khattak* (2016), Raza Rumi has appropriately noted the remarkable reach of Khattak's poetry which brings him closer to the great South Asian tradition of inclusiveness, coherence, and assimilation. He wrote:

> Essentially, the subalterns of Pakistan, not unlike much of North India, are united through a few common threads: folk heritage and syncretic South Asian spiritual traditions that overlap and nourish each other, creating a peculiar secular culture where religious creeds are tolerated for local harmony and to preserve community bonds. Khattak, a poet, administrator, warrior and a rebel of Mughal India—is a torchbearer of this rich tradition. (vii)

In appreciating these aspects of Khushal's poetry, we may contextualize him in the greater South Asian tradition. Rumi has further noted:

> India underwent a slow but significant transformation from the eleventh century onwards when the Muslim Sufis interacted with their Hindu counterparts. During what is known as Bhakti era, the poetries and folklore acquired newer dimensions of inter-communal understanding, Khattak even hints at such interactions and cultural dialogue in his poetry. And this fiercely professed and guarded object of co-existence—between Hindus and Muslims—is striking. (vii)

Apart from its relevance in the South Asian context, Khushal's poetry is more germane to the Indian subcontinent. He emerges as a poet of catholic preoccupations and liberal perceptions. Rooted in the tribal history and culture of Afghanistan, Khushal communicates like a poet of the Indian subcontinental location. He represents the prominent marks of shared history and culture of Afghanistan and India. His poetry is a historic account of a non-historian and the saga of a tribal poet trying to write a national history, howsoever perfunctorily. Khushal's poetry spells out the politics involved in the game of retaining power, and it annotates the meaning of success and failure in a philosophical matrix. This makes him a poet of broader appeal and larger relevance.

Endnotes

1. As it has been generally spelt in most of the historical and literary accounts, 'Khushal' is a combination of *khush*, which means happy, and *haal*, which means condition. However, a possible way of spelling this lexical item of two phrasal nouns with greater clarity and precision could have been 'khush-haal', which has not been the practice in the sources on this warrior-poet. Following the usual practice, I have chosen to follow the established practice rather than use another way of spelling this name, as I have suggested before.
2. Associated in its origin with Israelites and Greeks, Khattak was one of the oldest Afghan tribes, which was further divided into Borak, Akori, Yusufzai, and Soghari Khattak tribes. Prominent Khattak chiefs, Malik Akoray and Malik Shahbaz Khan, who were Khushal Khan Khattak's grandfather and father respectively, served the Mughal emperors Akbar and Shah Jahan with great distinction, and contributed towards protecting the Grand Trunk Route which extended to Kabul in Afghanistan beyond the Khyber Pass.
3. His books of poetry include *Divan*, a collection of about sixteen thousand *sher*s; *Sahat-u-Badan*, a poetical treatise on human body; *Tib Nama*, a discourse on folk medicine and health; *Fazal Nama*, a treatise on religious matters; *Farrukh Nama*, a dialogue between sword and pen; *Firaq Nama*, an account of suffering in exile; and *Swat Nama*, an account of his visit and appreciation of Swat valley. He also wrote on a rich variety of subjects and translated extensively in prose. His *Baz Nama* is a book on falconry, *Tarjuma Hadia* deals with Hanafi jurisprudence, *Zanziri* discusses principles of composition, *Dastar Nama* lays out the behavioural aspects expected of a leader, and *Aaina* is a translation of a book on jurisprudence from Arabic to Pashto.
4. Some of the translations include: C.E. Biddulph, *Afghan Poetry of the Seventeenth Century: Being Selections from the Poems of Khush Hal Khan Khatak* (London: Kegan Paul, Trench, Trübner & Co, 1890); Evelyn Howell and Olaf Caroe, *The Poems of Khushhal Khan Khattak with English Verse Translations* (Peshawar: Pashto Academy, University of Peshawar, 1963); D.N. Mackenzie, trans., *Poems from the Divan of Khushal Khan Khattak* (Australia: Allen & Unwin, 1965); Khushal Khan Khattak, *The Book of Falconry*, trans. Sami ur Rahman (Pakistan: Pangraphics, 2014); Sami ur Rahman, trans., *Rubaiyat of Khushal Khan Khattak* (Islamabad: Rainbow Graphic, 2016); H.G. Raverty, *Selections from the Poetry of the Afghans: From the Sixteenth to the Nineteenth Century* (London: Williams and Norgate, 1862); Paul Smith, *Khushal Khan Khattak: The Great Warrior-Poet of Afghanistan: Selected Poetry* (Victoria, Australia: New Humanity Books, 2012); and Faragh Bukhari and Raza Hamdani, trans., *Khushal Khan Khattak ke Afkar* (Peshawar: Naya Maktaba, 1952).

References

Biddulph, C.E., ed. and compiled. 1890. *Afghan Poetry of the Seventeenth Century: Being Selections from the Poems of Khush Hal Khan Khatak.* London: Kegan Paul, Trench, Trübner & Co. [Downloaded]

Farhadi, Ravan. 1970. 'Khushhal Khan Khatak.' *The Encyclopaedia of Islam.* 2. C – G 1 (1–2). Brill Archive. Retrieved on 1 March 2013.

Rahman, Sami ur, trans. 2016. *Rubaiyat of Khushal Khan Khattak.* Islamabad: Rainbow Graphic.

Raverty, H.G., trans. 1862. *Selections from the Poetry of the Afghans: From the Sixteenth to the Nineteenth Century.* London: Williams and Norgate (see PDF of digital commons).

Smith, Paul, trans. 2012. 'The Life, Times & Poetry of Khushal Khan Khattak.' In *Khushal Khan Khattak: The Great Warrior-Poet of Afghanistan: Selected Poetry.* Victoria, Australia: New Humanity Books.

An Evolving Text: Tahmima Anam's *A Golden Age*

Locating *A Golden Age*

The four-line epigraph to *A Golden Age* (2007) that Tahmima Anam draws from the major Bangladeshi poet Shamsur Rahman's (1929–2006) 'Shadhinota Tumi'[1] calls for our attention for more reasons than one. Rahman represents freedom in metaphorical terms and configures it in the images of nature. He identifies it in multiple ways as 'an arbour in the garden,' 'koel's song,' and 'glistening leaves,' which together find their place in his 'notebook of poetry.' In doing so, he projects freedom as a site of pride and celebration. Beginning with such an epigraph, Anam chooses to go backwards and recreate the conditions of war which preceded freedom and represents it as a terrible means to a glorious end.

This epigraph provides Anam with a point of reference to entitle her novel as *A Golden Age*. In a sensitive review of this novel, Mandira Sen, a publisher, engages briefly with the relevance of the title, but she does not offer an explanation for Anam's choice. She writes: ' ... one wonders what "golden age" Tahmima Anam's title could possibly refer to. The onset of freedom? The gratitude of those who lived to tell the tale? The house named *Shona* (gold) that becomes a symbol of the rebels' heroism after guerrillas take it over? Anam leaves it to her readers to decide' (5). I would like to offer a possible answer by positing that on the surface, the title appears to be both ironic and enigmatic and sounds more like an oxymoron, but once initiated into the narrative, the reader may discover within the telling of this tale a realistic fictionalization of a people's history and their land of belonging. At a philosophical level, the title underlines the element of pride Anam seems to take in telling an abysmal tale, as does the poet whose lines she chooses for an epigraph. It should be relevant to mention here that it echoes Yeats's idea of 'terrible beauty' which he presented in his poem 'Easter, 1916' published in 1921.[2] As in Yeats, there is a sense of pity and pride in Anam's *A Golden Age* also. Remarkably enough, both the texts weigh and balance the pathos of life against the quest for honour with reference to national independence. In the last stanza of his poem, Yeats draws upon the poetic metaphors of night, death, dream, green, and human characters, which also extend into Anam's imagination in a fictional framework, where the same referents, with a similar magnitude, emerge as they did in Yeats. Let me consider Anam's narrative as one that maps a location and writes a history with reference to human agencies involved, who make a choice for what they do in the chain of events.

The years 1947 and 1971 that saw the partition of India and the liberation of Bangladesh, respectively, stay as the two major marks in the history of South Asia. These two consequential markers of history defined the predicaments of peoples and places like no other event in the history of the two nations. Being extremely significant in political terms, they have been the most engaging sites of scholastic engagements[3] and fictional representations[4] over the past decades. It may well be observed that the formation of modern history in the Indian subcontinent, which became a subject of greater academic interest after 1947 and 1971, had actually been a serious preoccupation ever since the beginning of the twentieth century with the partition of Bengal in 1905 itself. With the partition of India, however, it became a major intellectual concern, and the same could be traced in the climate of opinion created for the being and becoming of Bangladesh. Leaders and social thinkers of various shades of opinion, who had championed the case of Bangladesh,[5] called for its recognition as a nation with a political, cultural, and linguistic entity. All these scholastic and political engagements created a condition for the 1971 war of liberation of which *A Golden Age* emerged as a sensitive literary testament.

Mapping Location

It has been generally argued that *A Golden Age* is a novel that draws essentially upon the experiences of war and liberation. To develop a larger and more catholic view, I should like to posit that apart from drawing upon the idea and experience of war and liberation, this novel operates at two particular levels of time and space as it moves through the meandering motions of a historical period and the shifting locations in a given space. Even while it engages directly with Bangladesh, it also refers back and forth to two neighbours—India and Pakistan—that act as causes to many effects at the personal levels of the characters involved and the political levels of the countries in question. In a larger pursuit of creating a realistic fiction, Anam's account of war and liberation evolves as a historical saga situated in a given frame of time and place. This saga, which projects Bangladesh in a direct-indirect relationship with India and Pakistan, with all their parities and disparities, represents a major aspect of the contemporary history of the Indian subcontinent.

It may be argued further that as *A Golden Age* implicates multiple conditions ranging broadly from personal to communal, cultural to political, and historical to national, it develops a perspective on war which turns out to be a site of struggle for integrity and honour rather than for being condemned to disappointment and doom. In terms of these generic points of reference, Anam's novel annotates larger issues that relate on a physical level with struggle for freedom and the future evolution of a nation. It meanders through different locations and communities, as well as the rooted subjectivities of characters involved that impart a remarkable tension to the narrative. At a broader level, it annotates conditions concerning larger human predicament in a given space and frame of historical time.

With reference to Anam's representation of war as a landmark of history, one may ask whether her response is conditioned by her own choices, or it is based on material evidence afforded by contemporary politics played by three parties—Bangladesh in the middle and India and Pakistan on the two sides. Even a general reading of the novel would show that the latter would hold good, as the novel is essentially a realistic representation of time in fictional terms. Concrete references to Sheikh Mujibur Rahman, declaration of independence, and the general election of 1970 help her thin out the distinction between fact and fiction, which makes it possible for her to represent history in actual terms of literary historiography. As she does this, she also allows the novel to evolve on its own. This leads me to posit that there emerge points of intersection between her point of view and those of the characters involved. Rehana Haque, being the central character, tends her relationships with persons in and outside her home, which may be appreciated as her emotional responses to her family on the one hand, and political responses to others on the other hand. As such, this web of dual relationships may be appreciated in how she shares her personal anguish with her family that include Iqbal Haque, her dead husband, in whom she confides by visiting his grave and opening her heart to him; Faiz, her brother-in-law, and Parveen, his wife, who takes her children into their custody; and Sohail and Maya, her son and daughter. Her anguish acquires a different colour in her relationship with those outside her family like Mr and Mrs Sengupta, her tenants; Mrs Rahman and Mrs Akram, her sister-like friends; Sharmeen, Maya's friend; Mrs Chowdhury, her neighbour, as well as Silvi, her daughter and Sabeer, her fiancé; and very importantly, an unnamed army officer with whom Rehana develops a strange emotional relationship. All these characters, embroiled in different situations, are the victims of time, and they together constitute a complex of human relationships developed on the basis of shared misery. One may easily mark that these relationships also write the history of times, but these relationships represented in a literary narrative differ entirely from historians' concept of history and historiography.

In the backdrop of the earlier argument, it would be meaningful to see how Anam reconstructs history by developing her own chronology while keeping close to actual happenings. All the events and their sequences spell out the making of a revolution and its impact on the characters involved.

Divided into ten sections (and subsections within them), the novel constructs history in the following terms:

March 1959	Prologue
March 1971	Shona with her back to the sun
25 March 1971	Operation Searchlight
April	Radio Free Bangladesh
May	Tikka Khan, the Butcher of Bengal!
June	I loves you, Porgy
July	The red-tipped bird
August, September, October	Salt Lake
November	Take my affliction
16 December 1971	

As seen, Anam configures her narrative in terms of months and dates of the year 1971, except for the first chapter which looks back in time and links the past with the present. This implies that even though the plot develops and reaches its point of culmination in the present, it also harks back to the past in order to represent a historical continuity between the two phases of time. This may be testified with reference to Rehana's brief and poignant sharing of emotions with her late husband with which the narrative begins: 'Dear Husband,/I lost our children today' (3), followed by 'Dear Husband,/Our children are no longer our children' (5), and then 'My children are no longer my children' (5). With a delicate balancing of 'I', 'our', and 'my', the three sentences following each other like a refrain find their correlate at the end of the narrative: 'Dear Husband,/ The war will end today' (309). This is followed by equally poignant sentences like those she uttered at the beginning of the novel, and it is with these sentences that the narrative comes to an end: 'Dear Husband,/I came to tell you the story of our war and how we have lived./The war will end today. I have aged a thousand years. I am ugly and tired. But I live' (314). As Rehana shares these feelings, she sums up her life's ordeal not as one who has opted out of the journey midway, but as one who has finally succeeded in arriving. Between the two stages of Rehana's life, as represented in the first and the last chapters of the novel, we have the plot evolving in a sequential order from a despairing past to a reassuring present. The end spells out optimism and expresses a sense of quiet delight one experiences at the end of a gruelling journey. Between the first and the last chapters, Anam indulges in a sophisticated interweaving of plots and subplots related to simmering discontent leading up to the condition of war, massacre, homelessness, rescue, reunion, and faith in that order. All these stages involve characters, locations, and situations that may be classified into odds and evens in the life of a people questioning their independence. In simple and plain terms, *A Golden Age* represents the history of Bangladesh, which evolves slowly and develops, in this process, its geographical, political, linguistic, communal, and cultural markers.

Anam's representation of history may be appreciated with reference to the major turns of events that involve the characters, their location in the story, and their stances. These may be considered in relation to some of the important extracts from the narrative in a sequential order, as quoted later, since they stand linked together and chart out the essential plot and its pace. These, in turn, represent personal and communal histories as well as the history of a nation to be in the near future. The novel begins with Rehana parting with her children and their going away to Pakistan to be in the custody of her brother-in-law. There is a keen metaphoric representation of this parting as follows:

> Rehana watched them leave from an airport window made foggy by hair oil and goodbye fingerprints. She waved a small wave, wondering when the world would stop ending. ('March 1959: Prologue': 9)

This is the first major happening in the story of Rehana, who has chosen to stay back in East Pakistan near to her husband's grave. This makes way for other subsequent developments that start impacting individuals who together take the narrative forward. As the plot thickens, there comes a moment of discontent and veiled anger in the story when the exploitation of a people by a people finds a potent voice through Sohail:

> If you know anything about the country you would know that West Pakistan is bleeding us out. We earn most of the foreign exchange. We grow the rice, we make the jute, and yet we get nothing—no schools, no hospitals, no army. We can't even speak our own bloody language!'. ('March 1971: Shona with her back to the sun': 33)

This is an acerbic remark typically representing the sentiments of the oppressed, which, in a more general way, reflects the irredeemable dilemma of the powerless struggling to seek one's strength for survival. This dilemma finds its expression with a different reason in the case of Rehana. While Sohail complains of injustice meted out to East Pakistan, Rehana laments the loss of her language which is a definite cultural marker in her case:

> She spoke, with fluency, the Urdu of the enemy....She could not give up her love of Urdu, its lyrical lilts, its double meanings, its furrowed beat (55). By the end she found herself shouting *Joy Bangla, Joy Bangla, Joy Bangla* with the crowd ... ('March 1971: Shona with her back to the sun': 57–8)

Even though the native language remains a sign of identity for the speaker, the speaker also brings another language to his tongue, as required, which precisely happens here in the case of Rehana. She does this for a cause dear to her heart, in spite of all the sufferings that come her way. Soon, suffering makes its way into the lives of people after a proclamation made by Major Zia, provisional commander-in-chief of the Bangladesh Liberation Army, on behalf of Sheikh Mujibur Rahman regarding the independence of Bangladesh and its subsequent governance. While all nations are being called to get together in solidarity and condemn the genocide in Bangladesh, this proclamation leads to a pensive response in the narrative as it marks a new phase of struggle and survival:

> So this was it: a war had come to find them. Whatever was going to happen had already happened; now they would have to live in its shadow. Rehana wrapped her arms around herself and squeezed tight,

> willing the old strength to rise up within her again. ('25 March 1971: Operation Searchlight': 75)

Wars are known to spell disaster and put people to misery in general, but here Anam projects Rehana as a generic figure to bear its onslaughts. She represents inclusive consciousness and, on behalf of everyone else, she responds like a classic recipient of the consequences of war which spreads like fire and alters individual and communal histories:

> By the middle of April they began to realize that the attack on Dhaka was only the beginning. The army was making its way across the country, subduing one district after another, leaving behind a trail of burning villages. ('April: Radio Free Bangladesh': 84)

The narrative progresses with war being the leitmotif, and it engages all characters in its wake as different situations unfold one after another. It reaches a point of utter helplessness:

> 'Tikka Khan,' Maya shouted, as though she were making an announcement, 'the Butcher of Bengal!' And then she kicked at the tree again, reached up and hugged a ropy branch, looking as though she might swing from it, but then just stood there with her arms raised and her face pressed against the bark.' ('May: Tikka Khan, the Butcher of Bengal!': 142)

As it happens in life, excess of pain is punctuated by momentary escape into relief. It happens in this narrative also, as it progresses further. Here comes a sequence when Rehana finds a sympathetic chord in a stranger:

> It was a woman. In every syllable Rehana could hear the delicate intake of her breath, the tongue caressing the palette and the slow, tender piano in the background, and, as the song built, she could hear melancholy, and a low, guttural moan and stretched-out vowels. Her voice was a thousand years of sorrow. Rehana tried to make out the English words. I loves you, Porgee. ('June: I loves you, Porgy': 165)

In one of the subplots which relates with Sabeer's misery and his release, following hectic efforts by Rehana, Anam develops yet another aspect of suffering that marks the essential nature of her narrative. The following narration brings out how relief, following misery, helps towards the realization of a distant dream. It is like a fantasy turning into a reality as well as reality turning into fantasy:

> When the guard finally brought Sabeer out, Rehana thought she might be dreaming. She jerked herself upright, ignoring the ache in her arms from where her head had rested. The thana was a dim memory. ('July: The red-tipped bird': 227)

This interplay of dream and reality continues further. Rehana once again finds herself in yet another role as a sympathetic server to one who is unable to redeem himself and has to be rescued in death, as in life:

> SABEER DEAD STOP TRIED OUR BEST STOP/COULDN'T SAVE STOP GOD BLESS MRS C
>
> Rehana folded the telegram, neatly, making sure the edges lined up. She felt weak and shaky and her fingers trembled, but she continued to fold, until it was a tiny sliver of paper that she could tuck into her blouse, like loose change. All the way to Salt Lake she felt her heart beating against it. ('August, September, October: Salt Lake': 269)

Having resolved the crisis of language, which is regulated by the conditions of her life, Rehana seeks relief in dreaming once again, as she had been doing incessantly:

> Do you want a song, Ma? Rehana was taken aback by the offer. 'Really? I would love that. Sing 'Amar Shonar Bangla'. ('November: Take my affliction': 291)

The end, after all terrible happenings, captures a moment where life is approached afresh with a mixed feeling of delight and exhaustion after a long and arduous journey. After a description of joy with selling of flags, waving and craning of necks, sailing of coloured papers, waving of fists in the air, dancing, playing flute, beating of dhol by a woman, there is the final moment of reconciliation:

> The roads are flat and dusty; we are spellbound, love-bound, home-bound, singing *'How I love you, my golden Bengal.'* The sky is pale and iridescent and today the war has ended, and today I will clutch my flag, hold my breath and wait for our son./I know what I have done./This war that has taken so many sons has spared mine. This age that has burned so many daughters has not burned mine./I have not let it. ('16 December 1971': 315)

Anam's narrative is sensitive to the core and essentially poetic in the treatment of human emotions. All through the narrative, one is again and again struck by the use of language for representing the experiences of pain and pathos, as well as the interplay of reality and fantasy into which the characters find themselves intermittently placed. The language acquires its strength from the images and metaphors she executes to create an atmosphere for her narrative, which distinguishes itself as a narrative of struggle created both with sympathy and clinical detachment.

A Golden Age that recalls the past and develops under its shadow in the present ends on a quiet note of resignation and resolution, which reflects a silent arrival at a destination sought for a long period of time. What had been brewing up for ages saw its point of culmination in the year 1971, which turns into a time of all times, where dreams nourished result in dreams realized. The year 1971 thus emerges as an intersection time for a people and their homeland in symbolic terms. It maps the locations of pain and redemption, and alternates between states of dreaming, struggling, and finally arriving at a location with its own identity in the community of nations.

Locating Maps

A Golden Age evolves through a web of events and interpersonal relationship of characters and situations. We come across Hindus and Muslims as well as Indians and Pakistanis, who figure out Bangladesh and Bangladeshis as a people in dire need to rescue themselves and seek a land of their own. In the midst of these, we also have the personal evolving into communal, and the communal into national. As the narrative evolves, it problematizes larger issues concerning gender (man/woman), language (Bangla/Urdu), and location (Bangladesh/Pakistan/India). All these cumulatively contribute towards the evolution of the narrative in multiple avatars as a period narrative, a historical narrative, and a paradigmatic narrative that keeps on evolving through different chapters.

In the way this narrative evolves, it may be read from two broad perspectives of how the characters develop and how they contribute towards the making of history. Since war emerges as a kind of thematic refrain, it has led Shahnaz Parvin to say that it acts as a 'catalyst' (116) towards the self-discovery of Rehana. I would extend it further by positing that this discovery comes to her at a huge cost of personal suffering. Beginning as one whose affiliations to the place are uncertain in the beginning, she finds Bangladesh as her ultimate location which is fully affirmed through her commitment to the cause of liberation, and through her larger human sympathy for the people located there. It is only after a monumental realization that she allows her children to join the liberation movement. As she matures further, she herself becomes the movement and takes part by providing little conveniences to those actively engaged in the liberation movement. Even if she is not at the forefront of the liberation movement herself, her offerings in terms of clothing, shelter, medical assistance, and rescuing a victim at great personal risk earn her respect, which, in reality, is a respect for the cause rather than the person which Anam wishes to underline.

Yet another aspect that relates with the gendered perspective has been noted by Louise Harrington: 'Just as Bapsi Sidhwa's *Ice-Candy Man* broke new ground for the discussion of women in Punjab in 1947, *A Golden Gate* exposes both the trauma and the triumph—to borrow a familiar phrase—of women in the 1971 War' (243). However, the point is carried too far in the statement in that being located where she (Rehana) is, she 'must learn to fight the oppressive patriarchal society...' (243).

It should be added here that she, in fact, relates with everyone outside her family who constitute a motley complex of characters with different affiliations. This implies that she relates liberally with persons involved in the macabre drama of times rather than intentionally connect with women who also constitute the scenario as men do. A widow and a mother of two, Rehana operates in a small world of her own and responds to situations as a human rather than a woman. It would only be proper to posit that she fights oppression irrespective of her gender and seeks deliverance as everyone else in the narrative does. Mandira Sen offers a reasonably balanced account in saying that the ' ... book's tone matches Rehana's personality: gentle but firm, reserved, outwardly conventional, and as the war unfolds, astonishingly courageous, even heroic—though Rehana would not identify herself thus' (5).

In addition, I should like to posit that apart from being a novel of war and liberation, as it appears to be on the surface, *A Golden Age* projects the most significant question of identity which poses itself at multiple levels. The novel problematizes the identity of the self as well as of the other. While in one way, it relates with the individual identities of the characters who cumulatively constitute one identity of the oppressed, in another it concerns the identity of those who may be identified as oppressors. It is the dynamics of the oppressor and the oppressed that characterizes the novel as a novel of identity politics. This problem of identity extends further to multiple levels and relates with three locations—Bangladesh, Pakistan, and India; two languages—Bangla and Urdu; and two communities—Hindus and Muslims. It may be easily noted that all these identities rooted in languages, locations, and communities are posed against each other as markers of difference, and they together constitute a discourse with regard to identity politics. The issue of identity is further related with the choice of language that Anam makes for writing this narrative. It must be noted that this story of Bangladesh is not written in Bangla but in English, which must be taken as a liberal act on the part of the author to move beyond linguistic and geographical frontiers and reach out to a wholly different group of readers with an aim to attract broader participation in the postcolonial act of redefining power dynamics and identity politics. This struggle for identity also situates the novel in the larger schema of decolonization, which concerns directly with the questions of who we are, what language we speak, where we seek our strength from, and how we constitute a part of a larger world.

Along with the problem of identity that this narrative projects, it is important to note that in spite of all their ambiguities and disparities—their living split lives and suffering ruptured consciousness—the people of East and West Pakistan, as well as India in the middle, have shared their histories and cultural practices. They suffered colonization together before they drew their boundary lines. All along, they have suffered hope and despair that contemporary history brought to them, but all the while they have been identified as parts of a greater whole of the larger Indian subcontinent. Anam's *A Golden Age* sublimates history in a given location, and it turns out to be a testament of hope and faith while redefining the terms of colonization and decolonization.

Endnotes

1. 'Freedom, you are/an arbour in the garden, the koel's song,/glistening leaves on banyan trees,/my notebook of poetry, to scribble as I please.' (trans. Kaiser Haq) (unnumbered page 8)
2. What is it but nightfall?/No, no, not night but death;/Was it needless death after all?/For England may keep faith/For all that is done and said./We know their dream; enough/To know they dreamed and are dead;/And what if excess of love/Bewildered them till they died?/I write it out in verse—/MacDonagh and MacBride/And Connolly and Pearse/Now and in time to be,/Wherever green is worn,/Are changed, changed utterly:/A terrible beauty is born. (86–7)
3. A huge amount of scholarly work is already available on the year 1947 in Indian history from historians and social scientists, which are often quoted in a variety of contexts and also may be seen separately. Apart from all others, it would be enlightening to approach the writings of M.K. Gandhi and Jawaharlal Nehru for a first-hand account of India's struggle for freedom leading to independence.
4. India's partition has been represented in the long and short fictions in English, Urdu, Hindi, and Bangla more prominently than in other languages. Some of the

most prominent writers, among many others, who made it their major concern include Khushwant Singh, Manohar Malgonkar, Bapsi Sidhwa, Salman Rushdie, and Amitav Ghosh in English; Intizar Hussain, Qurratulain Hyder, and Saadat Hasan Manto in Urdu; Bhisham Sahni, Yash Pal, and Kamleshwar in Hindi; and Sunil Gangopadhyay and Jyotirmoyee Devi in Bangla. Similarly, some of the notable ones who represent historical and fictional accounts of the liberation of Bangladesh include works by Selina Hossain, Mushtari Safi, Nilima Ibrahim, and Jahanara Imam in Bangla.

5. References may be made to leaders and politicians like A.K. Fazlul Huq, Sheikh Mujibur Rahman, Maulana Abdul Hamid Khan Bhashani, Tajuddin Ahmad, Syed Nazrul Islam, and Muhammad Mansur Ali, among others, who championed the cause of Bangladesh as an independent state based on the principle of natural justice.

References

Anam, Tahmima. 2011. *A Golden Age*. India: Penguin Books.

Harrington, Louise. 2011. 'An-Other Space: Diasporic Responses to Partition in Bengal.' *India and the Indian Diasporic Imagination*. Eds Rita Christian and Judith Misrahi-Barak. Montpellier: Presses universitaires de la Méditerranée, pp. 237–50.

Parvin, Shahnaz. 'War Mothers in a Non-Fiction and Two Fictional Works on the Liberation War of Bangladesh.' *Bangladesh Research Foundation Journal* 4(2) (2015): 113–19.

Sen, Mandira. 'The Language of the Enemy.' *Women's Review of Books* 25 (1) (Jan–Feb 2008): 5–6.

Yeats, W.B. *The Major Works: Oxford World's Classics*. Ed. Edward Larrissy (Oxford: Oxford University Press, 2001) [a revision of *Selected Writings* (1997) in the Oxford Authors series].

Acknowledgements

'Rumi and Kabir: Reading and Reception' was presented as a plenary talk at the thirteenth CLAI Biennial International Conference on *The Journey of Comparative Literature: India and Beyond*, Department of Comparative Literature, Jadavpur University, Kolkata, 17 January 2013.

'Love Songs to the Divine: Sufi Music in India and Pakistan' was presented in a special session on *Literary and Cultural Inter-relationships Between India, its Neighbouring Countries and the World* at the XXth ICLA Congress, Paris-Sorbonne, 22 July 2013.

'When Black Clouds Hang: Rethinking Kajri' was published as 'Rethinking Kajri When Black Clouds Hang', in Jasbir Jain, ed., *Narrative of the Village* (Jaipur: Rawat Publications, 2006), pp. 27–44.

'The Making of a Literary Culture: Patrons and Urdu Poets' was delivered as a plenary address at a national seminar on *Intersections: History and Literature*, Delhi College of Arts and Commerce, 11 March 2014.

'Language, Culture, Bombay/Mumbai Cinema: Cinematic Representations of Muslims' was presented as a plenary talk at an IRIS seminar, Jaipur, on *Representations of Muslim Culture in Indian Cinema*, 23 April 2010. It was later published as 'Language, Culture, Bombay Cinema: Reflections on Cinematic Representations of Muslims', in Jasbir Jain, ed., *Muslim Culture in India Cinema* (Jaipur: Rawat Publications, 2011), pp. 25–50.

'Discoursing Minority: Twentieth-Century Constructions of Indian Muslims' was presented as a plenary talk at the CLAI international Conference on *Minority Discourse Across Cultures*, Central University of Rajasthan, 27 February 2012. It was later published in Anisur Rahman *et al.*, eds, *Discoursing Minority: In-Text and Co-Text* (Jaipur: Rawat Publications, 2014), pp. 53–77.

'The Fall of the Romantic Ideal: Modernist Representations in Urdu Poetry' was originally published in Interdisciplinary Alter-Natives in Comparative Literature, Copyright 2013@ E.V. Ramakrishnan, Harish Trivedi, Chandra Mohan. All rights reserved. Reproduced with the permission of the copyright holders and the publishers, Sage Publications India Pvt. Ltd, New Delhi, pp. 158–74.

'The Problematic of Impact and Response: The Case of Faiz Ahmad Faiz' was presented as keynote address at an international seminar on *Internalizing Faiz in Twentieth Century*, Aligarh Muslim University, 20 January 2011. It was later published as 'Internalizing Faiz Ahmad Faiz: Problematic of Impact and Response', in Ali Refad Fatihi, ed., *Poetry of Protest: Internalizing Faiz Ahmed Faiz* (Germany: Lap Lambert Academic Publishing, 2014), pp. 17–40.

'On the Edge of Animation: Women Poets from Pakistan' was presented at an international conference on *Problematic of the Self and Multiculturalism,* Institute for Research in Multidisciplinary Studies, Jaipur, 27–28 December 2002. Subsequently, it was presented as a public lecture in Purdue University (USA) on 10 April 2007 and Rutgers University (USA) on 23 April 2007, and later published as 'On the Edge of Animation: Pakistani Women Poets in Their Own Voice', in Jasbir Jain, ed., *Dislocations and Multiculturalisms* (Jaipur: Rawat Publications, 2004), pp. 190–202.

'Counterposing Exotica and Stereotype: Sarojini Naidu's Text and Context' was published as 'Counterposing Exotica and Stereotype: Finding a New Context for Sarojini Naidu', in R. Azhagarasan, Bruce Bennett *et. al.*, eds, *New Bearings in English Studies* (New Delhi: Orient BlackSwan, 2008), pp. 178–93.

'Towards the Terms of Reference: Contextualizing Kamal Das' was published as 'Contextualising Kamala Das', in Smita Agarwal, ed., *Marginalized: Indian Poetry in English* (Amsterdam, New York: Rodopi, 2014), pp. 183–98.

'The Calligraphy of Coils: The Poetry of Agha Shahid Ali' was published in *The Journal of Indian Writing in English* 31 (1), pp. 48–59.

'Indian English Fiction: Multiple Receptions and a Rejoinder' was delivered as the inaugural address of a seminar on *Recent Trends in Indian English Fiction* M S College Motihari, 4 February 2012. It was later published in Md. Equebal Hussain, ed., *In Fictional Capital: New Perspectives on Indian English Fiction* (New Delhi: Creative Books, 2014), pp. 15–31.

'Premchand: Premises and Problems' was presented as a plenary talk at an international conference on *Premchand in Translation,* Department of English, Jamia Millia Islamia, 30 December 2012.

'Versions of Subversion: Michael Ondaatje's *Running in the Family*' was presented in a seminar on *Expatriate Writing: Theory and Practice,* University of Rajasthan, Jaipur, 7 December 1996. It was later published in Jasbir Jain, ed., *Writers of the Indian Diaspora* (Jaipur: Rawat Publications, 1998).

All essays and some of the titles have since been revised for this book.

I gratefully acknowledge the indulgence of the academics who reposed their faith in me for doing these essays for their seminars or conferences, and the publishers and editors of the volumes where some of these essays appeared. In collecting all these essays together, I also acknowledge the new-found interest of the international academia in South Asian Studies that took me along and helped me locate some of the sociocultural positions and paradigms that this volume tries to project.

I am deeply indebted to Nirmal Kanti Bhattacharya for promoting this project on the socioliterary cultures in South Asia, to Priyanka Misra for closely supervising its publication, and to Sukanya Sur for her understanding and meticulous editing.

Index

Note: Page numbers followed by 'n' represent endnotes.